I0759600

EMPIRICAL MODELS OF PHONOLOGICAL NETWORKS AND THEIR GROWTH IN ENGLISH

EVA MARIA **LUEF**

CHARLES UNIVERSITY
KAROLINUM PRESS, 2025

KAROLINUM PRESS
Karolinum Press is a publishing department of Charles University
Ovocný trh 560/5, 116 36 Prague 1, Czech Republic
www.karolinum.cz, redakcenk@ruk.cuni.cz

Set and printed in the Czech Republic by Karolinum Press
Layout by Jan Šerých
First edition

A catalogue record for this book is available from the National Library of the Czech Republic.

ISBN 978-80-246-5708-0
ISBN 978-80-246-5767-7 (pdf)
ISBN 978-80-246-5768-4 (epub)

The original manuscript was reviewed by Christiane Dalton-Puffer (University of Vienna, Austria), Eric Dwyer (Florida International University, USA) and Radek Skarnitzl (Charles University, Prague, Czech Republic).

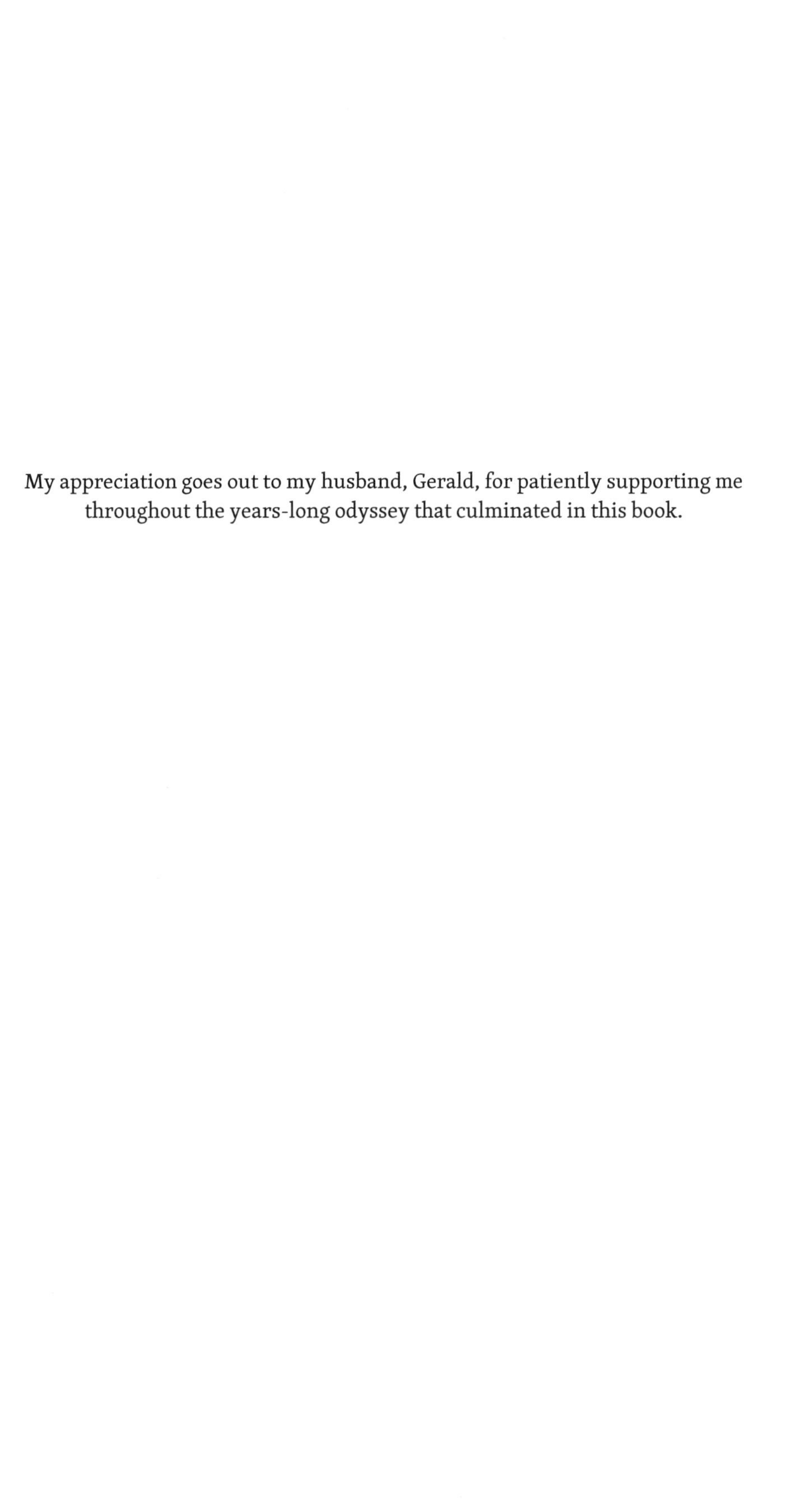

My appreciation goes out to my husband, Gerald, for patiently supporting me throughout the years-long odyssey that culminated in this book.

CONTENTS

PREFACE

Lexical knowledge is a crucial pillar of linguistic competence, upon which all other linguistic functions depend. Decades of psycholinguistic research have explored the cognitive representations of words in our minds and their internal organization, the so-called mental lexicon. Of particular interest have been the pathways of word acquisition and retrieval, the functional components of the mental vocabulary, and the interrelations between words encoded in the vocabulary. Research of the mental lexicon is voluminous and has significantly advanced our understanding of how the human mind processes words, both in first languages and those learned later in life.

To unravel the intricacies of the mental lexicon, researchers have primarily employed a "bottom-up approach" based on the reconstruction of linguistic processes, such as word recognition and lexical learning, by focusing on individual words and their formal and functional neighborhoods. This method has built a solid theoretical foundation to capture phenomena observed in experimental tests over decades. Recent advances in the mathematical domain of network sciences have opened up promising avenues for a "top-down" approach to studying the mental lexicon. This involves viewing words as parts of a vast, interconnected network. Novel insights into functional and developmental patterns can come from modeling the mental lexicon as a complex system, where the performance of one part relies on another, and the whole system is more than the sum of its parts. This bird's-eye view of the mental lexicon as a complex system facilitates the exploration of its grander structure, unveiling new patterns of hierarchical relationships and lexical access dynamics. Ultimately, it can lead to more predictive models of the factors that influence lexical processes.

The research field of lexical network science is relatively new, with studies primarily focused on a limited number of languages, mainly those involving first language users. Second languages have been underrepresented in this research. This book aims to address this gap by introducing readers to the methodology and utility of network science for second languages, specifically English as a second language[1]. To offer

1 The term "second language" will be used throughout this book in the psycholinguistic sense of any language learned after the first (native) language of a speaker, with the exception of bilingualism (see, e.g., Gass & Se-

a comprehensive perspective, the book will also present a lexical word form network of British English as a first language to allow for meaningful comparisons between the linguistic patterns of English as a first and second language. The focus of this book is on mathematical modeling of network-theoretical concepts within the phonological lexica of language users at various proficiency stages of English, their psycholinguistic implications, and the question of what network science can contribute to theories of word learning and lexical access. By approaching second language networks through the lens of evolving network theories, the book aims to provide insights into the developmental aspects of lexical learning in second languages. The ultimate goal is to offer a network-theoretical description of word form networks and their growth in learners of English as a second language. The structure of the book is designed as follows.

The opening chapter explores word form relationships within the mental lexicon, as outlined in widely accepted psycholinguistic theories of lexical access. At the core of this discussion is the notion of 'phonological neighbor', a measure of the relationship between word forms. Much explanatory weight of network science is placed on the quality and quantity of relationships between entities along known similarity dimensions, and phonological neighbors are the logical starting point for a network-theoretical approach to word forms. The chapter systematically surveys various concepts of network science and their application to the description of phonological networks. Special attention is given to the different levels of network organization, including micro, meso, and macro levels of analysis. Characteristics of individual nodes, small clusters of connected nodes (communities), and the overall topology of a lexical network all bear systemic relevance for network connectivity and can provide information about lexical processes. The chapter further explores theories on activation spreading in lexical networks. This is particularly important as patterns of co-activation are expected to align with network principles, potentially differing from predictions based on traditional models of lexical access.

Chapter 2 outlines the construction process of the phonological networks of English. Vocabulary data associated with different proficiency levels in second language English were collected, and phonological distances between word forms were calculated as the foundation of network creation. To provide a point of comparison, a separate phonological network with data from British English first language users was computed. The subsequent sections of the chapter describe network-mathematical analyses, covering all levels of analytical detail for the networks examined. Throughout, the implications that these findings hold for lexical processing are discussed.

In the third chapter, network growth algorithms that are of potential significance for phonological networks are reviewed. A specific focus is placed on scale-free networks and how new links can be accumulated in a way consistent with the scale-free assumption of phonological networks. A discussion of various factors influencing the growth of scale-free networks follows, including uniform and preferential attachment,

---

linker, 2008). The terms ESL or "English as a second language" and EFL or "English as a foreign language" will thus be used synonymously.

fitness models, and aging effects. The discussion extends to the application of these network growth algorithms in the second language networks, where vocabulary gains across proficiency levels are analyzed in terms of which network growth principle can best explain the observed patterns. Growth rates within distinct network parts, communities, and individual nodes are discussed. Additionally, the developmental trajectory of growth over the course of language learning at the micro, meso, and macro level of the evolving second language network is charted. Theoretical extensions of the Barabási-Albert evolving network model are tested in the networks.

The conclusion summarizes the findings and presents future directions for the application of network sciences to the study of the mental lexicon and word learning in second languages. The potential of network theoretical approaches to lexical organization and lexical access in language users is in its nascent stage, with ongoing development of new theories. Emerging hypotheses seek to integrate traditional knowledge about the mental lexicon with novel insights derived from the principles of network science.

Hopefully, this book will inspire researchers to apply network-mathematical concepts to the psycholinguistic study of word relationships in the mental lexicon. This integrated approach across research specialties can be intellectually fruitful and lead to a deeper understanding of the cognitive underpinnings of linguistic representations in the human mind. By embracing different theoretical perspectives and exploring innovative research questions, we can make significant strides toward elucidating the structural organization of human word memory.

1.
THE NETWORK REVOLUTION IN THE MENTAL LEXICON

1.1 VIEWS OF LEXICAL CONNECTIVITY

The mental lexicon is the human repository of lexical knowledge (Oldfield, 1966). It is the cognitive system that organizes lexical activity and forms the basis of expression by providing storage to all vocabulary items that are known by a language user (Dóczi, 2019). A lexical representation is believed to contain information about a word's form, meaning, and syntactic properties, which become accessible upon lexical access (Yelland, 1994). How words are represented and processed in the mental lexicon is crucial not only for theories on language acquisition and development but can more generally shed light upon universal principles by which humans mentally categorize language. The mental lexicon is best conceptualized as an ideal, abstract notion, rather than a mere catalogue of word knowledge (Aitchison, 2012; He & Deng, 2015). In essence, it functions as a dynamic memory system supporting linguistic processing, continually adapting in response to experience.

Virtually all psycholinguistic accounts of lexical processing acknowledge that information in the mental lexicon is organized according to phonological similarity (Buchwald, 2011; Schweppe, Grice, & Rummer, 2011; Vitevitch, 2002b). Studies have consistently revealed an advantage of phonologically similar word forms for word learning, underscoring the strong influence of phonology on lexical processing in first language acquisition and second language learning (e.g., Aitchison, 2012; Arutiunian & Lopukhina, 2020; Beckage & Colunga, 2019; Dell & Gordon, 2003; Fourtassi, Bian, & Frank, 2020; Gahl, Yao, & Johnson, 2012; Harley & Bown, 1998; Havas et al., 2018; James & Burke, 2000; Siew & Vitevitch, 2016; Vitevitch & Luce, 2016). Therefore, understanding the role of phonological similarity in the mental lexicon can illuminate processes involved in the organizational structure of lexical cognition.

1.1.1 PHONOLOGICAL NEIGHBORS

The phonological similarity bias in the mental lexicon is governed by 'phonological neighbors', a well-studied notion of lexical relationships (Goldrick, Folk, & Rapp, 2010; Landauer & Streeter, 1973). In their seminal study of lexical frequency in word recognition, Streeter and Landauer (1973) defined phonological (in their term "lexical") similarity as the distance of one piece of information (a phoneme or grapheme) between two words. What was referred to as "neighbors" and "similarity neighborhoods" have evolved into today's concepts of "phonological neighbors" and "phonological neighborhoods" (see, e.g., Vitevitch & Luce, 2016). Phonological neighbors are commonly considered to be words that share the majority of phonological segments and differ by just one segment through substitution, deletion, or addition (the so-called Hamming or Levenshtein distance, Landauer & Streeter, 1973; Luce & Pisoni, 1998). What lies at the core of lexical activation is competition for activation between segments and, consequently, among phonological neighbors. Activation of a target word, either through production or perception, leads to co-activation of other words sharing phonemes with the target. Since co-activation spreads through common phonology, the more phonemes are shared within a neighborhood, the more activation spreads within a neighborhood. This results in the "phonological neighborhood effect" on the lexical level (Vitevitch & Luce, 2016). The impact of the effect varies in speech production and in perception. In perception, competition among lexical candidates results in slower access to the target word (Luce & Pisoni, 1998; Magnuson, Dixon, Tanenhaus, & Aslin, 2007; Vitevitch, 2002a; Vitevitch & Rodriguez, 2004). In speech production the opposite is observable, and words from denser neighborhoods are produced faster and more accurately (Vitevitch, 2002b; Vitevitch, Armbruster, & Chu, 2004; Vitevitch & Sommers, 2003). In speech recognition, listeners have limited semantic information and rely solely on phonemic input to determine a phonological word form. In production, speakers have access to semantic information, which they can use to prevent co-activation of certain phonological neighbors. It has been proposed that in speech production, articulation-relevant features of phonological representations become strengthened through co-activation (Vitevitch, 2002b). Phonological neighborhood effects are well-documented phenomena in psycholinguistic research, observable across various languages and populations (e.g., Arutiunian & Lopukhina, 2020; Gordon, 2002; Marian & Blumenfeld, 2006; Stamer & Vitevitch, 2012). They constitute a central component of lexical processing (see Vitevitch & Luce, 2016, for an overview of neighborhood effects in perception and production).

Phonological neighborhoods play an important role in word learning. Words which find many potential neighbors or 'anchor words' in the vocabulary of a learner are more easily and rapidly integrated (Gaskell & Dumay, 2003; Storkel, Armbruster, & Hogan, 2006). Thus, dense phonological neighborhoods with numerous words connected via the one-segment distance can exert a pull-effect on new words sharing phonological features with these neighborhoods. Clusters of phonologically related words constitute particularly strong attraction points for new words (Stamer & Vitevitch, 2012; Storkel et al., 2006). Research indicates that adult word learning is facilitated by high-density neighborhoods, while challenges arise when target words belong to sparse neighborhoods (Storkel et al., 2006). The phonological homogeneity bias essentially skews the learner's perceptions and word memory in a way that favors accumulations of phonologically similar words. While most word learning research has focused on first languages (or ‘L1’), the phenomenon of phonologically guided word learning can also be found in second languages (‘L2’; see, e.g., Bialystok, 2010; Kaushanskaya, Yoo, & Van Hecke, 2013; Leach & Samuel, 2007; Smits, Sandra, Martensen, & Dijkstra, 2009; Stamer & Vitevitch, 2012; Yates, 2013). New L2 words that share phonological similarities with existing words in a learner’s L2 vocabulary are acquired more efficiently and retained more accurately (Dijkstra, Miwa, Brummelhuis, Sappelli, & Baayen, 2010). Conversely, acquiring and retaining new words that embed in sparse neighborhoods proves to be more challenging. The phonological similarity bias in learning is not restricted to one language but operates across different languages, as evidenced by parallel activation of L1 phonological forms when L2 is being processed (Broersma & Cutler, 2008). Phonologically similar L1 and L2 words are frequently co-activated, even when this activation is irrelevant to the task (Carrasco-Ortiz, Midgley, & Frenck-Mestre, 2012; Schulpen, Dijkstra, Schriefers, & Hasper, 2003). Third language (‘L3’) studies have yielded similar results, and L3 words tend to activate words from the first and second languages of speakers (Van Hell & Dijkstra, 2002), suggesting that similarity in word forms across languages can provide benefits for L3 lexical processing (Mulík, Carrasco-Ortiz, & Amengual, 2018). Co-activation between L3 and L1 words is commonly reported, but co-activation between L3 and L2 seems to be more dependent on the proficiency level of the learners (Mulík et al., 2018). This has implications for phonological pull-effects in word learning: higher L2 proficiency leads to increased L3 neighborhood effects. The typological and phonological relationship of L1, L2, and L3 languages certainly plays a role, too. Additionally, semantic relatedness of the similar phonological forms needs to be considered, as cross-language homophones and cognates can lead to different neighborhood effects (Carrasco-Ortiz et al., 2012; Dijkstra et al., 2010; Dijkstra, Timmermans, & Schriefers, 2000; Haigh & Jared, 2007; Midgley, Holcomb, & Grainger, 2011; Van Heuven, Dijkstra, & Grainger, 1998).

Perceived phonological similarity is tightly linked to the notion of phonological confusability and the question of how individual language users assess similarity of phonemes. Phonological confusability may extend beyond the one-segment neighborhood and encompass a broader spectrum of similarity relationships, including the PLD20, which gives the mean number of steps that are required to transform a word into its 20 closest neighbors (Suarez, Tan, Yap, & Goh, 2011). Suarez and colleagues demonstrated that co-activation extends to the wider neighborhood separated by more than one segment of distance between words (also see Chan & Vitevitch, 2009, for similar findings), even in the absence of one-segment neighbors. Their research uncovered what they termed “neighborhood effect without neighbors” (Suarez et al., 2011: p. 605).

The one-segment phonological distance has proven to be a useful concept for psycholinguistics over the last few decades. Over time, a more nuanced view of phonological neighbors has emerged. One line of research focuses on locus-oriented notions of phonological neighborhoods that consider the serial order of phonemes in words, suggesting that not all phonemes are equal when it comes to neighborhood construction (e.g., Desroches, Newman, & Joanisse, 2009; Simmons & Magnuson, 2018). Typically, word-initial phonemes are attributed a higher conceptual importance in the sense that stronger neighborhood connections exist between words that share onsets (so-called "cohort effects), such as *cat-cab*. In contrast, rhyme neighbors differing in the onset phoneme, for instance *cat-hat*, show weaker competition effects (Simmons & Magnuson, 2018). Another measure of phonological neighbors is captured by the so-called *P-metric* (or phonological neighborhood spread), which counts the phonemic possibilities for a word to form neighbors (Vitevitch, 2007). As exemplified by Vitevitch (2007), the English word *mop* has three phoneme positions where neighbors can form (P=3), e.g., *hop, map, mock*. Its phonological neighbor word *mob*, however, has only two phoneme positions for neighborhood formation (P=2), e.g., *rob, mock*. Conflicting findings regarding the phonological neighborhood spread exist in the literature. Yates (2009) found faster responses to words with numerous phonemic positions changeable for creating neighbors, while Vitevitch (2007) reported the opposite – faster recognition for words with smaller P-values, supporting assumptions of activation-competition theories. Fewer neighbor formation possibilities mean less cognitive effort involved in processing words. Higher degrees of certainty in word recognition (in the case of a smaller P) correlate with faster recognition rates, whereas more uncertainty due to a higher rate of variation probability (in the case of a larger P) slows down processing. These findings indicate that the probability of phonemic overlap with neighbors across different phonemic positions effects on lexical processing and potentially the structural organization of word forms in the mental lexicon.

Phonological similarity can also be described across different phonological dimensions, as shown by feature-based analyses measuring the closeness of phonological neighbors (Bailey & Hahn, 2001). For instance, the phonological distance between voiced and unvoiced variants of a consonant is arguably closer than that between a vowel and a consonant, as seen in examples like *bat-pat* vs. *ball-boy*. A study by Fricke, Baese-Berk, and Goldrick (2016) shows that the English word *cod* has a multitude of neighbors (27 overall) with which it shares different phonological features: *God* differs only in the voicing parameter of the word-initial plosive, while the word-initial sibilant in *sod* represents a larger phonological distance to the target word *cod*. The authors demonstrated that considering position-specific similarity of segments can predict the spreading of activation in a phonological neighborhood (in their case, in word-initial position). These findings underscore the importance of further quantifying phonological neighbors for understanding crucial aspects of lexical processing.

Phonology-based models of lexical access tend to view the mental lexicon as "a collection of arbitrarily ordered phonological representations and the process of lexical retrieval as a special instance of pattern matching" (Chan & Vitevitch, 2009: p. 1934). The majority of current models of spoken word recognition share the assumption that phonological overlap is the central force driving competition and activation in lexical processing (Weber & Scharenborg, 2012). Phonemic input activates all similar phonemes within a phonological neighborhood and words containing those shared phonemes compete for overall activation. The way phonological connections between words can further or hinder activation spreading is a crucial question in theoretical models of lexical access.

1.1.1.1 SPOKEN WORD RECOGNITION

Models of spoken word recognition rely on various notions of phonological neighbors. One of the earliest models, the cohort model of lexical access, focuses on word-initial segments (Marslen-Wilson, 1987; Marslen-Wilson & Warren, 1994). The model predicts co-activation based on temporal phonemic overlap, starting from the initial phoneme and progressing with each succeeding, similar phoneme in a sequential manner as speech unfolds in time. In this context, phonological neighbors are those words sharing onset phonemes, and non-onset phonological neighbors are excluded as candidate words early in the chronological perception of phonemes. The cohort model operates under the assumption that the human brain, and consequently the mental lexicon, follows the principle of greatest efficiency (Marslen-Wilson & Welsh, 1978). Initially, a broad range of lexical candidates is considered (with activation of the first few phonemes). However, this range quickly narrows, and mismatches are excluded from the candidate list. For example, upon hearing /s/, the whole cohort of s-initial words is activated, and gradually, with each subsequent phoneme, different words are dismissed until the target word is identified. Recognition occurs when a word reaches a unique identifying phoneme, such as the English phonemic string /fɛb/, which unmistakably identifies the only English word that begins with it, *February* (Weber & Scharenborg, 2012). Following this initial access process, the integration stage checks for syntactic and semantic suitability of a word, removing contextual mismatches from the cohort.

The structural organization predicted by the model resembles a computerized feed-forward string-matching process. However, it is unclear how different strings (=words) are related to one another. Since cohorts are formed based on the initial phoneme, each word-initial phoneme in a lexicon constitutes the first layer of its cohort. Word-initial biphones, triphones, and so forth each form their own cohorts. This means that each word is a member of different cohorts; for example, *bean* belongs to the /b/-cohort, the /bi/-cohort, and the /bin/-cohort). The likelihood of belonging to various cohorts increases with phonemic length of a word. However, cohort size decreases simultaneously.

The special status of the word-initial phonological portion for lexical processing has been consistently highlighted by numerous studies (e.g., Friedrich, Felder, Lahiri, & Eulitz, 2013; Treiman & Danis, 1988; Vitevitch, 2002a). High onset density or a high number of phonological neighbors sharing the same onset phoneme generally slow down lexical processing, as a large number of competitor words become activated (Vitevitch, 2002a). Interestingly, no similar effect has been observed for rhyme neighbors, emphasizing the sequential left-to-right activation of phonemes in speech recognition (Sevald & Dell, 1994; Vitevitch, 2002a). Competition remains high at word onsets but decreases as more phonemes are added to the word selection process (Chen & Mirman, 2014). In the cohort model, competition is restricted to phonemic access but it is not explicitly postulated that words in a cohort compete with one another. According to Marslen-Wilson (1987, p. 84), "the timing of word-recognition processes is not affected by the number of alternatives that need to be considered." Thus, the speed and accuracy of word retrieval are not influenced by the number of competitors. The cohort model has been challenged by findings that (English) listeners can rarely uniquely identify a word before its offset (Bard, Shillcock, & Altmann, 1988; Luce, 1986). As a consequence, the idea of onset matching as the singularly most crucial mechanism of lexical access has been questioned (Weber & Scharenborg, 2012).

Alternative models of word recognition acknowledge a contribution of non-initial phonological segments to neighborhood formation. One notable activation-competition model of spoken word recognition, the Neighborhood Activation Model (or NAM, Luce & Pisoni, 1998) and its connectionist counterpart PARSYN (Luce, Goldinger, Auer, & Vitevitch, 2000), posit that phonological co-activation occurs within a group of words that share the majority of phonological segments but differ in a minimal number (N=1) of segments. In the original NAM model, neighborhoods can be established through any segmental position in a word, and differences in phonemic neighborhood formation do not impact the strength of a neighborhood. An addendum to the model recognizes different variations in acoustic-phonetic distances between phonological neighbors, affecting neighborhood strength. As demonstrated by Goldinger, Luce and Pisoni (1989), phonologically close neighbors have an amplifying effect on phonemic competition, inhibiting word recognition (see Gahl et al., 2012; Scarborough, 2013; Suarez et al., 2011, for similar findings). For example, *cap* and *cab* are more influential neighbors and share more activation (and competition) compared to *cab* and *fab*.

In general, NAM assumes that competition arises between the co-activated lexical candidates from which the best-fitting word is then chosen for final selection. As lexical selection is inherently competitive, words with strengthened activation, resulting for instance from high frequency rates, facilitate word recognition (Frisch, 2011). The neighborhood probability equation is defined as follows:

$$p=(\text{target} * \text{frequency}_t) \mathbin{/} (\text{target} * \text{frequency}_t)+(\textstyle\sum(\text{neighbors}_j * \text{frequency}_{Nj})$$

Here, the activation level of the target word *t*, the sum of neighbor word probabilities (=neighbors$_j$, i.e., the overall level of activity in the lexical neighborhood), and lexical frequency information are considered (Chan & Vitevitch, 2009; Luce & Pisoni, 1998). Low-density neighborhoods with few neighbors experience less competition, resulting in faster recognition rates for the target word. As a result, words with fewer neighbors are responded to and recognized more quickly than those with a high number of neighbors. Numerous studies have validated the predictions of NAM for word recognition, solidifying its prominent place in spoken word recognition (e.g., Goh, Suarez, Yap, & Tan, 2009; Luce et al., 2000; Vitevitch, 2002c; Ziegler, Muneaux, & Grainger, 2003). Figure 1 illustrates the connectivity of phonological neighborhoods as conceived by NAM.

Luce and Pisoni (1998, p. 1) explicitly acknowledge a "structural organization of the lexicon" based on "similarity relations among the sound patterns of spoken words". However, they do not provide hints regarding any larger structural design beyond linking words in one-segment neighborhoods. It is a logical assumption that each of

Figure 1: Phonological neighborhood structure according to NAM. Node size corresponds to lexical frequency rate, with larger nodes representing more frequent words. Link strength corresponds to phonological distance, with thicker links indicating closer neighbors.

the neighbors of *way* in Figure 1 also has a neighborhood, with potential implications for further spreading of co-activation outside of the immediate neighborhood. Ultimately, a large number of words in a lexicon could be interlinked in one large web. NAM does not address this issue, nor does this idea factor into the NAM account of activation spreading. The central tenet of activation spreading in this model revolves around the immediate, one-segment-distance neighborhood of target words.

These two classical models of spoken word recognition make different predictions about the spread of co-activation in the mental lexicon. Both NAM and the cohort model posit that activated candidate words do not interact at the lexical level. Instead, these models propose decision rules that determine which lexical entry received the most activation relative to the other activated candidate words. The models specifically make predictions about immediate phonological neighbors, separated by a minimal number of phonological segments, and how they influence and compete with each other. However, they do not make predictions concerning activation spreading in neighbors of neighboring words. The larger organizational design of a full lexicon and the phonological relationships between all words contained in it remain unaddressed.

1.1.1.2 SPOKEN WORD PRODUCTION

A salient feature of phonological neighborhood effects is that they fulfil dual functions. In spoken word recognition, neighbors inhibit lexical processing, while in spoken word production, neighbors facilitate the process (Chen & Mirman, 2012; Dell & Gordon, 2003). Explanations for this discrepancy can be found in models of speech processing, in particular interactive models where lexical and phonological levels of word recognition provide feedback to each other. This interaction is captured by Dell's interactive two-step model of lexical access and retrieval (Dell, 1986; Dell, Schwartz, Martin, Saffran, & Gagnon, 1997), where lexical and phonological retrieval are distinct and ordered categories but interact through bi-directional spreading of activation. This means that semantic information can influence phonological retrieval, and phonological information can affect lexical retrieval (Dell, Martin, & Schwartz, 2007). In word production, the first step is lexical selection, mapping the conceptual representation of a word to a lexical representation (the 'lemma', Foygel & Dell, 2000). Phonological information is not required at this point (Levelt, Roelofs, & Meyer, 1999). Subsequently, phonological encoding is initiated, retrieving the phonemes used to form the target word. Phonological encoding is the process of constructing the phonological form of a target word before articulatory gestures can be prepared in spoken word production (Caramazza, Costa, Miozzo, & Bi, 2001; Dell, 1986; Levelt et al., 1999). Phonological components (phonemes) of target words are sequentially activated after speakers have selected words (Oppermann, Jescheniak, & Schriefers, 2010), mostly independently of the whole word representation (O'Séaghdha & Frazer, 2014; Roelofs, 2006). In word production, the initial semantic activation provides a baseline, further boosted by the activation of phonological neighbors. In contrast, word recognition begins with the activation of phonological segments, boosting activation of all phonological neighbors, including the target word. As a result, activation spreads more evenly within the phonological neighborhood in recognition and is less focused on the target word. This leads to the well-known effect of greater lexical activation competition in word recognition than in production (e.g., Vitevitch & Luce, 2016). Figure 2 depicts the interactive-feedback model proposed by Dell (1986).

An unresolved issue in speech production models concerns the flow of information from the semantic to the phonological domain and whether it can be characterized as discrete, cascading, or fully interactive (Schriefers & Vigliocco, 2015). This has direct implications for neighborhood activation. In discrete serial models of lexical access, the target lemma and a set of semantically related lemmas are initially activated. After exclusion of the non-target lemmas, phonological encoding of the target is initiated,

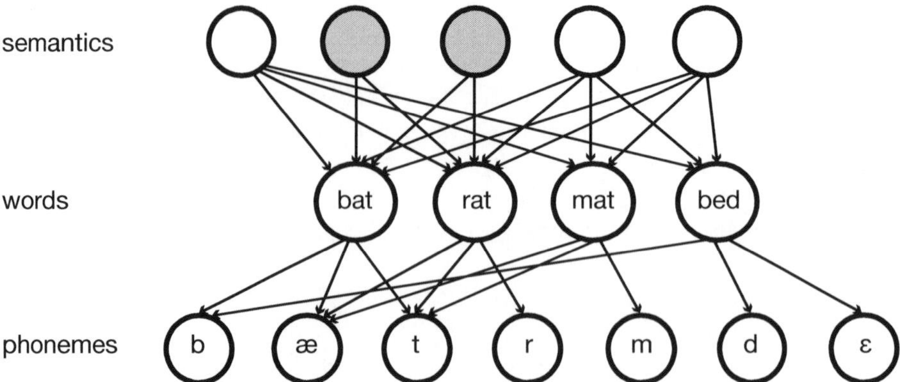

Figure 2: An interactive model of speech production.

and non-targets are not phonologically encoded (Levelt, 1999). In cascading models (e.g., Peterson & Savoy, 1998), the activated set of initial lemmas sends some activation to phonological encoding before the final target lemma is selected, thereby spreading phonological activation among competing lemmas. Interactive models (e.g., Dell, 1986) assume feedback spreading between the phonological and the lemma level, a process through which activation will be spread among competitor lemmas at the lemma stage, in addition to the phonological forms sending activation back to the lemmas and thus spreading co-activation among phonologically similar forms. There is some evidence that semantic competitors receive co-activation, as predicted by cascading and interactive models. For instance, phonological activation has been shown to spread between near-synonyms like 'couch' and 'sofa' (Jescheniak & Schriefers, 1998; Peterson & Savoy, 1998). However, some argue this may be a special case of activation spreading rather than the rule (Levelt, 1999; Schriefers & Vigliocco, 2015). The assumption of feedback from the phonological to the lemma level has been supported by the 'lexical bias effect', which refers to the fact that phonemic errors tend to lead to existing rather than non-words (Nooteboom, 2005). Feedback spreading from phonological segments to the higher lemma level can explain this phenomenon, while discrete serial models would predict independence of phonological errors from an existing word.

1.1.2 THE "CAULDRON OF LEXICAL SOUP"

The concept of phonological neighborhoods is essential to any theory of speech production or perception, given that the mental lexicon is organized along phonological similarity. While psycholinguistic models may differ in how they quantify and qualify phonological neighbors, the prevailing notion for predictions in theories of lexical access involves one-phoneme difference measurements and a metric of phonological distance. The traditional spoken word recognition models take into account only the nearest neighborhood of a word but disregard the larger structure linking different neighborhoods together, which may have an effect on activation spreading, as demonstrated by phenomena such as neighborhood effects without neighbors (Suarez et al., 2011).

Although lexical access models of speech production and perception vary in their basic architecture, they are united by the prediction that phonological pattern matching serves as the guiding principle. As Chan and Vitevitch (2009) put it, the mental lexicon is envisioned as a "cauldron of lexical soup" (p. 1944), where similar phonological forms compete for selection. This means that the lexical models are able to account for neighborhood density effects by virtue of phonological matching without explicitly investigating (or acknowledging) any non-arbitrary phonological structure underlying the entirety of words present in the mental lexicon. Psycholinguistic models are generally focused on acquisition, recognition, and production of words, but the matter of how language-related information is represented in the mental lexicon, including the relationships between stored words, has received limited research attention. Word memory itself is an issue separate from (albeit intertwined with) the processing-centric bias in contemporary cognitive psychology (Vitevitch, 2021).

1.1.3 COMPLEX SYSTEMS APPROACH TO THE LEXICON

Multi-agent systems, comprised of numerous constituent parts, can exhibit collective behaviors at the holistic level of the entire system, which may be unpredictable based solely on the interactions of individual constituents (Siegenfeld & Bar-Yam, 2020). Such systems are characterized as complex systems (Boccara, 2010). In contrast to reductionist modeling, which focuses on a part or a small-sized model of a system, the complex systems approach considers the dependencies, relationships, competitions, and other forms of interactions among local constituents. The emergence of global behavior in a complex system is intricately linked to these interactions. A complex system is more than just "the sum of its parts" (Kane & Higham, 2015), as novel behaviors appear when individual parts come together to form larger structures. There are parallels to Chaos Theory (Rickles, Hawe, & Shiell, 2007), and language viewed as a complex system may explain phenomena such as self-organization and emergent principles at the macroscopic level (Hohenberger & Peltzer-Karpf, 2009).

The mental lexicon has been described as a complex system (Siew, 2013; Vitevitch, 2008; Vitevitch, Chan, & Roodenrys, 2012). While most studies of the mental lexicon have focused on specific and localized lexical neighborhoods within a given lexicon, Aitchison (2012) acknowledged that a larger structure of word relations beyond the immediate neighborhood must exist and refers to the mental lexicon as a "gigantic multidimensional cobweb." However, the functional principles or structural organization underlying this extensive web are not further explored by Aitchison.

An effort to understand a complex system entails the theoretical ability to model it, and network science has emerged as a popular methodological approach for describing and analyzing complex systems (Turnbull et al., 2018). Applying the tools of networks science (or graph theory) to phonological connections between words in the mental lexicon permits the modeling of the organizational structure of lexical entries in the mental lexicon from a holistic, "top-down" perspective. Although this line of research is relatively new, studies have indicated that cognitive networks of the mental lexicon can predict lexical processing, making them psycholinguistically valuable concepts (e.g., Benham, Goffman, & Schweickert, 2018; Chan & Vitevitch, 2009; Lara-Martinez, Quintana-Obregon, Reyes-Manzano, Lopez-Rodriguez, & Guzman-Vargas, 2021; Levy et al., 2021; Luef, 2022b, 2023; Neergaard, Luo, & Huang, 2019; Shoemark, Goldwater, Kirby, & Sarkar, 2016; Siew & Vitevitch, 2016, 2020a; Turnbull, 2021; Turnbull & Peperkamp, 2017; Vitevitch, 2008, 2021). Through network science, the connectivity of words in a given lexicon can be modeled globally, patterns of interactions within and between lexical sub-groups can be correlated with emerging behaviors at the lexical level, and fundamental principles underlying the organization (and constant reorganization through learning) of the system and its growth can be studied.

1.2 PHONOLOGICAL NETWORKS

Networks science has been a presence in cognitive psychology for some time (Kauffman, 1993; van Hemmen & Schulten, 1995), and its utility for the study of linguistic processes in the human mind was recognized early on (Estes, 1975; Feather, 1971; see Siew, Wulff, Beckage, & Kenett, 2019, for a review). With network science, the structure of cognitive dyadic relationships can be modeled, and the influence of the structure on cognitive processes can be mathematically quantified (Castro & Siew, 2020; Cong & Haitao, 2014). This is akin to connectionism, which investigates the processing of information in human cognition and behavior from the viewpoint of large networks of interactive units (see Joanisse & McClelland, 2015). Connectionism models processes, including memory categorization or pattern recognition, whereas network theory models the relationships between cognitive units, such as words. The two approaches are largely distinct.

In the network sciences, the primary concepts are *nodes* (or vertices) and *edges* (or ties), and their relationships to one another constitute the essence of network connectivity. A fundamental assumption about networks is that the transmission of information can only occur between connected nodes. To which and to how many neighbors a node passes its information (or a portion of it) is restricted by the number of neighbors and the strength of the relationships between nodes (Wang et al., 2011). Describing the mental lexicon as a network of phonological word forms necessitates an understanding of how information (i.e., lexical activation) flows within networks and the role that structural properties at different levels of network analyses (micro, meso, macro) play.

Studies of word relationships have employed graph theoretical architecture, even if not explicitly acknowledged. For instance, Quillian (1967) and Collins and Loftus

(1975) devised semantically based representations of the mental lexicon, depicting words as nodes and the relationships between them as edges (see Figure 3). Collins and Loftus conceptualized word relationships as two-fold: semantic and phonological (referred to as "lexical" by the authors). Phonological word relationships were assumed to be organized along phonemic similarity, with phonemic properties specified according to their position in a word. Closeness of word relationships was expressed via edge length, with a shorter line between two nodes indicating a closer semantic or phonological relationship.

Since the late 2000s, there has been a growing application of network-theoretical approaches in lexical research (Gruenenfelder & Pisoni, 2009), leading to the emergence of phonological word form networks (Vitevitch, 2008). In these networks, nodes are words and in case of a phonological relationship between two words, an edge is placed between them. Most commonly, the relationship measure is the one-segment distance, and words are linked if they differ by one phoneme (Vitevitch, 2021).

Research on semantic and phonological networks has demonstrated that network-theoretical models of mental pathways can effectively predict word acquisition (Beckage & Colunga, 2016; Beckage, Smith, & Hills, 2011; Carlson, Sonderegger, & Bane, 2014; Hills, Maouene, Maouene, Sheya, & Smith, 2009b; Luef, 2022b, Vitevitch & Castro, 2015), storage (De Deyne, Kenett, Anaki, Faust, & Navarro, 2017; Storkel, 2002; Vitevitch, 2008), and retrieval (De Deyne et al., 2017; Ferrer-i-Cancho & Solé, 2001; Vitevitch & Castro, 2015). The use of network science in studies on word

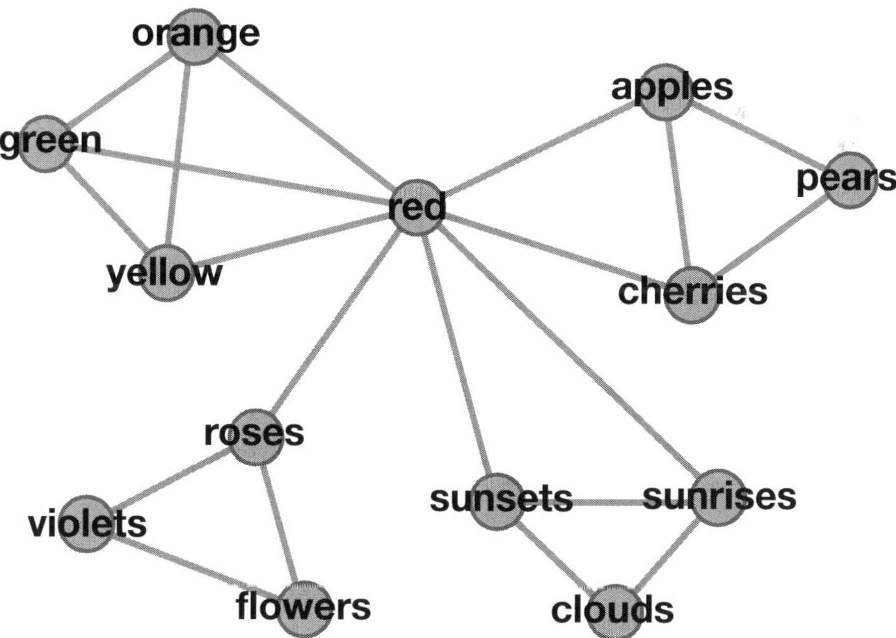

Figure 3: A semantic network, adapted from Collins and Loftus (1975).

learning has gained popularity in recent years, with a surge in network-theoretical studies exploring phonological relationships in the mental lexicon (e.g., Castro & Vitevitch, 2022; Nguyen et al., 2022; Siew, Chern, & Castro, 2023; Vitevitch & Sale, 2023).

What follows now is an overview of the most important network measures, their application to phonological networks, and their meaning for psycholinguistic processes. This will be followed by mathematical modeling of these measures in phonological networks of English-as-a-second-language ('ESL') learners.

Network measures can relate to different slices or aspects of a network. In macro analysis, the focus is on the entire network and its overall design. Meso analysis delves into sub-groups of nodes or communities in a network, while micro analysis focuses on the individual constituents (nodes).

1.2.1 MICRO-LEVEL ANALYSIS

One way to understand network cohesion is to look at the role of individual nodes in it, and the location of nodes can be estimated with centrality (Scott, 1991). Node centrality is a crucial property influencing dynamical processes such as activation spreading, synchronization, and information transmission between nodes. Various metrics quantify aspects of node centrality in networks (see, e.g., Rodriguez, 2019). The ones with known or potential implications for phonological networks are discussed below (for mathematical details refer to Barabási, 2016; Rodriguez, 2019; Wasserman & Faust, 1994). Figure 4 illustrates how network positions of nodes are defined by the various centralities.

1.2.1.1 DEGREE CENTRALITY

This measure counts the number of links of a node and relates it proportionally to all other links in a network. It is equivalent to the notion of phonological neighbors in phonological networks. Degree centrality can be calculated with the following equation:

$$C_D(u)=\sum_{v\in V\setminus\{u\}} a_{uv}$$

where N is the total number of nodes in the network, *v* represents a particular node, and *u* is the node for which degree is measured. If the two nodes are linked, the adjacency matrix value a_{uv}=1. Degree centrality of a node is calculated by starting with 1 and adding values up to N. A node can potentially have a degree of up to N-1 if it is linked to all other nodes in a network.

In weighted networks, nodes are connected through edges with varying strengths, and the notion of degree centrality has been expanded to include the sum of all edge strengths between each node and its neighbors (Roberts, 1976). In phonological networks this can represent the phonological or phonetic distance between phonological neighbors (Luef, 2023). Words with numerous phonologically close neighbors (e.g., *bat*: pat, bad, bag) exhibit higher weighted degree centralities compared to neighbors with greater phonological distances between them (e.g., *fog*: dog, fig, for). The equation for weighted degree is expressed as:

$$C_D(u)=\sum_{v\in V\setminus\{u\}} w_{uv}$$

with *w* being the weighted adjacency matrix, in which $w_{uv}>1$ if nodes *u* and *v* are linked, and the value representing the exact weight of the edge (see Opsahl, Agneessens, & Skvoretz, 2010).

1.2.1.2 CLOSENESS CENTRALITY

This measure accounts for the length of the shortest paths from a given node to all other nodes in a network, providing an estimate of the speed of information flow from one node to all others. Closeness of a node is defined as:

$$C_{Cl}(v)=1/\sum_{w\in V} d_{v,w}$$

The distance matrix value $d_{v,w}$ represents the shortest path between nodes v and w, and the sum of path lengths from node v to all other nodes is considered. Closeness centrality scores range from 0 to 1, with 1 indicating that a node is close to all other nodes (Metcalf & Casey, 2016). While there are conceptual similarities to degree centrality, closeness centrality is a mathematically different measure and not correlated with degree centrality (Ko, Lee, & Park, 2008). In highly-connected networks, a large number of nodes may show similar closeness centralities, making the measure best suited for sub-groups of nodes in a network (Salavati, Abdollahpouri, & Manbari, 2019). Eccentricity is the opposite of closeness centrality and measures the maximum distance of a node from any other node in the network. The maximum eccentricity value is the graph diameter.

Phonological word forms that show high closeness centrality can efficiently spread co-activation in phonological networks, as they have short path distances to numerous other nodes. Studies have reported an impact of closeness centrality on lexical processing (Goldstein & Vitevitch, 2017; Iyengar, Veni Madhavan, Zweig, & Natarajan, 2012; Nguyen et al., 2022), but some effects seem counterintuitive to standard lexical processing theories. Goldstein and Vitevitch (2017) found a recognition advantage for words with high closeness centrality. Contrary to the many-neighbors-disadvantage postulated by models of word recognition, words close to many others in the lexicon were retrieved faster and more accurately. The authors explain their findings by hypothesizing an accumulation of partial activation benefits over time that strengthens cognitive representations of central words with high closeness centrality scores, even-

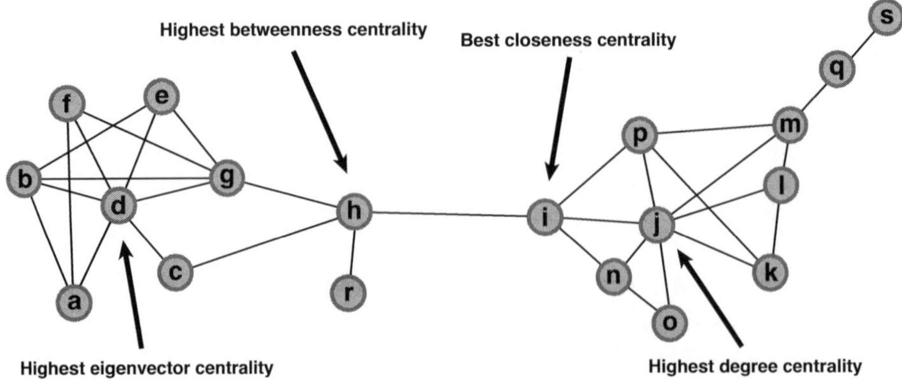

Figure 4: Degree, closeness, betweenness, and eigenvector centralities in a network.

tually leading to a lexical access advantage. This accrual of partial activation through activation of neighbors may occur over time as the lexicon ages. Specifically, Goldstein and Vitevitch (2017) state that the "accrued partial activation can yield processing benefits in the future" (p. 8). It may be assumed that during the course of vocabulary build-up, words with high closeness centrality scores become strengthened, benefit from a lexical processing advantage, and play a more central role in the growth of a phonological network.

1.2.1.3 BETWEENNESS CENTRALITY

Betweenness measures the times a given node lies on the shortest path between other nodes; specifically, it calculates the percentage of shortest paths that pass through a node (Goldbeck, 2015). Nodes with high betweenness centrality function as 'bridges' linking groups of nodes. They represent crucial points that govern the information flow in a network. The following equation yields betweenness scores:

$$C_B(v) = \sum_{s \neq v \neq t} (\sigma_{st}(v)/\sigma_{st})$$

where σ_{st} stands for the total number of geodesic distances from node *s* to node *t* and $\sigma_{st}(v)$ is the number of those paths that lead through *v*. Weighted networks take into account edge weights, and a node's betweenness score in a weighted network is given by the sum of the weights of its adjacent edges

$$C_{wB}(i) = \sum_{j=1}^{N} a_{ij} w_{ij}$$

where a_{ij} and w_{ij} are adjacency and weight matrices between the nodes *i* and *j*. A higher betweenness score is assigned to a node with many strong (high weight) edges. In phonological networks, certain words occupy key positions with higher betweenness centrality. Previous research suggests that words in strategic key positions of a phonological network are strengthened by repeated co-activation (or partial activation) received through nearby word activation, leading to lexical processing advantages (Vitevitch & Goldstein, 2014). Words with high betweenness centrality play an important role in the community structure of a network (i.e., sub-grouping of nodes according to similarity) and foster cohesion between phonological sub-groups in the network (Gerometta, 2015).

1.2.1.4 EIGENVECTOR CENTRALITY

This centrality measure scores nodes based on their influence in a network by considering the number of neighbors and their centralities (Bonacich, 1972, 2007). Highly-connected nodes (=high degree centrality) that are linked to other highly-connected nodes are deemed most influential in a network. Eigenvector centrality is a suitable measure when assuming that a node's status is positively influenced by the status of its neighbors (Bonacich & Lloyd, 2015). Various mathematical algorithms, accounting for features like edge centrality (Xu, Feng, & Qi, 2021), different interaction patterns between nodes (Carreras, Miorandi, Canright, & Engo-Monsen, 2007), the number of interactions between nodes ('Katz centrality': Katz, 1953), and link quality between nodes ('PageRank': Page, Brin, Motwani, & Winograd, 1998) can be used to calculate eigenvalue and eigenvectors for networks. Generally, neighbors with high-scoring eigenvector centrality will contribute more to the eigenvector centrality score of the target node than links with low-scoring nodes, following the logic that not all neighbors are equal. The information that is available to a node is limited to what the neighbors pass on, and highly central neighbors possess more information. In phonological networks, high eigenvector centrality of a node indicates more efficient activation spreading through highly-central node connections. Vitevitch et al. (2011) and Chan and Vitevitch (2009) propose that eigencentrality-centered search algorithms, akin to those described by Griffiths, Steyvers, and Firl (2007) for semantic search, could facilitate lexical retrieval.

1.2.2 ASSORTATIVITY BY DEGREE

Another graph-theoretical concept that has been shown to have an effect on phonological networks is assortativity by degree, also known as 'assortative mixing by degree' or 'homophily' (see Peel, Delvenne, & Lambiotte, 2018). It refers to the extent to which nodes link to other nodes that have similar degrees within a network. It is calculated as a correlation between two node degrees, often expressed as Pearson's assortativity coefficient, also known as degree correlation r (Newman, 2002). Positively assorted networks show clustering of high-degree nodes, whereas negatively assorted networks (=disassortative networks) show a propensity for high-degree nodes to link up with low-degree nodes. Assortativity by degree is generally high in phonological networks (r=0.56 – 0.76, in Arbesman et al., 2010; Luef, 2023; Vitevitch, 2008). This implies that high-density neighborhoods tend to link to other high-density neighborhoods, and low-density neighborhoods tend to link to other low-density neighborhoods (see Gravino, Servedio, Barrat, & Loreto, 2012; Van Rensbergen, Storms, & De Deyne, 2015, for similar findings in semantic networks). Vitevitch (2008) proposes that assortative mixing in phonological networks presents advantages for lexical processing: if disassortative mixing is the rule, the distribution of highly connected nodes throughout the network will result in wide activation spreading among a large number of nodes. This means that numerous lexical competitors would have to be processed for each word recognition event, leading to slower and more laborious speech recognition. In highly assortative networks, activation spreading and lexical competition remain more localized, facilitating more efficient and quicker lexical retrieval. The implications of high degree assortativity and lexical processing are twofold. Accumulation of phonological neighbors in confined areas of a phonological network facilitates production but inhibits retrieval of words (Chen & Mirman, 2012; Dell & Gordon, 2003). With speech perception being generally slowed by co-activation of numerous neighbors (Luce & Pisoni, 1998; McClelland & Rogers, 2003), Arbesman et al. (2010) argue that low rates of degree assortativity in phonological networks strengthen lexical representations and reduce retrieval errors. Conversely, high assortativity in phonological networks could indicate a lexical organization that favors production processes, potentially speeding up speech production.

Assortativity also has implications for network robustness, and networks with positive assortative mixing are less vulnerable to targeted removal of high-degree nodes (Newman, 2002). If one highly connected word is lost in an assortative network, it has only a minor impact on the overall connectivity and activation spreading patterns within a network (McClelland, Rumelhart, & Hinton, 1986). If one highly connected node is lost in a disassortative network, major implications arise for overall connectivity, with network break-down as a likely outcome (Newman, 2002). This prediction aligns with findings from a study on misperceived words, so-called "slip of the ear" errors, in American English. Vitevitch, Chan, and Goldstein (2014) identified a correlation between neighborhood density/node degree produced by speakers and those misheard by listeners. The observation that the misheard word and the correct word were from similar assortative neighborhoods indicates that speech recognition relies on assortative patterns governing a phonological neighborhood.

1.2.3 MACRO-LEVEL ANALYSIS

1.2.3.1 NETWORK COMPONENTS

Macro analyses of networks traditionally deal with a range of graph theoretical constructs, such as the *giant component*, *islands*, and *singleton nodes* or hermits (Barabási, 2016). Of significant interest in network science is the giant component, which is the

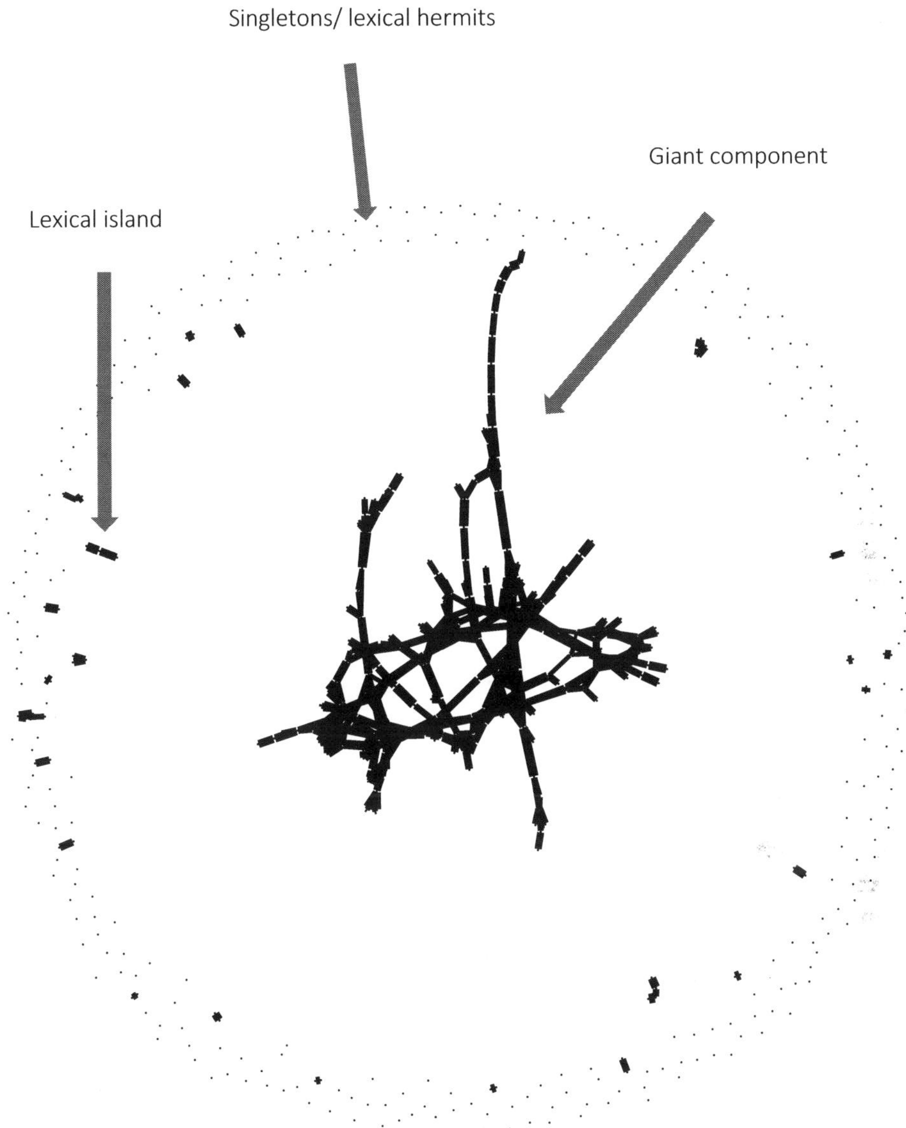

Figure 5: The giant component of a phonological network is located at the center and is surrounded by lexical islands (=smaller linked components) and singleton words (=gray dots). Yifan-Hu visualization in Gephi.

largest connected portion of a network (see Figure 5) that allows each node to reach any other node by "traversing a suitable path of intermediate collaborators" (Newman, 2004, p. 5202). The size of the giant component determines the shortest (geodesic) distance between two random nodes (Barabási & Albert, 1999), and provides information about the topological structure of a network. Giant component formation is not necessarily related to the number of nodes in a network, and small networks may have large giant components. Assortative mixing influences giant component growth. Positive assortative mixing by degree can contribute to the enlargement of the giant component over time, as high-degree nodes tend to link to other high-degree nodes (Newman, 2002). Disassortative mixing by degree may result in the dynamic where high-degree nodes are less likely to join the giant component, maintaining smaller components in the network.

Islands, referred to as "lexical islands" in language networks, are smaller, interconnected components that are not part of the giant component (Arbesman, Strogatz, & Vitevitch, 2010). Singleton nodes, or "lexical hermits", are isolated nodes with no connections. Figure 5 depicts the macro level network components of a phonological network.

1.2.3.2 CONNECTIVITY

The beta index (β) is a simple connectivity measure that represents the ratio of edges to vertices within a network (Arbesman et al., 2010). It is expressed by the relationship of the number of edges (e) over the number or nodes (v), equaling $\beta = e/v$. This index is a valuable indicator of network efficiency (Linehan, Gross, & Finn, 1995). Beta values greater than 1 signify more complex connectivity (Haggett & Chorley, 1972), while $\beta=1$ indicates circular connectivity, and $\beta<1$ suggests a tree-like dendogrammatic network. An efficient network with a high β value links a large number of nodes together, minimizing average path lengths and geodesic distance. An efficient network where nodes can easily link to one another and exchange or spread information is also characterized by short path lengths between nodes and a small network diameter (which is defined as the longest path of the shortest paths across a network; Latora & Marchiori, 2001). The mean path length (ℓ) is the average of all path lengths in a network and is estimated as:

$$\ell = 1/[N(N-1)] \sum_{i \neq j \in V} d_{ij}$$

where N is the number of nodes in a network and d_{ij} denotes the shortest distance between nodes *i* and *j* (see Watts & Strogatz, 1998). The network diameter δ is found by calculating all the shortest paths between all nodes following the equation

$$\delta = \max\{s(i, j)\}ij$$

with $s(i,j)$ being the number of edges in the shortest path from node *i* to node *j*. The longest of all paths is then chosen as the network diameter.

In phonological networks, path length and the diameter of the giant component are crucial measures indicating how densely words are distributed in phonological space in a lexicon. Words are connected beyond their immediate neighborhoods, and even distant words linked to a target via multiple paths, can become lexical competitors (Suarez et al., 2011). Vitevitch, Goldstein, and Johnson (2016) found that phonological associations more frequently involved words from distant neighborhoods when the target word had a sparse neighborhood (low-degree target word). Here, activation was suggested to spread out from the immediate neighborhood, as only a few near neighbors contained the activation diffusion close to the target word. This is analogous to the notion of near and distant neighbors in semantic neighborhood analysis. Near semantic neighbors are thought to exert inhibitory effects, but distant neighbors facilitate semantic processing (see Mirman & Magnuson, 2008). This is explained by a competition effect, where semantically similar words (=near neighbors) heighten competition, while distant neighbors create a graviational gradient that helps identify the correct attractor (=target word) without subsuming excessive activation which would slow down recognition. Vitevitch and colleagues argue that this dynamic may also apply to phonological processing.

1.2.3.3 NEIGHBORHOOD CLUSTERING

Many networks have a tendency to form links between neighboring nodes, a process known as clustering. Node clustering is quantified by the clustering coefficient (CC), calculated using the equation:

$$CC = 2e_n/(k_n(k_n-1))$$

with k_n being the number of neighbors per node (n) and e_n the number of connected pairs between all neighbors (Watts & Strogatz, 1998). Hence, CC=0 if none of the neighbors of a node are linked, and CC=1 if all are. Figure 6 illustrates neighborhood clustering in the phonological neighborhood of the English word "mass". In probabilistic terms, the clustering coefficient expresses the likelihood of a connection between two arbitrary neighbors of a node. Clustering coefficients in phonological networks assess the number of phonological neighbors of a target word that are also neighbors of one another (Goldstein & Vitevitch, 2014).

Words with low clustering coefficients (i.e., low-C words) have been found to be recognized faster and more accurately in spoken word recognition (Chan & Vitevitch, 2009; Luef, 2025; Yates, 2013), similar to the effects of neighborhood density on word recognition (e.g., Luce & Pisoni, 1998; Vitevitch & Rodriguez, 2004). Neighborhood density and clustering coefficient are distinct measures, with neighborhood density accounting for the number of neighbors and the clustering coefficient accounting for neighborhood connections between neighbors. The two measures are generally not correlated (Chan & Vitevitch, 2009; Yates, 2013). In the realm of word production, the clustering coefficient behaves differently compared to neighborhood density, with low-C words being produced faster and more accurately (Chan & Vitevitch,

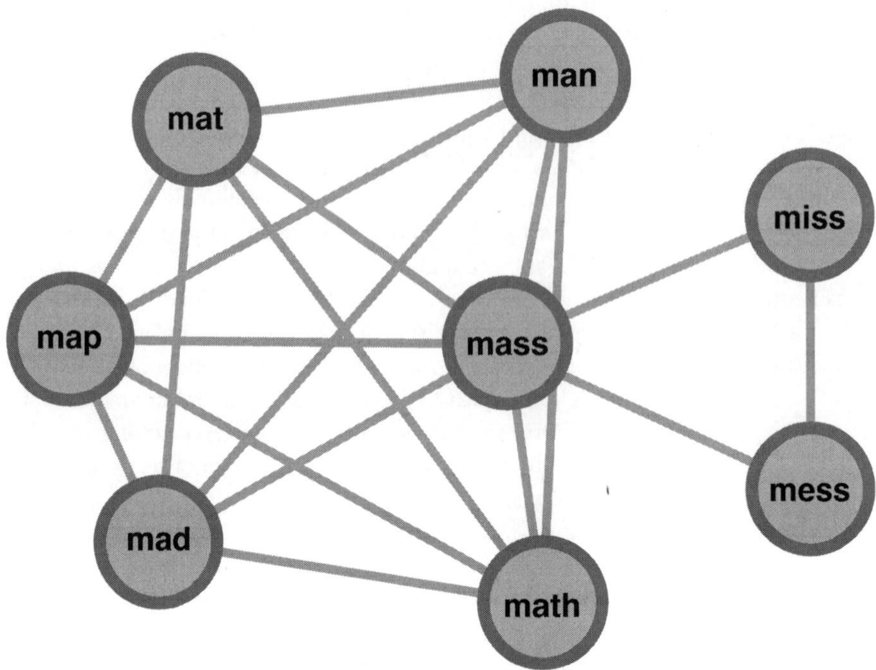

Figure 6: Links between neighbors of the target word can be quantified with the clustering coefficient, which equals 0.52 for the mass-neighborhood.

2010). High clustering coefficients of phonological neighborhoods seem to influence lexical recognition and production, a finding potentially linked to the diffusion of activation across a lexical network. Regarding language acquisition, clustering coefficients have been shown to be indicative in children acquiring the semantics of their first language. Normally developing children exhibit higher clustering coefficients in their semantic networks than those who were delayed in their semantic development (Beckage et al., 2011).

A macro-level network measure closely related to the clustering coefficient is transitivity, which represents the probability of adjacent nodes being connected (Luce & Perry, 1949; Newman, Strogatz, & Watts, 2002). Values for transitivity are bounded between zero and one, with higher values indicating better transitivity. While conceptually similar, transitivity differs mathematically from the clustering coefficient and typically leads to different values (Schank & Wagner, 2005). Specifically, the consideration of triangles (or triads) of nodes constitutes a crucial difference in the two measures. Triads are subgraphs between three nodes in a graph, which can all be linked to one another (the triangle), not linked at all (the null triad), or show some links (e.g., one-edge-subgraph). The clustering coefficient takes into account the ratio of the number of triangles of a node in relation to the number of potential triangles that could involve that node. Transitivity accounts for the total number of triangles in a network divided by the total number of triads (Estrada, 2016). A transitive triad is a group of three nodes which are completely interconnected; an intransitive triad may only have two edges. The transitivity equation is as follows:

T=3t/P_2

where t represents the triangles in a network and

$P_2 = \sum_{i=1}^{N} k_i(k_i - 1)/2$ (see Wasserman & Faust, 1994)

Network transitivity is commonly applied in undirected graphs (Newman et al., 2002). Both clustering coefficient and transitivity have been computed for phonological networks (Arbesman et al., 2010; Chan & Vitevitch, 2009). In the present work, global transitivity will serve as an indicator of network connectivity across the whole network, whereas clustering coefficients will be determined for individual nodes, estimating the interconnectedness of a node's immediate neighborhood.

1.2.3.4 SMALL-WORLDNESS

Networks characterized by short average path lengths and high clustering coefficients (or transitivity) are known as small-world networks (Watts & Strogatz, 1998). Such networks exhibit exceptionally dense connectivity patterns, enabling fast and efficient information propagation (see Figure 7). The small-world coefficient σ proposed by Humphries and Gurney (2008) compares the ratio of network transitivity (T) and path length (ℓ) to their equivalents in a random network. The conditions for a small-world network are defined as $T \gg T^{rand}$ *and* $\ell \approx \ell^{rand}$, which results in $\sigma > 1$.

Phonological networks display features of small-world structuring (Gerometta, 2015; Vitevitch, 2008). They are optimally designed for rapid and robust lexical retrieval processes (Goldstein & Vitevitch, 2014), as the short distances between words in a small-worldish lexicon offer advantages for lexical search. Kapatsinski (2006) argues that small-worldness and/or short average path lengths are not required for efficient lexical retrieval, as lexical search is generally restricted to small localized neighborhoods that share sublexical similarity features. In this context, short path lengths across the giant component or the overall network play a minor role.

Small-world networks naturally spread lexical co-activation more widely, encompassing a larger number of neighbors and neighborhoods. As a target word becomes activated and neighbors become co-activated, their neighbors also receive some of the co-activation. This cycle of activation bouncing back and forth within the tightly interlinked neighborhood can trap activation within it, potentially resulting in delays in word recognition.

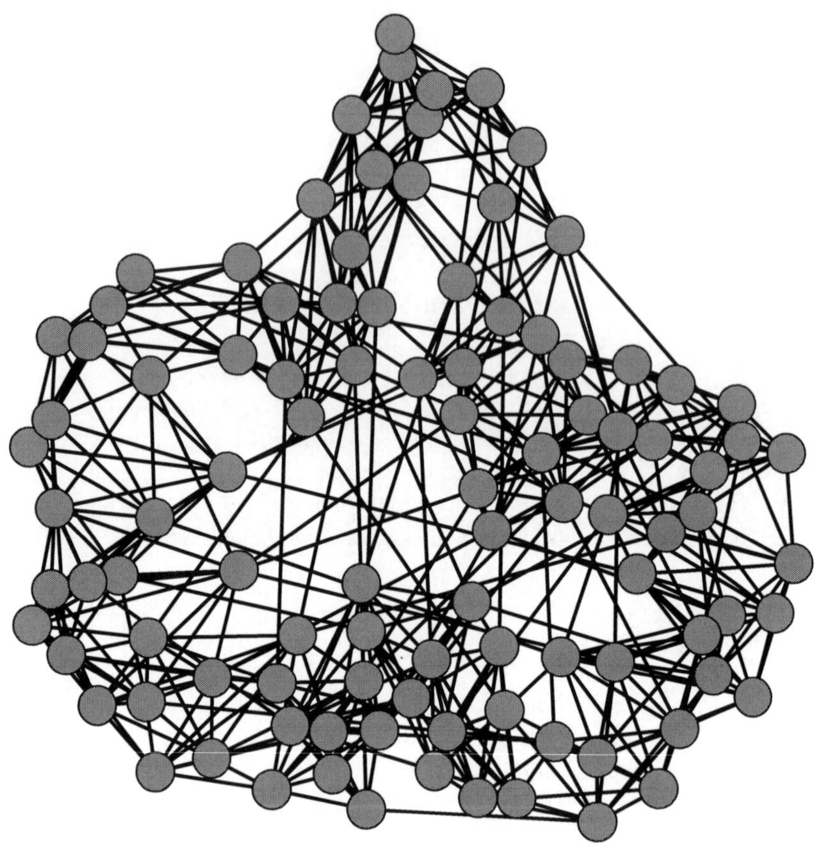

Figure 7: A small-worldish network where numerous nodes are connected. Constructed with the function "watts.strogatz.game" of the R package "igraph".

1.2.4 MESO-LEVEL ANALYSIS

In addition to the macro and micro level analyses that are commonly performed on networks, another layer of mesoscopic dimension exists between the two. Here, the focus is on smaller sub-graphs embedded within the larger network, a natural tendency of nodes to cluster together in so-called *communities* (Ravasz & Barabási, 2003; see Figure 8). Communities are groups of similar nodes in a network. They can play an important role for network structure (Barabási, 2016). Complex networks become partitioned into smaller and more interpretable parts. Mesoscopic analysis provides the means to uncover coarse-grained network interactions and relations related to community behavior (Hoffmann, Peel, Lambiotte, & Jones, 2020).

In graph theoretical terms, communities are characterized by the interconnectedness of their nodes, where each node must be linked to every other node or be ac-

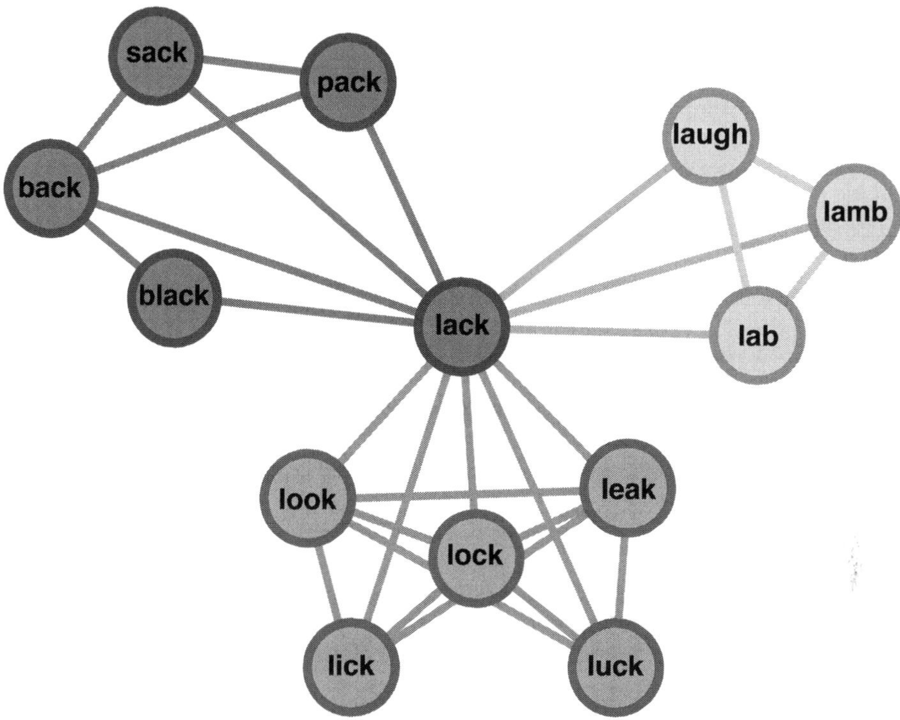

Figure 8: Communities in the phonological neighborhood of "lack".

cessible through other nodes in the community. Moreover, nodes belonging to a community show a higher likelihood of being linked to other nodes within that same community rather than nodes outside of it (Porter, Onnela, & Mucha, 2009). Nodes with high betweenness centrality play a pivotal role in community formation by serving as bridges that link different sub-groups together. There are various methods for community detection, including modularity (Newman & Girvan, 2004). The starting point here is maximization of difference between actual number and expected number of edges in a community, which undergoes repeated optimization. One of the most popular optimization methods is the so-called Louvain algorithm (Blondel, Guillaume, Lambiotte, & Lefebvre, 2008) and it has proven useful in community detection in phonological networks (Siew, 2013; Siew et al., 2023). A modularity value Q quantifies the density of links within communities in comparison to the density of links between communities (Newman, 2006). It is mathematically defined as

$$Q=\sum_{i=1}^{k}(e_{ii}-a_i^2)$$

with e_{ii} representing the probability that edge e is in module i, and a_i^2 representing the probability that a random edge would be classified into module i. Q ranges from -1 to 1. A high Q value close to 1 indicates that more edges are found within a module than would be expected by chance (Schaub, Delvenne, Rosvall, & Lambiotte, 2017). It is a good indicator that community structure is well optimized within a network. The Louvain method (a so-called 'greedy heuristic', Blondel et al., 2008) first puts each node in its own cluster and then repeatedly merges two clusters that increase modularity by the largest amount. The process ends when all merges lead to reduction of modularity (or Q).

Few studies have explored communities within phonological networks. Siew (2013) found that community size can predict various lexical characteristics of words in the lexicon of American English first-language users. Large communities tend to include phonemically shorter and more frequent words of higher node degree. They are acquired relatively early during childhood language acquisition (see Siew, 2013). This has implications for language learning/acquisition: the early stages of language learning may be geared toward building robust communities as a foundation for future lexical expansion. Supporting this notion, a phonological network analysis of British English child-directed speech revealed a higher prevalence of larger communities compared to an adult-directed network (Luef, 2024). These findings imply that infants might benefit from exposure to larger phonological communities, potentially influencing their preference for acquiring words within those communities.

In 2023, Siew, Chern and Castro conducted a comparative analysis of community structure in phonological networks across various (European) languages. Their findings indicate that these languages display robust community structures in their phonological lexica. Specifically, the languages tend to group shorter and more frequent word forms with numerous phonological neighbors within larger communities. Community structure in phonological networks is suggested to influence the flow of lexical activation among neighboring words and communities: communities can effectively contain activation, thereby limiting the phonological search space and reducing lexical competition (Siew, 2013). By keeping activation within a community with minimal spill-out, each word within the community receives a larger share of the activation, excluding competitor words from the activation loop. Community formation is suggested to play a crucial role in activation-competition restriction and optimization of lexical retrieval. There is undoubtedly great utility of the network community concept for phonological networks in terms of word learning and the efficiency of lexical access in the mental lexicon.

1.2.5 ACTIVATION SPREADING IN THE PHONOLOGICAL NETWORK

Diffusion theory, also known as diffusion dynamics, is the analysis of how an innovation or a bit of information spreads through an interconnected network. Various diffusion models have been proposed in the network literature (e.g., Dearing, 2008; Gomez-Rodriguez, Leskovec, & Krause, 2012; Ren, Yang, Yang, Xu, & Yang, 2012; Rogers, 2003; Zhang & Gan, 2018). Diffusion processes typically comprise three components: the population where they unfold, the mechanisms governing their evolution and development, and the content of the diffusion (Milli, Rossetti, Pedreschi, & Giannotti, 2018). There are two main branches of diffusion modeling, each characterized by different predictions for overall network behavior: (1) purposeful information spreading and (2) non-selective information spreading (Wang et al., 2011). Purposeful spreading refers to the nodes' ability to suppress information transfer. For instance, humans tend to spread information purposefully in their social networks – not every individual will share information with all those they interact with. Such selective spread of information is complex to model, requiring consideration of various factors that explain people's motivations to share information selectively (see, e.g., Alexy, George, & Salter, 2013). Non-selective spreading, on the other hand, follows the simple rule that each node 'infects' all of its neighboring nodes (e.g., Keeling & Eames, 2005). While a number of factors can influence spreading patterns, nodes generally lack the ability to prevent the transmission of information to another node upon interaction. Non-selective network propagation models originated from viral spreading models (including computer viruses, Kephart & White, 1991), but there are crucial differences when applying them to activation spreading in phonological networks. In viral spreading, social agents or computers do not always transmit the virus due to factors like physical proximity or anti-virus software. In phonological networks shared phonemes reliably become co-activated by neighboring words during lexical processing. There is no mechanism making a neighboring node resistant to activation reception. Thus, activation of phonological word forms consistently leads to co-activation of shared phonemes with neighbors in a phonological network, absent inhibitory mechanisms (see Berg and Schade, 1992a, 1992b; Kleinman and Gollan, 2019).

Two categories of virus propagation models are commonly recognized: homogeneous and heterogeneous models. In homogeneous networks, all nodes are fully interconnected, and viruses propagate without dependence on network typology (Zhu & Cen, 2017). Heterogeneous networks are not fully interconnected, and their typological structure plays an important role in determining how viral infection can spread between nodes (Kjaergaard, Brander, & Poulsen, 2010). Not all nodes can reach all others, and viruses may remain localized to specific parts of the network. Phonological networks are characterized as heterogeneous: singleton nodes, lexical islands, and the giant component cannot spread information to one another.

A number of network-relevant measures have been implicated in activation spreading in phonological networks, chief among them the overall network typology. The sizes of the giant component and the islands, as well as the ratio of singleton nodes all have influence on the ability of individual nodes to exchange activation. Larger giant components result in more and more wide-spread diffusion of activation, encompassing a broader array of words (Siew & Vitevitch, 2016). Networks containing many small islands and/or unconnected singleton nodes will experience minimal activation diffusion. In terms of lexical processing, the latter scenario leads to less lexical competition as there are fewer co-activated words. This can have great lexical retrieval benefits (Siew & Vitevitch, 2016). Clustering coefficients of network parts, together with the small-worldness of the entire network, have a crucial impact on activation diffu-

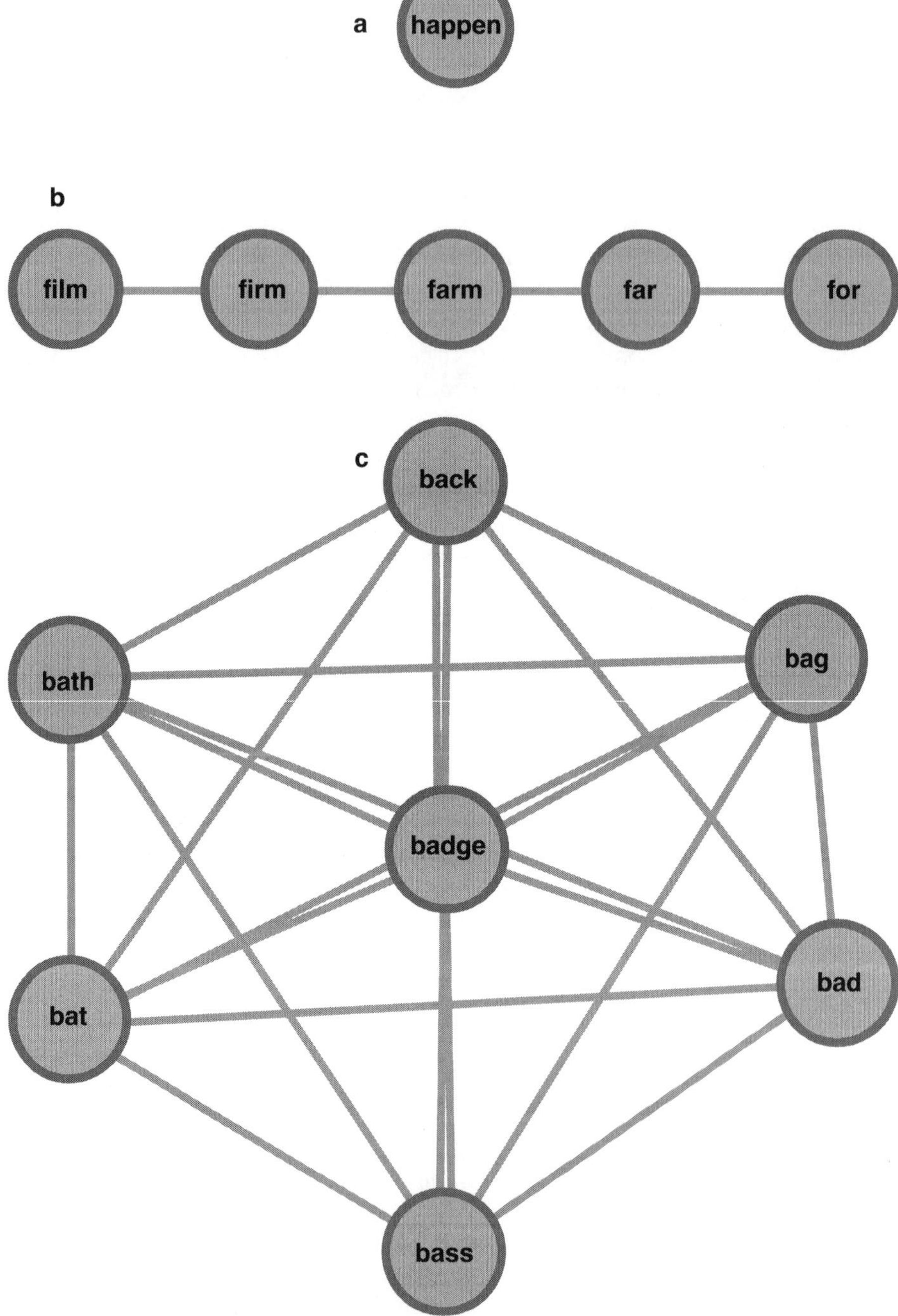

Figures 9a–c: Activation-restricting network parts are smaller, less-connected entities (a, b). Activation-propagating network parts are larger, interconnected entities (c).

sion. Networks with low clustering coefficients generally exhibit a wider spread of information because there are fewer densely (or exclusively) interconnected regions. In contrast, networks with high clustering coefficients restrict information transmission to the interconnected regions, which are in turn less strongly linked to other areas of the network (Naug, 2008; Newman, 2003a). Lexical neighborhoods can either restrict or propagate activation. Figures 9a-c illustrate how activation can be localized to singleton nodes or less densely connected neighborhoods, and how it can be propagated by a highly interconnected neighborhood.

An activation diffusion theory for phonological networks was proposed by Chan and Vitevitch (2009) and further developed by Vitevitch and colleagues (2011). Activation starts with a node and spreads along phonological similarity paths to neighboring words, extending further to neighbors of neighbors. Some of the activation spreads back to the originally activated node, giving it an additional activation boost. Over time, activation accumulates in a specific node, which is ultimately retrieved as the target node. The more interconnected the neighbors are (such as in Figure 9c), the more activation bounces back and forth in the neighborhoods. The "badge" neighborhood displayed in Figure 9c, characterized by high interconnectedness and a high clustering coefficient (see Chan & Vitevitch, 2009), diffuses activation across all neighboring words, making it more difficult for listeners to resolve the lexical competition. In the case of the neighborhood shown in Figure 9b, the activation of "firm" spreads to "farm", with some rebounding to "firm" and some extending to "far". The overall activation received by "firm" surpasses that of any word in the 9b neighborhood, leading to faster and more efficient lexical recognition.

The diffusion model bears direct implications for lexical processing of words distributed across different parts of the phonological network. Words situated within the giant component are hypothesized to pose a greater challenge for retrieval due to the extensive activation that is perpetuated through the greater neighborhood. This heightened difficulty in retrieval was proven by Siew and Vitevitch (2016), who found that words in lexical islands and singleton nodes are more easily retrieved. When a node resides within the giant component, the activation diffuses to a greater degree, with each node in the giant component receiving a diminished share of the activation. Consequently, lexical retrieval is rendered more difficult and time-consuming (Siew & Vitevitch, 2016). A similar study by Vitevitch and Castro (2015) reports higher accuracy in the picture naming of words residing in islands and singleton words. Hence, lexical islands and singleton words possess a lexical retrieval advantage compared to words within the giant component (Siew & Vitevitch, 2016). In light of these findings, it would be anticipated that the giant component's size in a phonological network is an important determiner for speed and accuracy of lexical access. Furthermore, the network diameter seems relevant; longer distances in the giant component may result in faster dissemination of activation, reaching fewer distant neighbors. By contrast, a shorter diameter in the giant component allows for the diffusion of activation to extend farther, potentially encompassing more distant neighbors of the target word. The findings presented by Vitevitch and his colleagues (2015, 2016) are difficult to reconcile with psycholinguistic models of lexical processing, which would predict a processing advantage in the highly interconnected giant component that contains shorter and more frequent words (Siew & Vitevitch, 2016). Considering the correlation between word length and lexical frequency (Zipf's law) and the known lexical processing benefits that frequent words entail (see, e.g., Brysbaert, Mandera, & Keuleers, 2017, for a review of the word frequency effect), it is expected that giant component words are retrieved more efficiently. The diffusion model of lexical activation spreading offers a framework to explain the discrepancy between anticipated and actual findings concerning lexical access in giant component words. This highlights the imperative need to integrate a network-scientific approach into theories of lexical access.

Vitevitch and colleagues' (2011) diffusion model for lexical activation in phonological networks suggests an initial surge of activation at a target word. This node retains a proportional share of the activation and transmits the rest to its nearest neighbors. The transmitted activation is evenly distributed among all neighbors, and they, in turn, pass on activation to their neighbors while holding onto a portion of it. Computational simulations of this simple model by Vitevitch and colleagues successfully replicated lexical retrieval delays for highly connected words, as observed by Siew and Vitevitch (2016) in their experimental study. In a similar vein, Siew (2019) developed a simulation model based on the spreading patterns proposed by Vitevitch et al. (2011) and was able to reproduce the earlier results. Even though the activation diffusion model is preliminary and based on 24 mini networks (Vitevitch et al., 2011), it nonetheless offers an intriguing perspective on lexical processing, suggesting a potential analogy to diffusion dynamics. One significant caveat of the assumptions underpinning this diffusion model pertains to the distance between the phonological neighbors and the varying degrees of relatedness among them. Given the fact that closer phonological distances facilitate activation spreading, the lexical diffusion probability within phonological networks should be different for close and distant phonological neighbors.

Figure 10 illustrates the impact of phonological distances on lexical activation and how it can modify diffusion dynamics within a network. In Figure 10, the edges are labeled with numbers that represent similarity scores between phonological neighbors. These scores were computed using a feature-weighted phonological distance measurement, a method developed for comparative linguistics by Kondrak (2000) and Downey et al. (2008). In this scoring system, values range from 0 (indicating no similarity) to 100 (representing identical phonology).

Despite the relatively equal sum of all phonological distances in the two neighborhoods ("ache"=1228, mean=73, "a"=1239, mean=68), the "ache" neighborhood is characterized by a larger number of close relationships between words. Specifically, in the "ache" neighborhood, nine words exhibit phonological distances greater than 79, whereas in the "a" neighborhood, only five words share such close phonological proximity. Conversely, the "a"-neighborhood accommodates a higher count of words that are phonologically more distant from the target word (N=13), while the "ache"-neighborhood has fewer of these words (N=7). According to the diffusion account of pho-

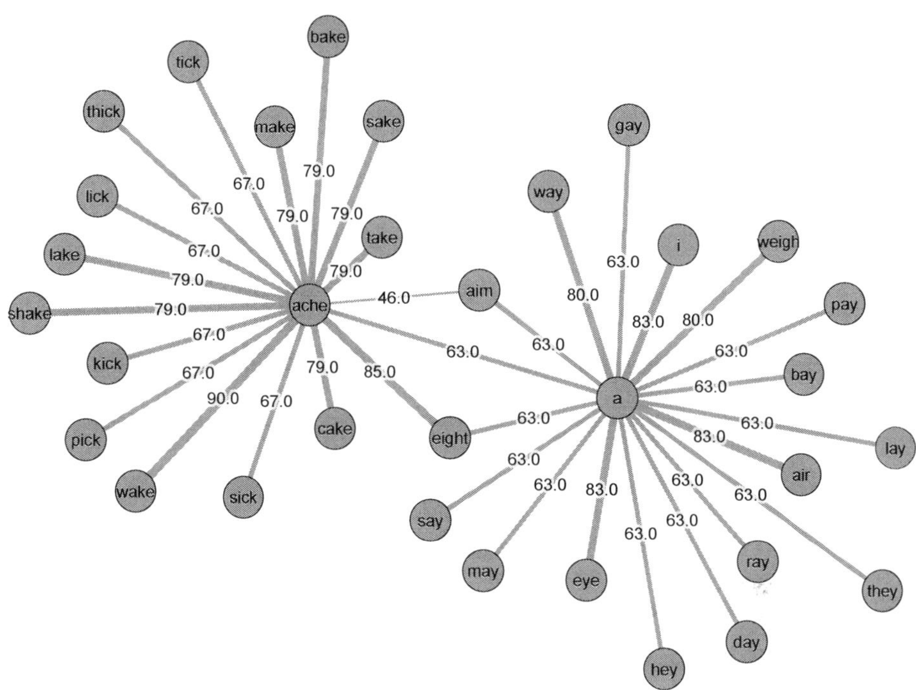

Figure 10: Phonological neighborhoods of "ache" (left) and "a" (right). The phonological distances are indicated by edge strength, and thick lines link close neighbors.

nological processing proposed by Vitevitch and colleagues (2011), activation diffuses similarly through both neighborhoods and is primarily restricted by the number of neighbors (i.e., node degree), which is comparable in the two neighborhoods (k"a"=18, k"ache"=16). However, it is plausible to assume that phonologically closer neighbors may share a larger portion of the overall activation, or, at the very least, activation spreads more rapidly through phonologically closer neighbors. This would naturally result in more nuanced diffusion patterns. For instance, more activation is assumed to spread from "ache" to "a" than vice versa, since "ache" passes on more activation to "eight", which then, in turn, transmits a portion of that to "a". Considering such detail in activation patterns can help refine the diffusion account of lexical spreading in phonological networks.

In the diffusion model, activation is assumed to "spread unimpeded between connected nodes" (Vitevitch et al., 2011: p. 11) without decaying over time. This, however, could lead to what has been referred to as "heat death problem" (Berg & Schade, 1992a), where an excessive activation of too many (irrelevant) words could lead to inefficient processing. As memory naturally decays with time, so too might node activation levels. The initial burst of activation in a phonological neighborhood might not persist until the activation cycle in the neighborhood concludes. For a target node to be selected as the lexical candidate, it must retain the largest share of the activation, and this accrual of activation can be hindered by activation decay. A spreading activation model by Bock and Levelt (1994) proposes a similar procedure but incorporates activation decay. In their model, activation signals spread through the mental lexicon along associations (both semantic and phonological), bounces back between associated words before ultimately converging on the target word. Many network diffusion theories integrate a time component, predicting that activation transmission will diminish over time (Liu & Kuan, 2016; Rogers, 2003). This temporal aspect recognizes the dynamic nature of activation processes in the spreading of information within a lexicon.

Vitevitch and colleagues (2011) identified several network measures that can serve as predictors for activation spreading: degree, clustering coefficient, and network density. Words with a low degree (i.e., few neighbors) and a low clustering coefficients in their immediate neighborhood tend to receive a larger proportion of overall activation in their neighborhood. Denser networks with more interconnected neighborhoods diffuse activation in a manner where target words only accumulate enough activation after a significant delay. The authors suggest that their model of activation spreading can effectively explain observed word recognition patterns in phonological networks, as seen in previous studies like Chan and Vitevitch (2009). This sheds light on how the structural characteristics of the network influence the dynamics of word activation and recognition.

1.2.6 OUTLOOK

Recent research has shown that network science can be useful to gain knowledge on lexical processing by extending beyond the localized measure of neighborhood density and providing a global perspective on the phonological word form lexicon. The diffusion hypothesis exemplifies that lexical activation for a target word is not solely contingent on its immediate neighborhood but also on the larger, interconnected network components of which the neighborhood is a member. The embedding of phonological neighborhoods within a larger network structure has opened up new research avenues that may potentially explain some of the discrepancies observed in past studies on phonological neighborhood density. Notably, studies on Spanish and Russian revealed contrasting effects compared to what is known for English. In these languages, words in dense neighborhoods impede word production but facilitate recognition (Arutiunian & Lopukhina, 2020; Vitevitch & Stamer, 2006; also see, e.g., Neergaard, Britton, & Huang, 2019; Sadat, Martin, Costa, & Alario, 2014; Vitevitch & Rodriguez, 2004, for conflicting results on phonological neighborhood density in relation to lexical retrieval/production in various languages). This contradicts findings in English and introduces complexity to the understanding of the phonological neighborhood effect. Future studies exploring predictions derived from a global network perspective of different lexica may contribute to explaining these effects and identifying common linguistic universals concerning neighborhoods and lexical processing.

An underexplored area within linguistic network sciences is the inquiry into how second language learners construct and grow their phonological networks. Studies have investigated semantic and syntactic word associations among second language learners of different languages, creating networks based on elicited words in experimental settings with both first- and second-language users of French (Wilks & Meara, 2002; Wilks, Meara, & Wolter, 2005) and English (Jiang, Yu, & Liu, 2019; Schur, 2007; Tanaka & Takahashi, 2019). Results from Wilks and colleagues indicate a higher semantic network density in the first language as compared to the second language, which influences linguistic performance in word-association tasks. The authors advocate for an inclusion of network theoretical notions in the investigation of second language word acquisition in the semantic domain. The exploration of phonological networks in the mental lexicon of second language learners is a more recent endeavor (Luef, 2022b, 2023). Given that phonological networks have yielded crucial insights into the study of the first-language lexicon, particularly regarding lexical processing and the acquisition of word form associations, extending this knowledge to second languages holds great potential for the study of L2 lexical processes. The subsequent sections of this book will explore phonological network structure in English as a second language across various proficiency levels and with a special emphasis on network growth and its utility for the study of L2 vocabulary learning. The presented findings aim to illuminate how the English L2 word form lexicon is organized and the potential implications this structure may have on lexical cognition at different stages of language learning.

2.
MODELING NETWORKS

2.1 CONSTRUCTING PHONOLOGICAL NETWORKS

The construction of phonological networks hinges on accurate vocabulary lists that closely align with language users' lexical knowledge. In prior studies, phonological networks of L1 English were based on dictionaries, such as the 'Hoosier Mental Lexicon' (see Nusbaum, Pisoni, & Davis, 1984), the 'Merriam-Webster Pocket Dictionary' from 1964, or the 'Webster Collegiate Dictionary' from 1967, which served as samples of English vocabulary known by adult native speakers (Arbesman et al., 2010; Siew, 2013; Vitevitch, 2008 & 2021; Vitevitch & Castro, 2015). In addition, language corpora - collections of English language material by native speakers in various contexts - have been utilized to construct phonological networks, drawing on resources like the CELEX database, 'WordNet', or the "British National Corpus' (e.g., Arbesman et al., 2010; Levy et al., 2021; Shoemark et al., 2016; Stella & Brede, 2015). Moreover, empirical data collected through lexical experiments, such as phonological associations tasks, have also served the foundation for English phonological networks (Castro & Vitevitch, 2023).

In order to investigate the various stages of a developing lexicon, phonological networks of L1-learning children have been constructed based on age of acquisition norms for English. These norms, such as those found in the MacArthur-Bates Communicative Development Inventory (Dale & Fenson, 1996), define lexical entries per age group and inform about which words children acquire at which age (see Beckage et al., 2015, Fourtassi, Bian, & Frank, 2020). Siew and Vitevitch (2020a) used the age-of-acquisition norms reported by Kuperman and colleagues (2012) for constructing snapshots of a developing English phonological network. Researchers often integrate these norms with language acquisition corpora of child speech, such as the 'Chicago Corpus' (see Carlson, Sonderegger, & Bane, 2014), or 'Wordbank' (see Fourtassi, Bian, & Frank, 2020).

Compiling the complete vocabulary of English as a second language learners at various proficiency stages is more complex than it is for English as a first language. Unlike first language knowledge, which can be defined according to dictionaries, there is a lack of such resources for second languages. This limitation leaves corpus data as the primary avenue for constructing lexica that represent lexical knowledge of English learners at different proficiency stages. It is important to note that usage-base learner corpora can hardly reflect the entire lexical knowledge of a learner. The tasks with which the corpus data was collected can only elicit a limited number of known words of the learners (Gráf, 2017). This inherent corpus-study problem equally applies to all types of linguistic corpus research but is particularly pronounced in a study that intends to describe a lexicon. To alleviate this issue, it becomes essential to obtain large-scale vocabulary data of different proficiency stages of language learning.

The present study utilized data from the Cambridge Learner Corpus (CLC), the largest corpus of English as a foreign language. The corpus comprises student exams and was collaboratively compiled with the Cambridge English Language Assessment. It contains linguistic data from over 180,000 students of English from approximately 200 countries and 138 different first languages. Designed to articulate English learners' competencies at various stages of the language learning process (McEnery, Brezina, Gablasova, & Banerjee, 2019), the CLC follows the proficiency guidelines set by the 'Common European Framework of Reference for Languages', ranging from the lowest proficiency stage A1 to the highest C2. While the raw data of the CLC is not freely accessible, the consortium overseeing the corpus publishes websites where specific aspects of the corpus data are made available to interested researchers. The *English Vocabulary Profile* (or 'EVP') is the online resource on vocabulary of L2 English learners in the corpus (English Vocabulary Profile, n. d.) and it documents vocabulary knowledge for the six CEFR stages of language proficiency in English as a second language. The data in the EVP does not only stem from the corpus itself but is also augmented with data from leading coursebooks, vocabulary references, and standardized examination vocabulary lists (Key English Test or KET, Preliminary English Test or PET). The vocabulary lists within EVP include sub-categories for American British English varieties. The EVP is the most comprehensive resource on the lexical knowledge of ESL learners. Much of language acquisition research relies on the EVP vocabulary lists, and they form a reasonable basis for the construction of phonological networks of English learners.

2.1.1 ESL LEXICA

The British English vocabulary data for each proficiency level was extracted from the EVP website and organized in a spread sheet. Since the EVP word lists only include base words, manual sorting and correction efforts were minimal. Several cleaning processes were applied to enhance the quality of data:

- Removal of duplicate word forms that convey the same meaning, for instance "address"-noun, "address"-verb. Semantically unrelated homophones, such as "four" and "for" or "see" and "sea" were also merged.
- Dissolving of phrases in constituent parts (e.g., "think", "about", "something").
- Removal of abbreviations (e.g., "Dr", "Mrs"). Acronyms, such as "p.m." or "CD" were retained in the final data set.

- Removal of inflected word forms, except for all forms of the verbs "be" and "have" (e.g., "is", "had").
- Splitting of clitics into separate words (e.g., "it's" → "it", "is").

The data cleaning aimed to lemmatize and streamline the vocabulary data, ensuring its accuracy and coherence for purposes of analysis. Table 1 shows the resulting vocabulary size for each proficiency level.

Table 1: Vocabulary estimations for each CEFR proficiency level based on the English Vocabulary Profile. These networks are referred to as "ESL networks" or "learner networks".

A1	A2	B1	B2	C1	C2
606	1483	2901	4621	5632	6714

In a next step, the phonological transcriptions of the word forms, as provided by the EVP website (set to *British English*), were collected for all words across the proficiency level vocabularies. Vowel length symbols and stress indicators were removed from the IPA transcriptions. This was followed by further transcribing all IPA word forms into X-SAMPA ('Extended Speech Assessment Methods Phonetic Alphabet' or machine-readable phonetic transcriptions) using the online *Phoneverter* tool (Phoneverter, n. d.). The X-SAMPA transcriptions were necessary for determining one-segment neighbors in all six vocabularies in an Oracle database. Approximately 10% of the automatic X-SAMPA transcriptions were compared to manually coded transcriptions according to the SAMPA coding scheme developed by Wells (1997), and correspondence was 98%.

Phonological neighbors are defined as pairs of words that differ in only one segment via additions, deletions, and substitutions of phonemes (Levenshtein, 1966; Turnbull & Peperkamp, 2017; Vitevitch, 2008). To establish these relationships, Levenshtein distances were calculated pairwise for each word and with each other word in a proficiency lexicon. For instance, in the A1 network of 606 words, the phonological distance of each of the 606 words to each of the other 605 words was determined. This resulted in a very large number of possible combinations to be calculated and displayed that necessitated the use of an *Oracle* database, a multi-modal database management system capable of handling millions of rows of data. In Oracle 12c (see Bryla, 2015), the function "Edit Distance" (or "Levenshtein Distance") was employed to compare string similarities of paired X-SAMPA-transcribed words, such *'board'/ bOd* and *'aboard'/@bOd* in the A1 network. The output provided the number of character changes (so-called insertions, updates, and deletes) required to transform the first string into the second. This number is referred to as the "edit distance", and only edit distances of "1" were extracted for further analysis, as these represented the phonological neighbors.

Following the identification of phonological neighbors for each proficiency level word list, the phonological distances between phonological neighbors were further quantified. To achieve this, an alignment algorithm was computed to calculate phonological similarity scores for pairs of phonological neighbors. The *aline* algorithm, developed by Kondrak (2000) for the comparison of phonological similarity in language typology and evolution research, compares (weighted) features associated with phonological segments in word pairs. The R package "alineR" (Downey et al., 2017) is based on the *aline* algorithm and considers twelve features: syllabic, voice, lateral, high, manner, long, place, nasal, aspirated, back, retroflex, and round. The input in *alineR* are pairs of IPA-transcribed words for which a similarity score ranging between 0 (=indicating no distance between two words) and 1 (representing maximal phonological distance) is then calculated. The *alineR* results were subsequently transformed to reflect percentage agreement between two words: the values were reverse scaled and multiplied by 100. In this transformation, 0 reflects the least similarity, while a value of 100 reflects the greatest similarity between two segments. For instance, a value of 0.3 in *alineR* was transformed to a value of 70, signifying 70% similarity. Essentially, the *alineR* output of a distance score was converted to a similarity score. This rescaling was crucial for obtaining more intuitive edge strengths for the phonological networks: thicker edges indicate a closer relationship between two words, thinner edges indicate a more distant relationship. This approach provides a valuable measure of phonological distance between phonological neighbors, offering finer-grained distance measurements to test their relevance to lexical processing.

Several lexical variables were computed for each word at every proficiency level. First, lexical frequency rates of the words were obtained from the online British National Corpus and log-transformed using the formula *LOG(x+1)* to account for frequency rates of zero. The resulting values were then normalized by a factor of 100 and converted to integers for better clarity in network visualization. Second, the phonological lengths of the IPA-transcribed words were determined using the Microsoft Excel function "len", which counted the number of IPA symbols comprising the phonological transcription of a target word, excluding stress and length symbols. Third, phonotactic probabilities were calculated using the *Kansas University Phonotactic Probability Calculator* for English (Phonotactic Probability Calculator, n. d.). For this, each word was manually transcribed in computer-readable 'Klattese' (Vitevitch & Luce, 2004) before being processed by the software. Because the calculator is based on an American English database, all words had to be transcribed in American English as well (using *Tophonetics*). The Kansas University phonotactic probability calculator computes the sum of all positional probabilities of each segment per word, along with the sum of all biphone probabilities. A Pearson's correlation between the averages of both measures in the ESL dataset yielded r=0.6. The average biphone probabilities per word were selected as the variable "phonotactic probability" in the analysis.

2.1.2 L1 BRITISH ENGLISH NETWORK

The British National Corpus (or BNC, 2007) is a compilation of around 100 million words gathered from written and spoken language samples, specifically chosen to represent a broad cross-section of British English from the latter part of the 20th century. Its most recent release was in 2007.[2]

A word list containing all words in the BNC was downloaded and processed in a manner identical to that described for the learner corpus (including removal of duplicates and abbreviations, lemmatization, etc.). The final word count for the British vocabulary was 5376. Notably, the L1 British vocabulary was smaller than that of learners at the C1 and C2 levels (C1=5632 words, C2=6714 words). This difference is likely attributed to the fact that the majority of the ESL data stems from testing contexts, such as specific vocabulary or grammar tests, whereas the BNC data of the L1 British speakers was collected from naturally occurring speech and texts.

Similar to the ESL word lists, the BNC word list underwent IPA and X-SAMPA transcriptions, and phonological neighbors were determined with the Oracle database. Furthermore, for each BNC word, a log-transformed lexical frequency rate was calculated, phonological length per word (based on IPA transcriptions) was counted in Excel, and phonotactic probabilities (biphones) were computed. Lastly, phonological distances were established using the *aline* algorithm.

2.2 NETWORK PROPERTIES

Networks of learners' lexica and the L1 British users' lexicon were constructed with *Gephi*, an open-source software for network and graph analysis, widely used in network analysis (Bastian, Heymann, & Jacomy, 2009), and the R packages "qgraph" and "igraph" (Csardi & Nepusz, 2006; Epskamp, Cramer, Waldorp, Schmittmann, & Borsboom, 2012). Six distinct ESL networks were created for each proficiency level (referred to as "A1 network", "B2 network" etc., up to "C2 network"), along with one for L1 British English ("BNC network"). The graphs were formulated as undirected networks, featuring equal links between neighboring nodes. Edges were weighted based on the phonological distance measurements obtained from the *aline* algorithm. The following network statistics were calculated for each network:

- network size (number of nodes)
- number of edges

2 Data cited herein have been extracted from the British National Corpus Online service, managed by Oxford University Computing Services on behalf of the BNC Consortium. All rights in the texts cited are reserved.

- β coefficient
  - calculated by dividing the number of edges by the number of nodes, once for the whole network and once for the giant component
- size of the giant component (number of nodes and edges, percentage of overall network size)
- number and size of the islands
- number of singleton nodes
- average path length ℓ (whole network, giant component)
- clustering coefficient per node
- degree centrality per node
- weighted degree centrality per node
- closeness centrality per node
- betweenness centrality per node
- eigenvector centrality per node

Using the R package "igraph" (Csardi & Nepusz, 2006), the following variables were calculated:

- network diameter
- Pearson's assortativity coefficient
- global transitivity of network

Small-world coefficients for each of the seven networks were computed using the "smallworldness" function of the R package "qgraph" (Epskamp et al., 2012), taking into account the global transitivity of the network (Newman, 2003b) with 1000 iterations per network.

Community detection within the networks was performed using the "Modularity" function in Gephi, which utilizes the Louvain method of community computation. First, modules were created with the resolution set to "2" (as recommended by Siew, 2013, for phonological networks), and edge weights were included. Singleton nodes were excluded from the analysis, as each of them constitutes their own community. Modularity values (Q) were obtained, and each node was assigned a modularity class. These modularity classes were then extracted to spread sheets, where their sizes and the average values of the investigated network measures (degree, clustering coefficient, etc.) were calculated.

Network comparisons are complicated by the influence of network size on centrality measures. Closeness centrality, for instance, is highly dependent on network size, with larger networks typically yielding lower centrality measures. This is attributed to the increased number of connections that must be traversed to move from one node to another in larger networks. Freeman (1979) suggested normalizing centrality values to mitigate the impact of varying network sizes. To ensure comparability across differently sized ESL and BNC networks, z-scores of all network variables were used in subsequent analyses.

Distributions of network statistics such as node degree are crucial considerations in the network sciences (see debate in Broido & Clauset, 2019; Zhou, Meng, & Stanley, 2020). Especially power law distributions are frequently the subject of network investigations, as they represent specific assumptions about network structure in general and growth possibilities in particular. In such distributions, the mathematical relationship between variables is such that changes in one variable lead to proportional relative changes in the other variable, independent of the initial size of the variable quantities (Clauset, Shalizi, & Newman, 2009). Power laws are mathematically represented with the function

$$y=cx^{-\alpha}$$

with α being the power law exponent, and c an overall scale (or normalization). With changes in x, y either decreases or increases. When power laws are calculated for distributions, the exponent α is positive, and y decreases as x increases (Milojević, 2010). This means that events with a high value of a quantity are typically rare. Power law distributions can represent what is known as the 'Pareto principle' or the '80:20 rule' stating that 20% of causes lead to 80% of phenomena (Sanders, 1987). Perline (2005) suggested three different variants of power law distributions: (1) a strong power law, with all values of a variable falling into the category of power law, (2) a weak power law, where only a part of the distribution follows a power law, and (3) a false power law, where a truncated part of the distribution can mimic a power law, such as for instance in log-normal distributions, where only the upper tail approximates a power law.

The probability of a distribution adhering to a power law is calculated by comparing distribution probabilities involving other heavy-tailed distribution types (e.g., discrete log-normal, discrete exponential) and selecting the best fit based on comparative tests. The procedure of distribution fitting in the ESL networks started with an investigation of good candidates among a small set of heavy-tailed distributions, including log-normal, log-logistic, log-gamma, weibull, exponential, Pareto, and Burr. Using the R packages "fitdistrplus" (Delignette-Muller & Dutang, 2015) and "actuar" (specifically for log-logistic, Pareto, and Burr fitting) and the "plotdist" function, plots of the empirical cumulative distribution function (CDF plot) and the histogram on a density scale were obtained per investigated network (i.e., proficiency level). In addition to these classical goodness-of-fit plots, a Q-Q plot emphasizing a lack-of-fit at the distribution tails and a P-P plot emphasizing a lack-of-fit at the distribution center were analyzed per network. Next, different goodness-of-fit statistics were calculated with "fitdistrplus" in order to compare the fit of best-seeming candidate distributions as judged by the plots. Goodness-of-fit statistics measure the distance between a fitted parametric distribution and the empirical distribution (between the fitted cumulative distribution function F and the empirical distribution function F_n). The following goodness-of-fit statistics were calculated with the R function "gofstat": Cramer-von Mises, Kolmogorov-Smirnov, and Anderson-Darling statistics (as recommended by D'Agostino & Stephens, 1986). Distributions were compared by classical penalized criteria based on the log-likelihood (Akaike Information Criterion or AIC and Bayesian Information Criterion or BIC), with lower values indicating a preference for a particular distribution (Delignette-Muller & Dutang, 2015). The smallest values per goodness-of-fit statistic and goodness-of-fit criteria (AIC, BIC) were selected as the best fitting distribution for a given network.

As power laws can be difficult to mathematically quantify due to the fluctuations in the heavy tail and the fact that not all values of a variable x may follow a power law, the R package "poweRlaw" specifically designed to detect power laws and differentiate them from other, similar heavy-tail distributions (specifically for continuous data: power law with cutoff, exponential, stretched exponential, and log-normal; for discrete data: Yule, exponential, Poisson) was additionally used. The package is based on Clauset and colleagues' (2009) approach, who propose a rigorous power law validation procedure with maximum-likelihood fitting methods and goodness-of-fit tests based on the Kolmogorov-Smirnov statistic and likelihood ratios (see Gillespie, 2014, for details). A Monte-Carlo bootstrapping p-value is then calculated to evaluate the plausibility of a power law; and lastly, the power law model is compared to a set of alternative models. In practice, heavy-tailed distributions as identified by the first distribution fitting procedure (with "fitdistrplus") were further subjected to specific power law calculations with "poweRlaw". If power law was the best-fitting of the distributions compared by the package, a power law distribution was assumed for the data. This power law fitting procedure has increasingly been used in linguistic literature on statistical distributions in recent years (see, e.g., Macklin-Cordes & Round, 2020).

When histograms indicated a bi- or multimodal distribution, the R package "diptest" was used, which utilizes Hartigan's dip test to determine whether a distribution has more than one mode (see Maechler, 2013). P-values of less than 0.05 indicate significant bimodality, and values greater than 0.05 but less than 0.1 indicate bimodality with marginal significance (Hartigan & Hartigan, 1985).

2.3 MACRO-LEVEL NETWORK STATISTICS

The ESL learner networks and the BNC network differ in several of the central network measures. The C2 and BNC networks share similarities in certain aspects (such as assortativity coefficient, average degree in giant component, transitivity and β of the giant component). The BNC network stands out in other aspects where it does not resemble the learner networks (for instance, in terms of giant component size). Table 2 summarizes the main macro level network statistics calculated for the ESL and BNC networks.

Table 2: Overview of network statistics in the ESL and BNC networks.

	A1	A2	B1	B2	C1	C2	BNC
Network size (number of words)	606	1483	2901	4621	5632	6714	5378
Connectivity (number of edges)	583	1784	3748	5889	6717	8129	4866
Giant Component size (%)	44%	42%	38%	35%	31%	30%	13.2%
Pearson assortativity coefficient r	0.57	0.59	0.65	0.67	0.68	0.68	0.71
Average degree	1.9	2.4	2.6	2.5	2.4	2.4	1.8
Average degree in GC	4.1	5.3	6.2	6.7	6.7	7	7.2
Edges in GC (%)	94%	93%	92%	90%	89%	88%	52.3%
Average path length	7.42	6.03	5.9	5.9	6	6	5.1
Clustering coefficient	0.42	0.37	0.35	0.34	0.34	0.34	0.38
Ratio of edges to vertices/β	0.96	1.2	1.3	1.3	1.2	1.2	0.9
Ratio of edges to vertices/β (GC)	2.04	2.6	3.1	3.3	3.4	3.5	3.6

2.3.1 NETWORK CONNECTIVITY

The A1 lexicon comprises 606 nodes (i.e., words) and 583 edges (i.e., links between words), resulting in a beta (β) value of 0.96. This indicates a relatively sparsely connected lexical network, in contrast to the adult native L1 American English network, which has a β value of 1.61 in a study by Arbesman, Strogatz, and Vitevitch (2010). About 94% of all edges can be found in the A1 giant component, and the β of the giant component is 2.04 (in adult L1 English β= 4.55, Arbesman et al., 2010). As the lexica expand, word increases initially lead to higher connectivity between the nodes (β increase from A1 to A2 to B1). However, connectivity trails off at later proficiency stages (β decrease/plateau from B2 to C1 to C2). The β value of the giant component steadily and proportionally increases, indicating a consistent development from A1 to C2. Despite this, the number of edges in the giant component decreases as the networks grow. Compared to the L1 American English network described by Arbesman et al. (2010), where β=4.55, the learner networks exhibit substantially lower β values in the giant components. The BNC giant component contains 52.3% of all network edges, with a β value of 3.6, the highest of all seven networks.

The high β index of 1.6 calculated by Arbesman and colleagues (2010) for American English and that of 4.55 for the giant component is not reached by even the most advanced ESL learner proficiency level, although the BNC network comes close. This shows that dense interconnections of a large number of phonological neighbors is more pronounced in networks of L1 English users (both American and British). The L2 English networks are more sparsely interlinked, even in the absence of differences in lexicon size (note that the BNC network is smaller than the C1 and C2 networks). The giant components of the L1 English networks are especially tightly knit units, a dynamic possibly resulting from their smaller sizes compared to the ESL networks.

2.3.2 GIANT COMPONENTS, LEXICAL ISLANDS, AND SINGLETON WORDS

Like most networks, phonological networks can be divided into discrete network parts: the giant component as the largest cluster of linked entities, the smaller linked entities called islands, and non-linked stand-alone phonological isolate words. Among these, the giant component plays an outsized role as it represents an expanded phonological neighborhood where all words are connected through multiple degrees of phonological neighbors. Phonological activation spreads not only within the immediate one-segment-distance phonological neighborhood but can reach farther, potentially activating neighborhoods multiple phonological segments away (Chan & Vitevitch, 2009; Siew & Vitevitch, 2016; Suarez et al., 2011). Therefore, the density of connections in the giant component of a lexical network, the overall diameter of the giant component (i.e., geodesic distance between farthest points), as well as the average degree of words in the giant component are crucial metrics providing insights into the patterns of activation spreading during the lexical processing of second languages. Figures 11a and 11b depict two same-sized networks differing in diameter. In 11a, activation can swiftly spread throughout the network, covering a larger number of nodes in a short time, whereas in 11b, activation spreading involves more steps to reach each node. These spreading dynamics can significantly impact word retrieval in the mental lexicon.

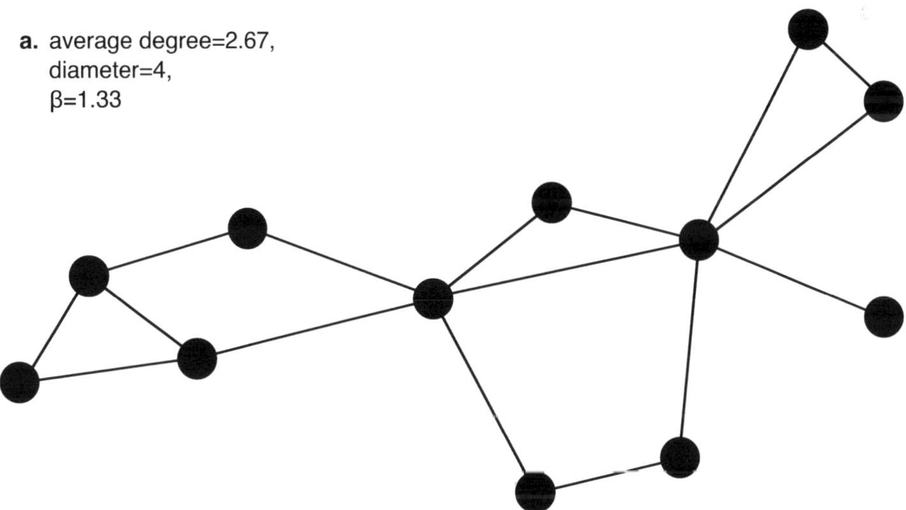

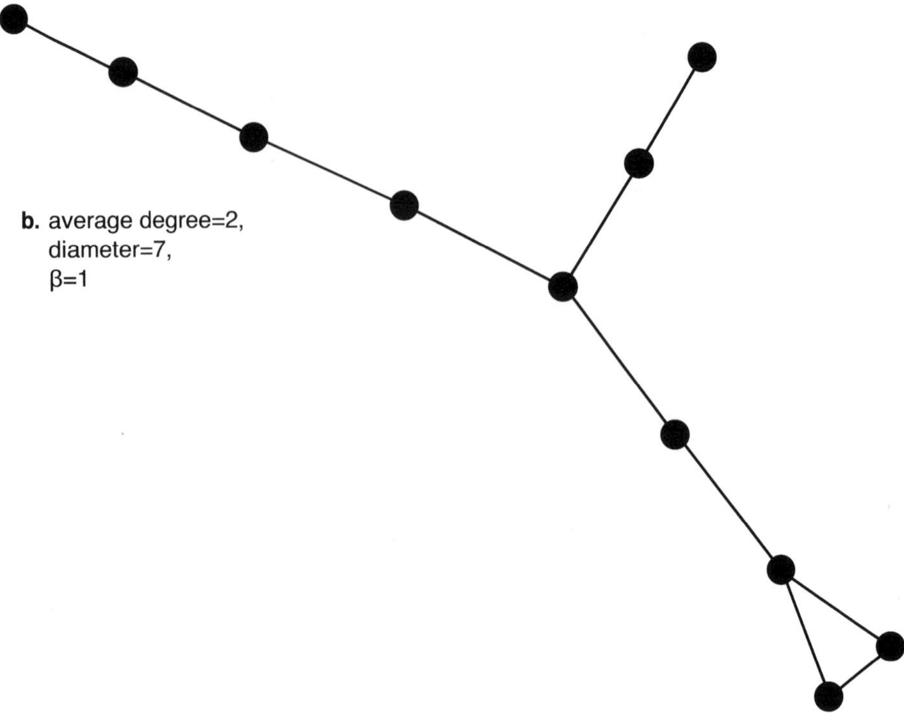

Figure 11: Two similarly sized networks differing in network diameter.

Giant component size is largest in the A1 lexicon, comprising 44% of the network nodes, accompanied by 25 islands (10%) and 279 singleton nodes (46%; see Figure 12a). Islands are small and range from 2 to 4 nodes with 1 to 3 edges. In the A2 network, the giant component size reduces to 42% of network nodes, with 77 islands (13%) and 664 (45%) singleton nodes. Island size and connectivity increase, ranging from 2 to 6 nodes with 1 to 6 edges per island. The giant component of the B1 network makes up 38% of the network, with 162 islands (15%) and 1371 (47%) singleton nodes. Islands vary in size from 2 to 18 nodes, involving 1 to 7 edges (see Figure 12b). In the B2 network, the giant component constitutes 35% of the network, accompanied by 328 islands 18%) and 2193 (47%) singleton nodes. Islands exhibit a broader size range, from 2 to 26 nodes, with 1 to 37 edges. The C1 giant component comprises 31% of all nodes, with 431 islands (21%) and 2751 (48%) singleton nodes. Average island size markedly increases, ranging from 2 to 70 nodes, with 1 to 88 edges. At the C2 level, the giant component proportion shrinks further and constitutes only 30% of the overall network. The proportion of islands and singletons increases to 527 islands (21%) and 3295 singleton nodes (49%; see Figure 12c). Islands in this lexicon vary in size and connectivity, ranging from 2 to 45 nodes, involving 1 to 52 edges. In the BNC network, 515 islands and 2791 singleton nodes (52%) were detected; islands range from 2 to 175 nodes (see Figure 12d).

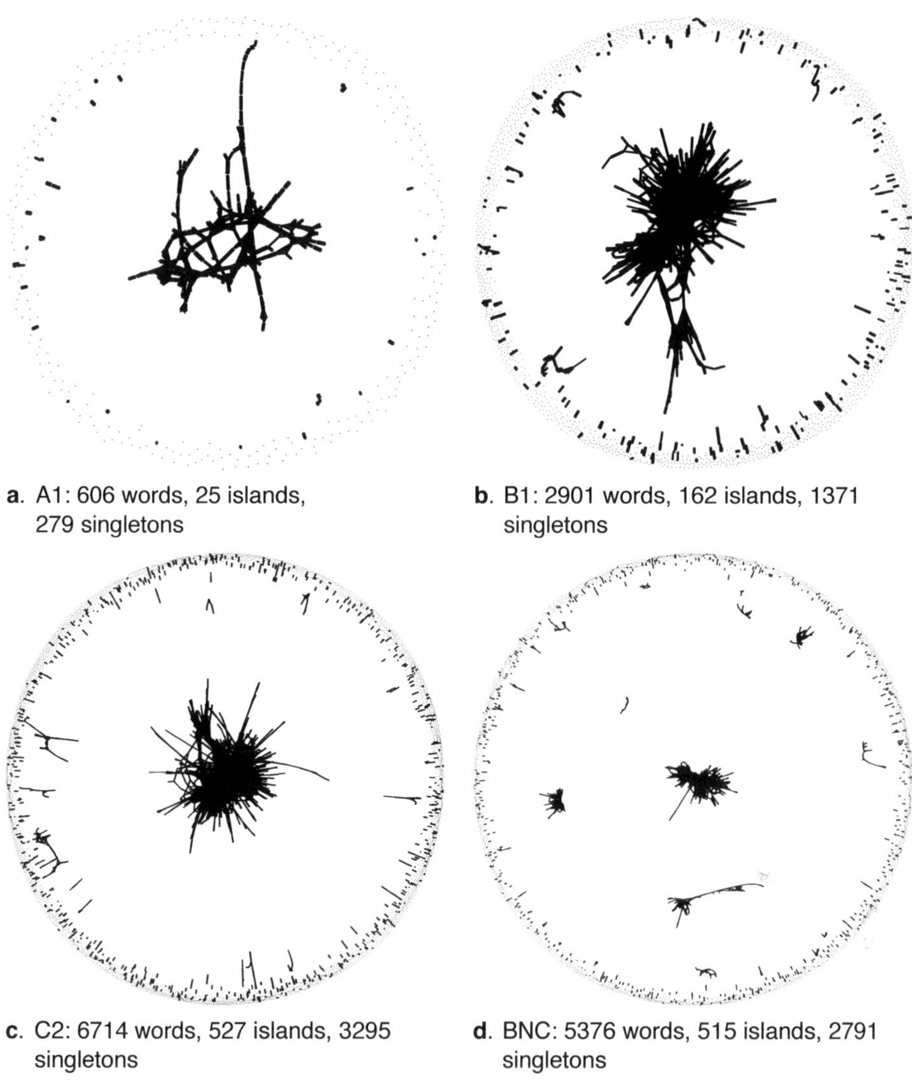

a. A1: 606 words, 25 islands, 279 singletons

b. B1: 2901 words, 162 islands, 1371 singletons

c. C2: 6714 words, 527 islands, 3295 singletons

d. BNC: 5376 words, 515 islands, 2791 singletons

Figures 12a–d: Phonological networks of the A1 (a), B1 (b), C2 (c), and BNC (d) lexica. The giant components are central and surrounded by lexical islands and singleton nodes (Yifan-Hu layout, Gephi).

The proportions of giant components within the learner networks decrease as proficiency increases, ranging from the highest percentage of 44% in the A1 network to only 30% in the C2 network. A study on giant component sizes in various languages by Arbesman and colleagues (2010) found that the giant component of American English was approximately 34%, the smallest among the languages investigated. For comparison, Spanish and Basque had giant component sizes of 37% and 35%, respectively, while Mandarin Chinese reached 66% (see Arbesman et al., 2010). In the current study, the BNC giant component accounted for only 13.2% of the network. A crucial caveat complicates a comparison between the findings of the present study and those of Arbesman and colleagues. The analysis of Arbesman et al. was not based on corpus data; instead, the authors constructed their American English phonological network with lexical data from the *Merriam-Webster Pocket Dictionary*, containing 19,323 words. While their study design is not directly comparable to the usage-based account of the present study, it is intriguing to note that the giant component sizes of the ESL networks closely align with those measured by Arbesman and colleagues. The findings of the present study support the hypothesis of small giant component sizes in English phonological networks, a notion further underscored by the very small giant component of the BNC network of first-language users of British English.

Most social, technological, and biological networks can accommodate an extraordinarily large number of nodes in their giant components, reaching up to 80-90% of the network's nodes (see Newman, 2001). However, large giant component sizes come with several disadvantages, such as low network robustness (Hu & Lee, 2020). In contrast, small giant component sizes are indicative of better resilience against accidental failures and targeted attacks on a network. Phonological networks, in particular, may be structured to maximize robustness (Siew & Vitevitch, 2016; Vitevitch, 2008). Arbesman and colleagues (2010) discovered that the phonological networks of several languages exhibit high resistance to network failures, primarily due to small giant component sizes coupled with high numbers of islands and singletons. If new words become preferentially attached to lexical islands and singletons, rather than contributing to the giant component, network stability is enhanced (Siew & Vitevitch, 2016; Zhao & Xu, 2009). Such a dynamic ensures the constancy of the structure and size of the giant component, where the bulk of lexical processing occurs. At the same time, it promotes growth in the overall network by supplementing smaller components (islands, singletons) with new words, without drastically impacting the overall functioning of the lexical network (Siew & Vitevitch, 2016).

In the A1 network, 44% of all words reside in the giant component, marking the highest proportion among all ESL networks. This indicates a stronger inclination for phonological clustering of words in the giant component during the initial stages of word learning. Studies have shown that phonological similarity significantly aids word learning in children (Hoover, Storkel, & Hogan, 2010; Storkel & Lee, 2011), and this tendency may be particularly pronounced when dealing with a small lexicon, be it in child language acquisition or second language learning. Starting from the A2 level, the giant components of the learner networks decrease in size, while the islands steadily grow, a trend that continues up to the C2 level. From a macro perspective of the lexical network, growth predominantly occurs in the islands, which expand at each proficiency level. This expansion begins at a proportion of 10% within the A1 network and increases to 21% in the C2 network.

The percentage of singleton, non-connected words is rather stable across all learner levels, ranging between 45% and 49%. Nearly half of the learner networks at all proficiency levels consists of singleton nodes, indicating a propensity to learn words even in the absence of phonological neighbors. A phonological network of American English described by Vitevitch (2008) also exhibited a substantial proportion of singletons (lexical hermits): 53% of the investigated words (see Gerometta, 2015, for comparable findings). In the BNC network, singleton nodes made up 52% of the network.

The network part to which a word belongs is of consequential nature for its lexical access. Giant components pose a processing disadvantage, as activation spreads more extensively, leading to the activation of a greater number of lexical competitors (see Siew & Vitevitch, 2016). The topological designs of the ESL networks reveal a gradual reduction in giant component proportion with each advancing proficiency level. This trend may reflect a cognitive development aimed at enhancing processing advantages and reducing lexical competition. During the build-up of the ESL lexicon, network resources (i.e., newly learned words) are gradually shifted more toward peripheral areas of the network, thereby avoiding concentration in the giant component. Smaller giant component proportions could represent an adaptation for improved lexical processing: with each successive proficiency level, a larger number of words must be navigated during lexical search, which imposes a burden on processing efficiency. Larger vocabularies require better organization for efficient navigation, and smaller giant component sizes may facilitate that.

2.3.2.1 LEXICAL CHARACTERISTICS OF ESL NETWORK PARTS

In the ESL networks, shorter words have a higher likelihood of residing in the giant component (see Siew, 2013, for similar findings in an L1 American English network). Across all learner networks, the phonemic length of words was found to be shortest in the giant components and longest in singleton nodes (Kruskal-Wallis: $\chi^2(2)=7791.3$, $p<0.001$; see Figure 13).

Words of higher lexical frequency displayed a tendency to cluster together in the giant component of the learner networks (Kruskal-Wallis: $\chi^2(2)=923.57$, $p<0.001$; Siew, 2013, reports a similar finding). Figure 14 illustrates the differences in lexical frequency across various network components in the six ESL networks.

Phonotactic probability was found to be lowest in the giant component words, while islands and singletons contained phonemic combinations with higher average probabilities (Kruskal-Wallis: $\chi^2(2)=392.57$, $p<0.001$; see Figure 15 for details).

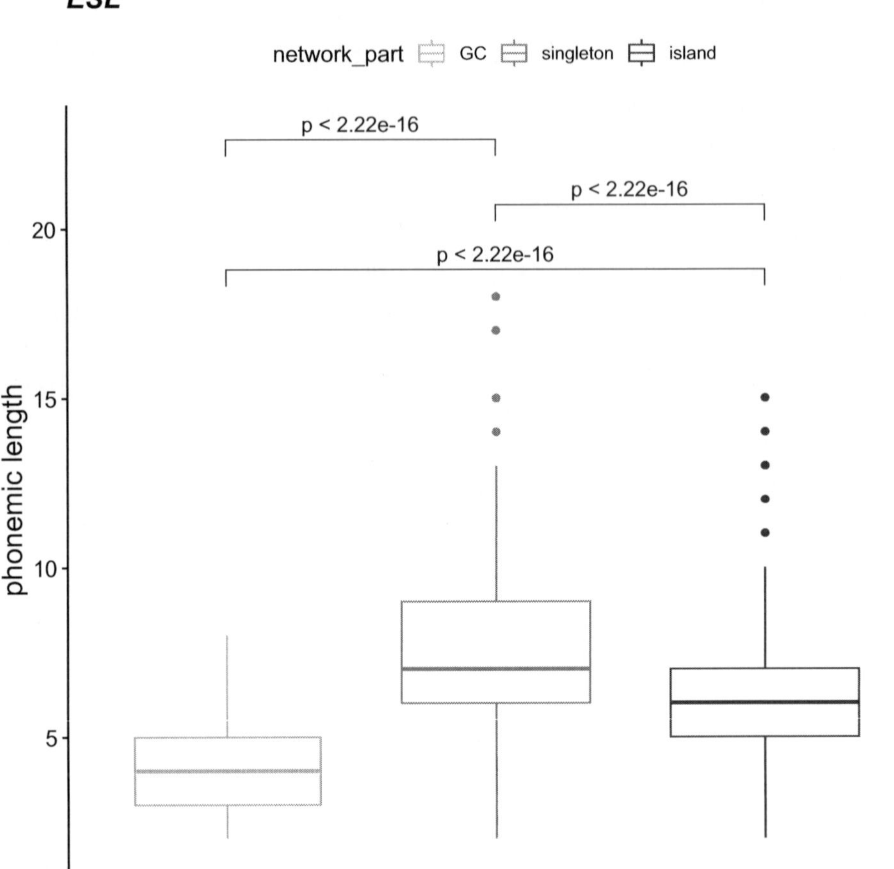

Figure 13: Phonemic length of words belonging to different network parts (giant component, island, singleton) across all ESL networks. The individual proficiency networks yielded identical patterns. Post-hoc Wilcoxon signed rank test results are indicated.

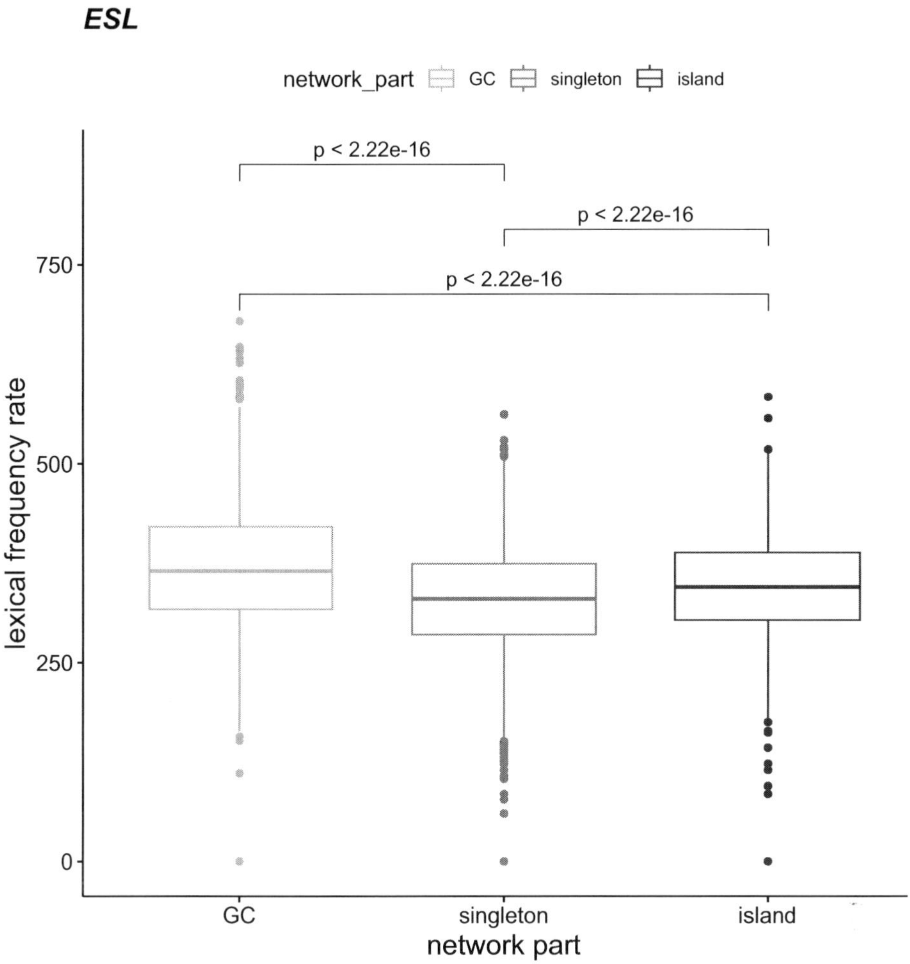

Figure 14: Lexical frequency rates of words belonging to different network parts (giant component, island, singleton) in the six ESL networks. The individual proficiency networks yielded identical patterns. Post-hoc Wilcoxon signed rank test results are indicated.

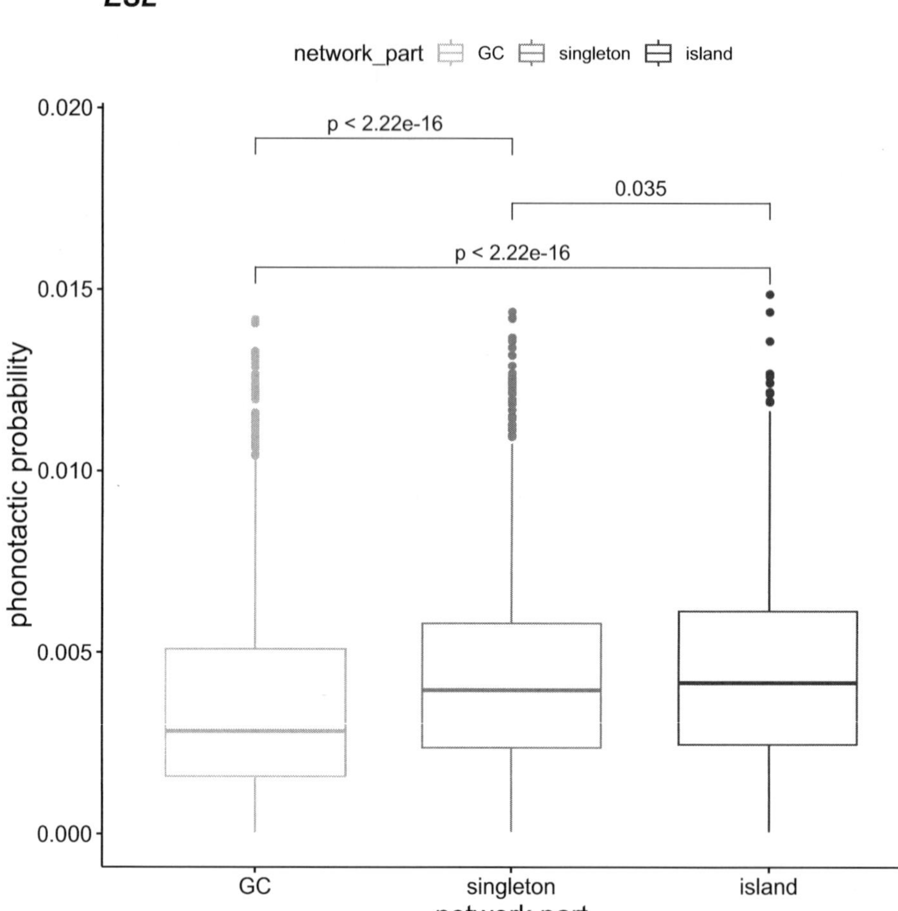

Figure 15: Phonotactic probabilities of words belonging to different network parts (giant component, island, singleton) in the six ESL networks. The individual proficiency networks yielded identical patterns. Post-hoc Wilcoxon signed rank test results are indicated.

2.3.2.2 LEXICAL CHARACTERISTICS OF L1 BRITISH ENGLISH NETWORK PARTS

Similar to the learner networks, phonemic length of words was longest in singleton nodes and shortest in the giant component (Kruskal-Wallis: $\chi^2(2)=1912.5$, $p<0.001$; see Figure 16).

The BNC giant component contained a higher concentration of high-frequency words than the island or singleton parts of the network (Kruskal-Wallis: $\chi^2(2)=156.4$, $p<0.001$), reflecting findings from the learner networks (see Figure 17).

Phonotactic probability was lowest in the giant component but highest in the singleton nodes (Kruskal-Wallis: $\chi^2(2)=812.3$, $p<0.001$; see Figure 18).

The BNC network and the ESL learner networks exhibit similar patterns with regards to network structure and the distribution of lexical characteristics. These patterns are in agreement with findings by Siew (2013) for an L1 American English network: shorter words of higher lexical frequency rate and low phonotactic probability possess a learning advantage and are acquired earlier in first and second language learning (also see, e.g., Ellis, 2002; Storkel et al., 2006). This tendency for such words to accumulate in the giant component highlights the importance of giant component

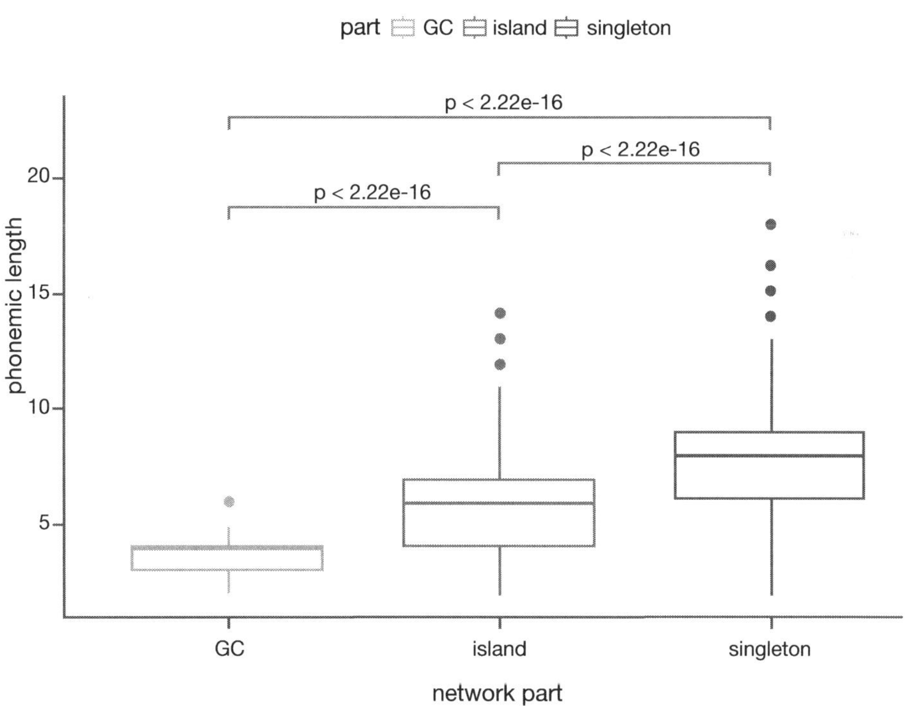

Figure 16: Phonemic length of words belonging to different network parts (giant component, island, singleton) in the BNC network. Post-hoc Wilcoxon signed rank test results are indicated.

formation for word learning. Over time, as language proficiency develops, the reliance on the giant component diminishes, while the importance of lexical islands grows. This is reflected in the macro-development of the ESL networks.

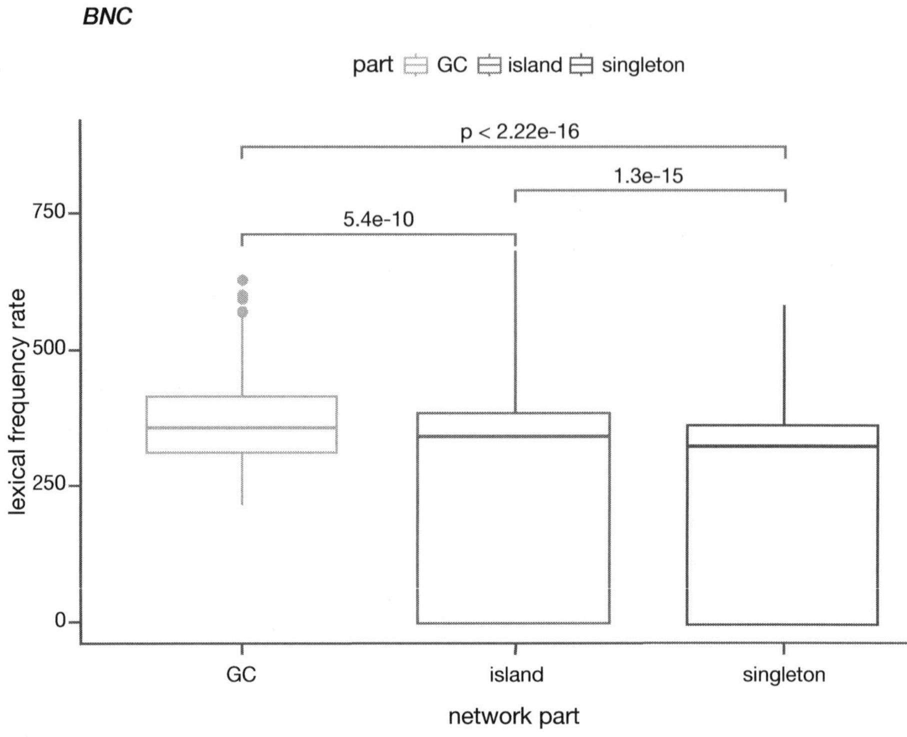

Figure 17: Lexical frequency rates of words belonging to different network parts (giant component, island, singleton) in the BNC network. Post-hoc Wilcoxon signed rank test results are indicated.

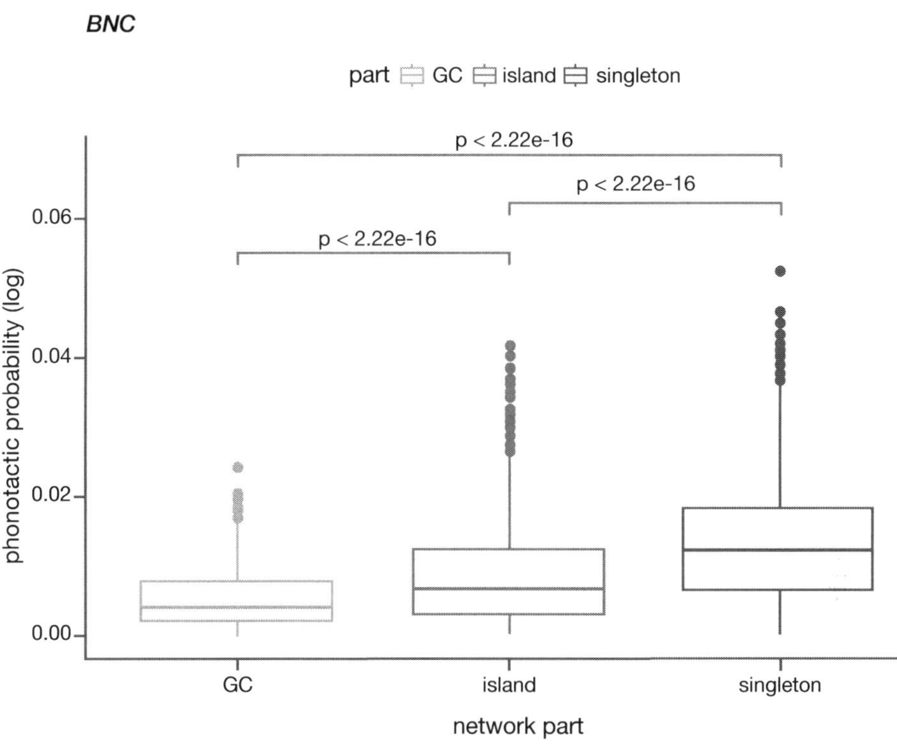

Figure 18: Phonotactic probabilities of words belonging to different network parts (giant component, island, singleton) in the BNC network. Post-hoc Wilcoxon signed rank test results are indicated.

2.3.3 ASSORTATIVITY BY DEGREE

As the learner networks increase from A1 to C2, degree assortativity in the phonological networks also rises. Assortativity by degree measures how likely nodes are to connect with other nodes that have a similar number of connections. In phonological networks, positive assortative mixing is recorded when $r>0.5$, a value exceeded by the BNC and ESL networks. Preferential neighborhood formation by degree makes it less likely that sparse neighborhoods can become linked to dense ones, in other words the neighborhood density distribution will inevitably be skewed. Arbesman et al. (2010) report $r=0.65$ for their L1 American English network, indicating a strong degree correlation among neighboring nodes (which is higher than typically seen in social networks with r commonly ranging from 0.1 to 0.3). Their analysis of Spanish yielded a very high assortativity score of $r=0.76$. The ESL learner networks were characterized by lower assortativity values, ranging from 0.57 to 0.68 (see Table 2) but with a clear tendency to increase degree assortativity with network growth. The L1 British English network yielded a particularly high r-value of 0.71, surpassing the levels found for the C1 and C2 proficiency levels ($r=0.68$ in both), and exceeding the Arbesman estimation for American English.

Figure 19: Assortativity in the giant component of the A1 network. Nodes tend to establish links with other similar-degree nodes (i.e., large nodes tend to be linked to one another, small nodes tend to be linked to one another).

Figure 19 displays assortativity patterns within the A1 giant component. Pearson's assortativity coefficient r equals 0.57, and the average node degree in the giant component is 4.1. The visualization makes it easy to observe groups of nodes with similar degrees (indicated through node size).

As the networks advanced from A2 to C2 levels, there was a noticeable increasing trend in the assortativity coefficient and average node degrees, both overall and within the giant components. The BNC network was characterized by r=0.71, indicating pronounced positive assortativity patterns. The average node degree across the entire networks was 1.8 but jumped to 7.2 in the giant component, suggesting that neighborhoods in the giant component are denser compared to those in the learner networks.

As denser and more tightly connected neighborhoods can impair lexical retrieval due to the higher level of activation diffusion and competition, the continuous enrichment of already "rich" neighborhoods cannot be an open-ended process in a lexicon. However, a network's resilience increases with higher positive assortativity levels, as noted by Newman (2002). The gradual increase in assortativity observed in the ESL networks suggests an inclination toward building a more robust lexical network, possibly at the expense of the immediate retrieval efficiency. This trend indicates a balancing act in language learning between creating a strong, resilient network and maintaining efficient access to words within that network.

2.3.4 PHONOLOGICAL DISTANCES: EDGE WEIGHTS

The strength of the connections between words, as indicated by edge weight reflecting phonological distances between the phonological neighbors, serves as an indicator of connectivity in the ESL and BNC networks. Typically, words in the giant component show closer phonological relationships than those in the lexical islands. As the ESL networks progress, the disparity in phonological distance between the giant component and the islands becomes more pronounced (see Figure 20).

Since the giant component words were typically of higher lexical frequency rates and shorter phonemic lengths than words in islands, correlations between the variables were evaluated. Results showed that lexical frequency and weighted degree were not correlated (average Pearson's r across all learner networks <0.33). However, phonemic word length and weighted degree showed a moderate negative correlation (average across all proficiency levels r=-0.58), implying that shorter word length is positively associated with higher weighted degrees in the ESL networks. Shorter words are known to have more phonological neighbors (Bard & Shillcock, 1993; Charles-Luce & Luce, 1990; Pisoni, Nusbaum, Luce, & Slowiaczek, 1985). The probability of phonolog-

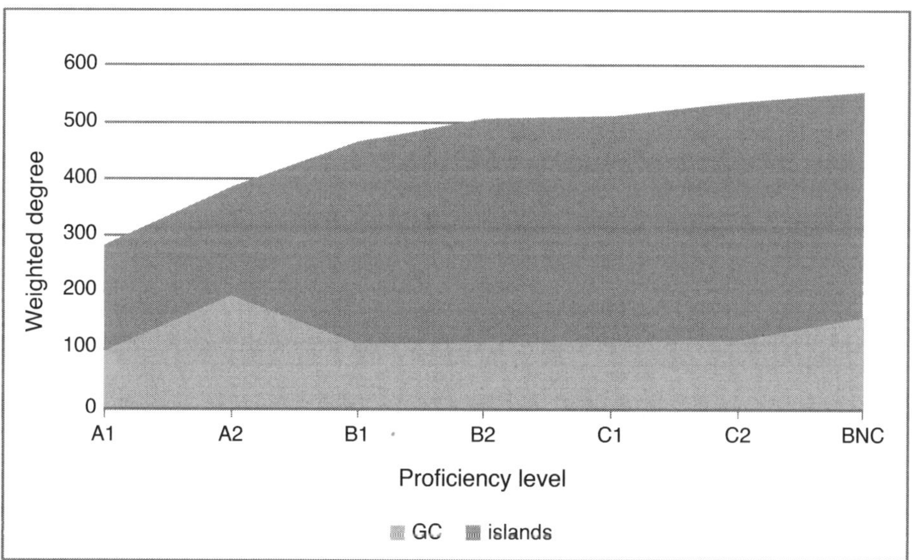

Figure 20: Edge strength (assessed through weighted degree centrality) increases in the giant component as the ESL networks grow but stays relatively constant in the islands.

ical neighbor creation in different segmental positions – the *P-metric* (Johnson & Pugh, 1994) – is notably higher in shorter words. This indicates that the spread of a neighborhood is more evenly dispersed in shorter words, making them more adaptable in creating neighbors across various segmental positions (Vitevitch, 2007). In terms of activation spreading, closely related phonological neighbors are assumed to take more of the co-activation within a neighborhood. In the diffusion activation framework, this could mean that phonologically close neighbors receive more and also pass on more of the existing activation to their own neighbors, potentially strengthening the phonological representations of themselves and their connections in the network.

2.3.5 DIAMETERS AND AVERAGE PATH LENGTHS IN THE GIANT COMPONENTS

The ESL networks displayed fluctuations in both network diameter and average path length in their giant components (see Figure 21). These measures were highest in the A1 network, subsequently decreasing in the A2 and B1 levels, followed by continued growth. These findings suggest a more loosely connected network at the outset of learning, evolving into a more tightly linked structure as proficiency advances. In the BNC network, the diameter of the giant component and average path length were comparable to the levels observed in advanced ESL levels.

Efficiency, characterized by factors such as shorter average path length, reduced diameter, and a smaller giant component, continues to enhance with proficiency progression in second language learning.

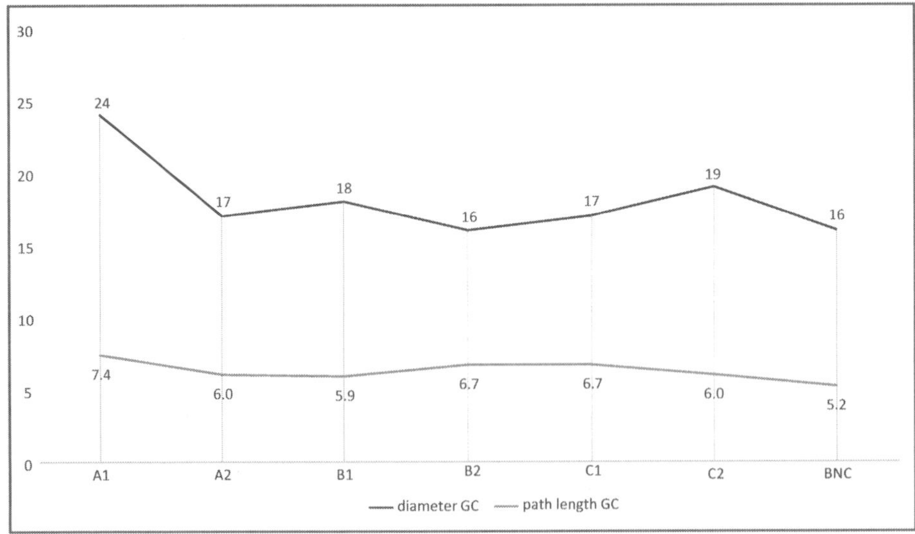

Figure 21: Average path length and diameter of giant components in the ESL and BNC networks.

2.4 MICRO-LEVEL CENTRALITIES

The average centrality measurements, as presented in Table 3, show similarities between the BNC and ESL networks. However, notable differences emerge in betweenness centrality and closeness centrality. Specifically, the BNC network shows lower average betweenness but higher closeness centralities. This discrepancy is likely attributed to the distinct topology of the BNC network, characterized by larger islands coexisting with a very small giant component.

Density analyses revealed heavy-tail distributions across all network measures and proficiency levels, as summarized in Table 4.

A power law distribution of node degree, often associated with scale-free networks, was not observed in the ESL networks (consistent with Vitevitch, 2008). This is not surprising, given the controversy surrounding power laws in scale-free networks (Broido & Clauset, 2019). Generally, a network is deemed scale-free if a fraction of its nodes follows a power law distribution $k^{-\alpha}$, with $\alpha>1$ (Broido & Clauset, 2019; Newman, 2010). It has been proposed that power law distributions are the only scale-free distributions in networks (Newman, 2005), and thus the terms "scale-free" and "power law distribution" are often considered as synonymous (Milojević, 2010). However, this claim has been challenged by numerous researchers who argue that scale-freeness can arise from other distribution types (see Li, Alderson, Doyle, & Willinger, 2005, for a short review). Clauset, Shalizi and Newman (2009) found that statistical tests rarely yield a power law distribution in networks, and Stumpf and Porter (2012) point out the suboptimal mathematical fitting commonly employed to determine power laws in networks.

Throughout the L2 development, there is a noticeable shift of degree centrality toward larger values in only a few prolific nodes (see Figure 22a). The skewness of node degree becomes more extreme with each proficiency level. In other words, few neighborhoods can increase their density during growth. Studies in child language acquisition found that children improve word learning when phonological neighborhoods start to emerge in their lexicon (Donnelly & Kidd, 2020). The developmental trajectory of node degree in the ESL learner networks could indicate a similar tendency, with denser neighborhoods facilitating lexical learning at more advanced stages of language acquisition.

A special case of neighborhood density effect in relation to language development was revealed by Karimi and Diaz (2020) in their study of child lexical acquisition. They compared lexical processing efficiency in words acquired at different acquisitional stages in L1 English-learning children and found that dense phonological neighborhoods facilitated the retrieval of early-acquired words but inhibited retrieval of late-acquired words. This effect was attributed to potentially weaker phonological representations in late-acquired words compared to the more strongly ingrained representations of early-acquired words. The activation level of a target word relative to its neighbors played a role: early-acquired words with strong phonological representation tended to dominate the activation in their neighborhood, especially when surrounded

Table 3: Mean network measures and their standard deviations across the networks.

	A1	**A2**	**B1**	**B2**	**C1**	**BNC**
Degree centrality	1.92±2.6	2.41±3.5	2.58±4.2	2.55±4.4	2.38±4.3	1.8±3.4
Weighted degree centrality	136.21±175	178.56±250	196.27±306	196.57±324	185.21±320	141.1±254
Closeness centrality	0.15±0.3	0.19±0.3	0.19±0.3	0.22±0.3	0.22±0.3	0.26±0.4
Betweenness centrality	380.35±962	670.6±1813	1040±3145	1362.19±4039	1391.7±4418	220.6±952
Clustering coefficient	0.16±0.3	0.14±0.3	0.13±0.2	0.12±0.2	0.11±0.2	0.1±0.2
Eigenvector centrality	0.046±0.1	0.047±0.1	0.043±0.1	0.032±0.1	0.029±0.1	0.03±0.1

Table 4: Best-fitting distribution per network measure (proficiency levels pooled).

	Degree centrality	*Weighted degree c.*	*Closeness centrality*	*Betweenness centrality*	*Clustering coefficient*	*Eigenvector centrality*
Best fit	Log-normal	Power law (Pareto)	Multimodal (dip test p: <0.001)	Multimodal (dip test p: <0.001)	Multimodal (dip test p: <0.001)	Log-logistic

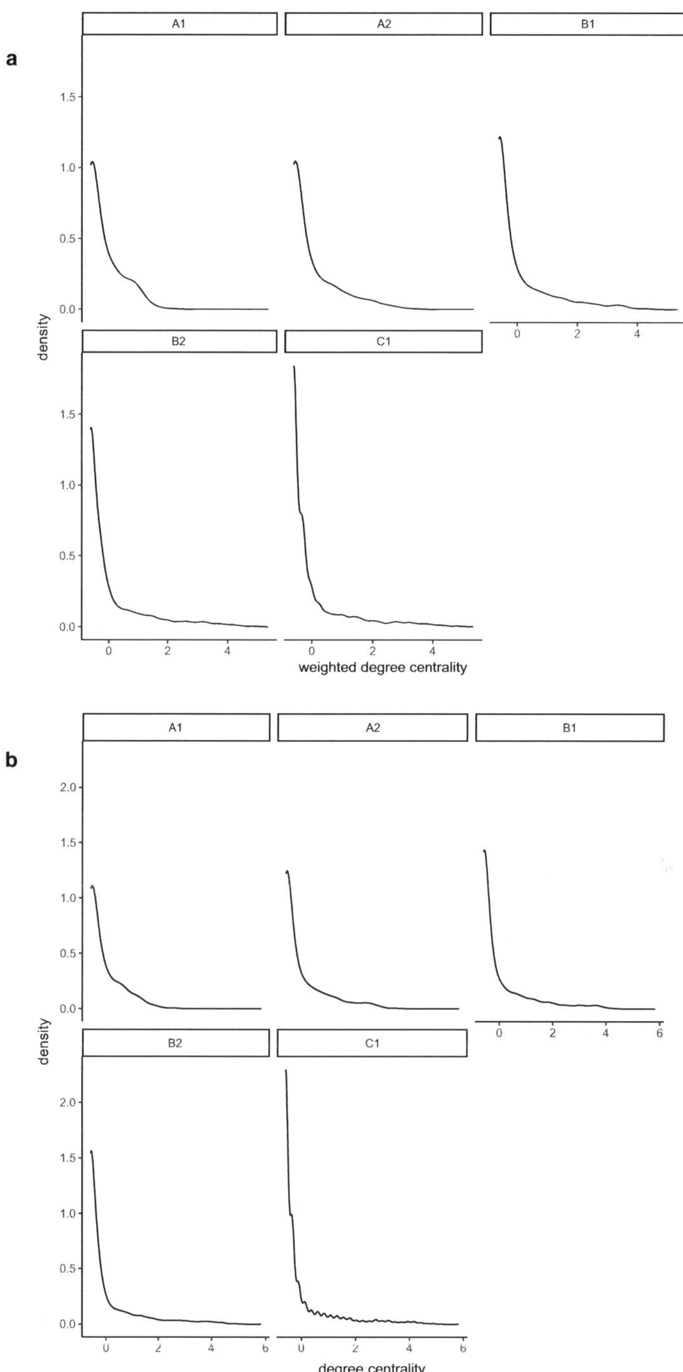

Figures 22a–b: Distributions of degree and weighted degree centralities (z-scored) in the ESL proficiency networks.

by late-acquired words with weaker representations. Even though Karimi and Diaz defined phonological neighbors more broadly than the present study, their findings bear implications for the learner networks examined here. In L2 learning, a similar age-of-acquisition effect could influence neighborhood activation. Early-learned words may possess stronger phonological representations, setting them apart from their immediate neighbors, thereby heightening discriminability and reducing lexical competition. This could shape the neighborhood structures at different stages of language learning.

On a more speculative level, lexical retrieval in more advanced learner lexica, which comprise a mix of old and new words, may not be impeded by dense neighborhoods. The varied strengths of phonological representations in old and new words could alleviate activation competition. This dynamic might allow denser neighborhoods to be formed, especially as the lexicon accumulates words. In the initial stages of language learning, where words are predominantly newly-learned, phonological neighborhoods might trend toward sparsity, facilitating lexical retrieval by minimizing activation competition. The evolving degree distributions observed over the course of learning (see Figure 22a) may suggest such a dynamic in the learner networks, with the dominance of numerous and moderately dense neighborhoods in the early stages, followed by the emergence of few dense and many sparse neighborhoods in the higher proficiency networks.

For various network measures, it can be observed that inequality increases as the networks grow (see Figures 22a–b and 23a–d). This is evident not only in degree but also in weighted degree, clustering coefficient, and eigenvector centrality. This could be a function of expanded network sizes and the associated mathematical probabilities inherent to differently sized networks. Alternatively, it might reflect an intrinsic characteristic of complex systems, wherein properties change in relation to emerging rules within an evolving system. In essence, these findings highlight that the ESL beginner network is not merely a scaled-down reflection of the more advanced lexicon but functions as a distinct system governed by its own set of rules.

The BNC network measures were distributed similarly to the ESL networks and the results are displayed in Table 5 and Figures 24 a–b.

Table 5: Best-fitting distribution per network measure in the BNC network.

	Degree centrality	*Weighted degree c.*	*Closeness centrality*	*Betweenness centrality*	*Clustering coefficient*	*Eigenvector centrality*
Best fit	Multimodal (dip test p: <0.001)	Bimodal (dip test p: <0.001)	Multimodal (dip test p: <0.001)	Burr	Multimodal (dip test p: <0.001)	Log-normal

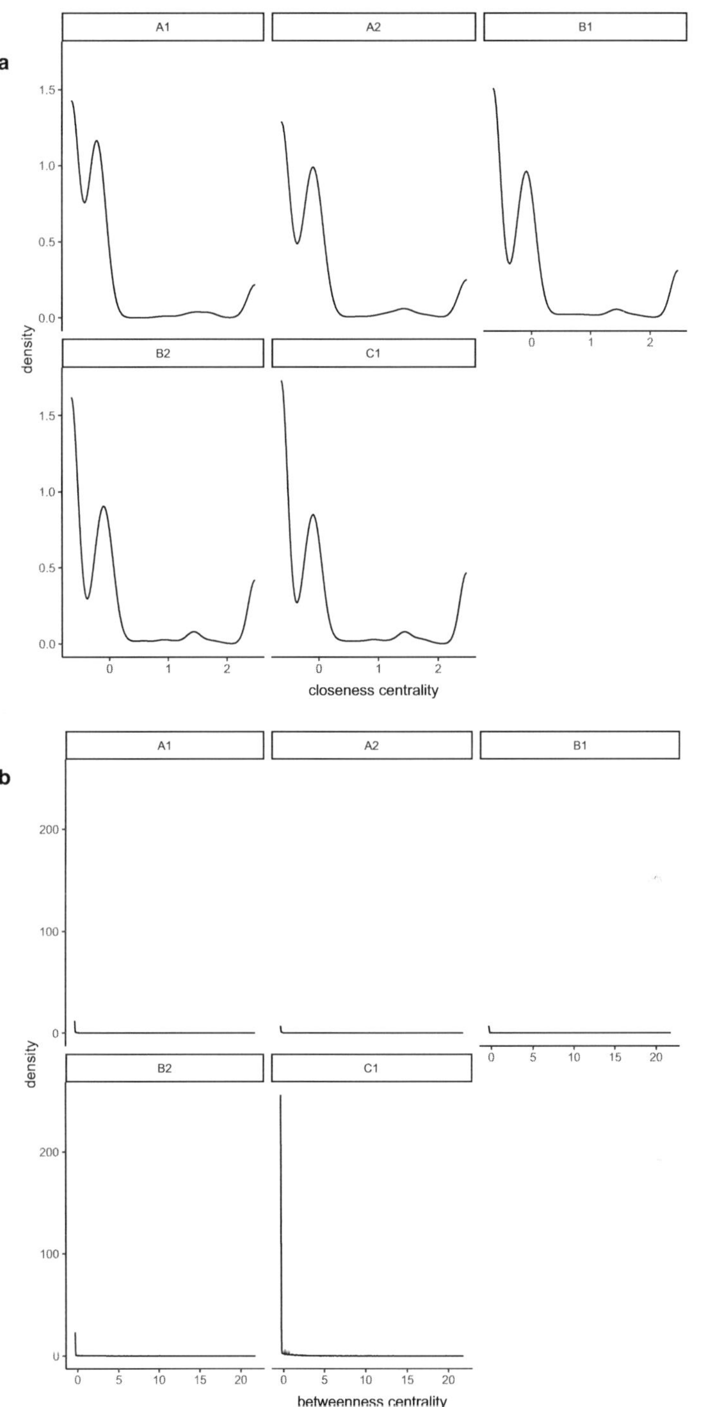

Figures 23a–b: Distributions of network measures in the ESL proficiency networks.

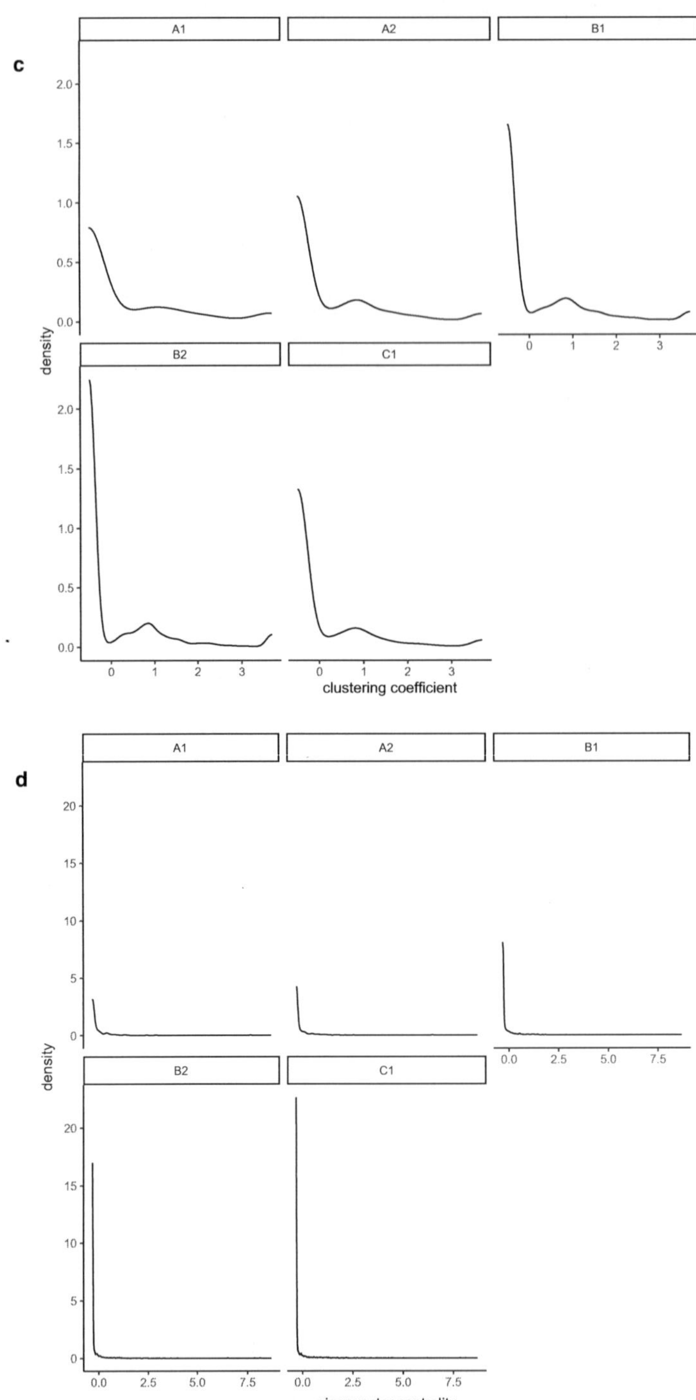

Figures 23c–d: Distributions of network measures in the ESL proficiency networks.

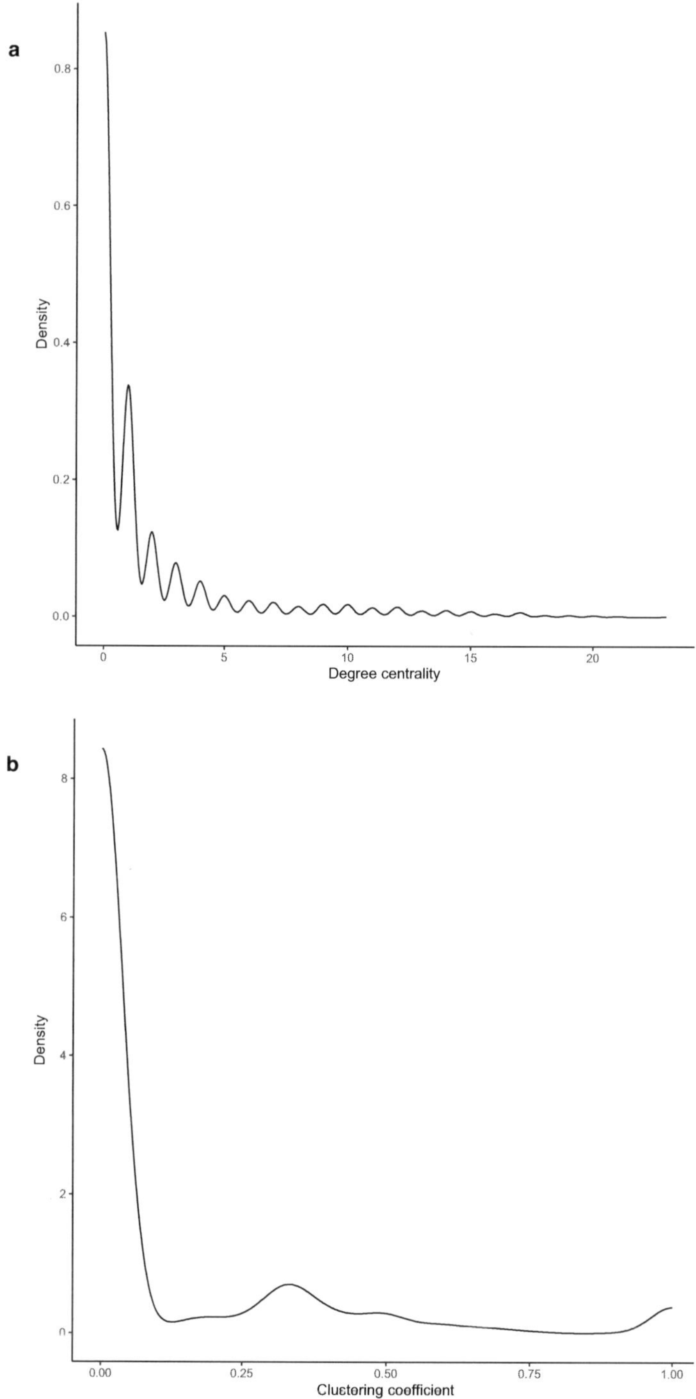

Figures 24a–b: Distributions of degree centrality and clustering coefficients in the BNC network.

In summary, all network statistics in both the ESL and BNC networks exhibited skewed distributions. The clustering coefficient and closeness centrality displayed the least skew, with high values dispersed across a larger number of nodes in the networks. High values in eigenvector and betweenness centrality were confined to very few prolific nodes, consistent with their expected roles in networks.

2.4.1 SMALL-WORLDNESS

All learner networks are characterized by high clustering coefficients in combination with relatively short average path lengths, indicating a tendency to incorporate small-world features. While the definition of small-worldness can be challenging (see, e.g., Telesford, Joyce, Hayasaka, Burdette, & Laurienti, 2011) and has been questioned in phonological networks (Gerometta, 2015), it holds relevance in understanding lexical competition (Levy et al., 2021; Vitevitch, 2008). The ESL networks demonstrate a development toward more small-worldness (see Table 6). Sigma values, used to establish the presence of small-worldness when $\sigma>1$ (Humphries, Gurney, & Prescott, 2006), compare path length and transitivity to a random network. The ESL networks start out with rather high σ values at the A1 level, which decrease in A2 and B1, and then rise again from the B2 level onwards. Small-worldness is rather pronounced in the upper proficiency levels and reaches even higher σ values in the BNC network. A major advantage of small-world networks is their improved searchability where inspection of a small number of interconnected nodes yields a high likelihood of success in locating a particular node in a system (Kleinberg, 2000). Lexical search in the adult and developing L1 lexicon can be greatly aided by such a structure (Arbesman et al., 2010; Carlson et al., 2014; Chan & Vitevitch, 2009).

Table 6: Small-world coefficients across the proficiency levels of the ESL and BNC networks.

	A1	A2	B1	B2	C1	C2	BNC
σ	5.19	4.22	4.25	5.72	6.87	6.96	7.9

The dense interconnectedness of neighbors leads to heightened co-activation rates within a neighborhood, potentially causing discrimination issues of the target word (Chan & Vitevitch, 2009, 2010; Goldstein & Vitevitch, 2014; Yates, 2013). Word learning in the ESL networks seems to be maximally facilitated at the initial-intermediate stages (A2, B1) when small-worldness is lowest. Given the relatively small vocabulary at these stages, small-worldness could have a pronounced impact on learning success. Following Goldstein and Vitevitch's (2014) proposal, word learning becomes more difficult as small-worldness increases in advanced proficiency stages. At this point, the larger vocabularies contribute to crowding in the phonological spaces, especially the giant component, making lexical processing more demanding.

The learner networks showed a clear tendency to decrease transitivity with each progressive stage (see Table 7). This trend may be linked to the increase in network size, as smaller networks and fewer nodes have an advantage in maintaining higher interconnectedness. As networks grow, it becomes increasingly difficult to sustain a larger proportion of interconnected nodes.

Table 7: Transitivity values across the learner and BNC networks.

	A1	A2	B1	B2	C1	C2	BNC
Transitivity	0.47	0.42	0.41	0.4	0.39	0.39	0.39

Transitivity values reported by Arbesman et al. (2010) for various languages range from 0.23 in Basque to 0.4 in Mandarin Chinese, with American English scoring 0.31, which ranges below those found in the BNC and ESL networks. Higher transitivity in the low-proficiency networks indicates a more tightly knit phonological network during the initial stages of language learning when vocabulary is limited. The transitivity values for the C1, C2, and the BNC networks are identical.

2.4.2 PHONEMIC INVENTORIES AND NEIGHBORHOOD FORMATION

During the course of learning English as a second language, phonological connectivity in the lexicon naturally increases with each successive proficiency level. Phonological neighborhood construction depends on the ability to form new words based on the phonemic inventory and phonotactic possibilities offered by English. Previous studies have shown that phonemic distributions within languages frequently follow a power law distribution (e.g., Zipfian or Yule), also in English (Tambovtsev & Martindale, 2007), implying that a small set of phonemes is used to construct a majority of English words.

In languages with a limited phonemic inventory, the likelihood of phonological neighbor creation increases since there are fewer possibilities to add, delete, or substitute phonemes. In fact, biased word formation processes are commonly observed, where highly frequent and probable phonemes are more likely to be used in word formation (Macklin-Cordes & Round, 2020). This "rich-gets-richer" dynamic on the phonemic scale could influence the bias in phonological neighborhood creation, favoring certain preferred phonemes over others. Figures 25a and 25b provide overviews of phonemic distributions across vocabularies of the ESL learners in comparison to the BNC data. Distributional skews are evident, with the A1 and A2 levels showing the largest phonemic skew, while the C1, C2, and BNC distributions display less skewness and longer tails.

Phonemic distributions were analyzed across proficiency levels using independent-samples Kolmogorov-Smirnov tests to identify differences in distribution.

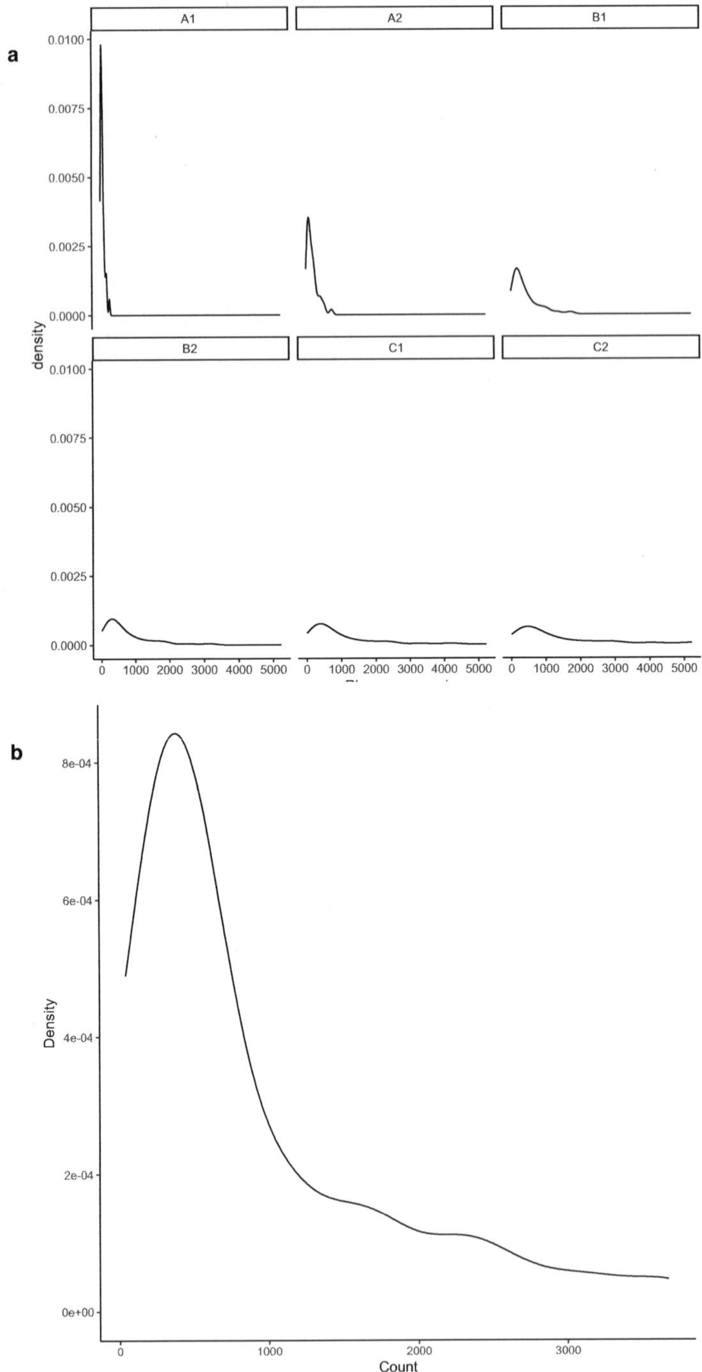

Figures 25 a–b: Phonemic distributions in the vocabularies of L2-English users (a) and L1-British English users (b).

Results showed that the A1 and A2 levels significantly differed from all other levels (A1: p values <0.001, D values range from 0.47 to 0.9, df=38; A2: p values <0.012, D range=0.37-0.66, df=38). The B1 distribution exhibited differences from C1, C2, and the BNC distributions (p values<0.045, D range: 0.32-0.34, df=38), while the remaining proficiency levels did not show different phonemic distribution patterns.

Power laws are intriguing for examining phonemic distributions in languages, as they suggest a correlation between growth and the "fitness" of particular phonemes – an explanation often cited for cross-language phonological differences (see, e.g., Macklin-Cordes & Round, 2020; Martindale, Gusein-Zade, McKenzie, & Borodovsky, 1996; Tambovtsev & Martindale, 2007). Such a phonological dynamic implies a tendency to reuse certain "fit" phonemes in word formation. The phonemic inventories of the ESL learners and the L1 British English users were tested for their underlying heavy-tail distributions (see Clauset et al., 2009; Gillespie, 2014; see Table 8).

Table 8: Phonemic distributions in the ESL and BNC networks.

	A1	*A2*	*B1*	*B2*	*C1*	*C2*	*BNC*
Best fitting distribution	Gamma (dip test p=0.8)	Gamma (dip test p=0.9)	Log-logistic	Log-normal	Log-normal	Log-normal	Log-normal

According to Piantadosi (2014), phonemic distributions have real-world implications for what they reveal about a language. Log-normally distributed phonemes in a lexicon indicate that the increase in phonemes is proportionally and predictably related. Entities in log-normal distributions increase in proportional amounts (the so-called law of proportional effect), rather than through disproportional accumulation, as in power-law distributions. Log-normally distributed phonemes reflect greater predictability, as each phoneme increases its presence in the lexicon based on its proportional share.

The skewed phonemic distributions observed in the initial ESL lexica suggest a more pronounced tendency for phonemic clustering to involve a few select phonemes during the early learning stages when the vocabulary is rather small. The vowels [ɪ] and [ə] and the consonants [t], [s], and [n] are the most prolific in the A1 lexicon, while phonemic distribution is more equal in subsequent ESL lexica and the BNC lexicon. It might be assumed that this distributional skew in A1 and A2 could reflect the fact that the A1 lexicon comprises the most frequent words, which are in turn characterized by frequent phonemes. However, the four identified phonemes are consistently the most frequent ones in all investigated lexica, including the BNC lexicon (see list below). This suggests that the phonemic composition in the initial stages of language learning follows statistical probabilities shown by the target language. Learners tend to preferentially acquire higher-frequency phonemes, a finding consistent with what we know from child language acquisition where infants are finely attuned to statistical frequencies of phonemes in their native language and prioritize high-frequency sounds (de Boysson-Bardies & Vihman, 1991; Velleman & Vihman, 2007). There are indications that second language phonology learning follows a similar principle.

Neighbor formation tended to involve different phonemes per proficiency level. The five most common phonemes involved in the creation of phonological neighbors (through deletion, addition, or substitution) are listed below (in order of frequency):

A1: / ɪ, t, a, n, k/
A2: / ɪ, t, l, e, k/
B1: /i, ɪ, t, n, l/
B2: /ɪ, t, n, s, e/
C1: /ɪ, t, l, n, s/
BNC: /ɪ, r, t, n, ə/

The phonemes /ɪ, t/ consistently emerge as the most frequent ones involved in neighbor formation at all proficiency levels, followed by /n, l/ and /k, s, e/. As mentioned above, /ɪ, t, n/ are among the most frequent phonemes to be found in all ESL and BNC lexica, underscoring the special status of high-frequency phonemes in a phonological inventory. The fact that not all phonemes are equally frequent within and across languages has long been recognized and formalized in the hypothesis of a universal phonological complexity hierarchy, which is rooted in the human articulatory and perceptual language apparatus (Greenberg, 1966; Jakobson, 1941/68). Simpler phonemes are acquired earlier by children and retained for longer, as evidenced in cases of language impairment (see Romani, Galuzzi, Guariglia, & Goslin, 2017, for an overview). Zipf (1935) recognized that the most frequent phonemes are simpler, and the least frequent ones tend to be more complex in articulatory terms (the "principle of least effort"). Recent studies have confirmed this principle, showing that easier phonological forms tend to be used and re-used, resulting in shorter words being more frequent and using sequences with higher phonotactic probabilities. A consequence is a higher degree of homophony and polysemy (Piantadosi, Tily, & Gibson, 2012). Phonological measures of simplicity and complexity are subject to debate (see, e.g., Maddieson, 2009), but markedness theory has played a role (see Trubetzkoy, 1939). The principle of least effort can be applied to phonological neighborhood formation, where more complex ("marked") phonemes have fewer opportunities to form neighbors due to their complexity and the fact that speakers try to minimize their articulatory or perceptual efforts. Consequently, the preferential accumulation of more frequent and articulatorily easier phonemes in the phonological space of the mental lexicon would be the logical result of such a trend.

2.5 MESO STRUCTURE OF THE NETWORKS: COMMUNITIES

Using the Louvain method of community detection in the giant component of the L1 American English phonological network (see Vitevitch, 2008), Siew (2013) and Siew and colleagues (2023) uncovered numerous differently-sized communities with distinct characteristics pertaining to phonological word form associations. While various lexical features were explored by these studies, the findings on phonemic word length, lexical frequency rate, and node degree are particularly relevant in the context of the present study. Notably, their research revealed that larger communities tend to comprise more frequent and shorter words. This is in agreement with Zipf's law (Zipf, 1935), which posits a negative correlation between word length and lexical frequency rate. Consequently, the mesoscopic community level of a phonological network mirrors the overall structure of a language. Ravasz and Barabási (2003) have proposed a compelling hypothesis suggesting that communities within a network are simply sub-graphs of the original network, reflecting characteristics and dynamics of the global network on a local scale. In this context, the largest community is analogous to the giant component, while smaller communities mirror the islands. The phonological networks investigated by Siew (2013) and Siew et al. (2023) seem to adhere to this rule.

Generally, high-frequency words are less prevalent, as languages tend to consist of many low-frequency words (Zipf, 1935). The fact that high-frequency words are predominantly located in large rather than small communities may suggest an unequal distribution of cognitive processing across different regions of the giant component (Luef, 2024; Siew, 2013). The retrieval of words in high-frequency clusters demands more cognitive effort compared to other sections of the phonological lexicon. Siew also found that large communities tend to harbor more high-degree nodes, indicating denser phonological neighborhoods.

2.5.1 ESL NETWORKS

Community detection in the learner networks closely followed the method outlined by Siew (2013). First, modularity values Q were obtained for each of the ESL networks to assess the reliability of community detection. Subsequently, the number of communities in each network (excluding singleton nodes) and within the giant component were calculated. Table 9 presents an overview of Q, communities and their sizes per network.

Generally, Q values are quite high, indicating robust community identification in the phonological networks. The number of communities increased with growing network size, but community sizes decreased with network expansion. Compared to the BNC networks, community sizes were rather large in the ESL networks. The C2 and the BNC networks were quite similar in terms of the number of communities they contain: 538 in the C2 network and 520 in the BNC network. Community sizes, denoting the number of words per community, were largest in the initial ESL networks

Table 9: Modularity (Q), number of communities, and their sizes in the ESL and BNC networks.

	A1	A2	B1	B2	C1	C2	BNC
Q	0.83	0.76	0.74	0.74	0.76	0.75	0.84
Communities (no singletons)	37	87	171	338	439	538	520
GC communities	11	10	11	12	11	11	6
Community size: mean, sd, range	9.1±12; 38	9.4±23.1; 137	8.9±34.6; 315	7.2±34.9; 429	6.6±34.2; 406	6.4±36.4; 673	4.9±22.5; 375

and decreased substantially as learning progressed. The fact that standard deviations increase indicates that the variability in community sizes became more pronounced in larger networks.

While community sizes varied across networks, potentially linked to network size, the number of communities per giant component remained relatively constant. Only the BNC network of L1 users had fewer communities, likely due to the small size of its giant component (approximately 13% of the overall network). In comparison, Siew's (2013) phonological network identified 17 giant component communities, with an average community size of 383 words (standard deviation: 250). Methodological differences (especially in data collection) between Siew's study on American English and the present study on British English have to be kept in mind when evaluating the present findings.

The giant component communities of the seven networks were explored in more detail, and the results are outlined in Tables 10 to 16. Communities were classified as *large* when they contained a number of nodes exceeding the 75th percentile of all communities, as *medium* size when they contained nodes between the 25th and the 75th percentile, and as *small* when they contained less than the 25th percentile in number of nodes.

Consistent with findings reported by Siew (2013), the larger communities within the A1 giant component comprised words of higher lexical frequency, shorter phonemic length, and denser neighborhoods. Additionally, clustering was less pronounced in larger communities compared to smaller ones. The community structure of the A1 network can be seen in Figure 26.

In the A2 giant component, no small communities could be detected. Results of the remaining communities differed from Siew (2013) and larger communities contained fewer high-frequency and generally longer words, as well as sparser neighborhoods with less node clustering (see Table 11 for details). This pattern, contrary to the L1 American English network detailed by Siew, persisted across all consecutive proficiency levels up to C1, and higher lexical frequency rates and shorter words were primarily found in smaller network communities. Both node degree and clustering coefficient showed an increase with community sizes for all networks (see Tables 11 to 14).

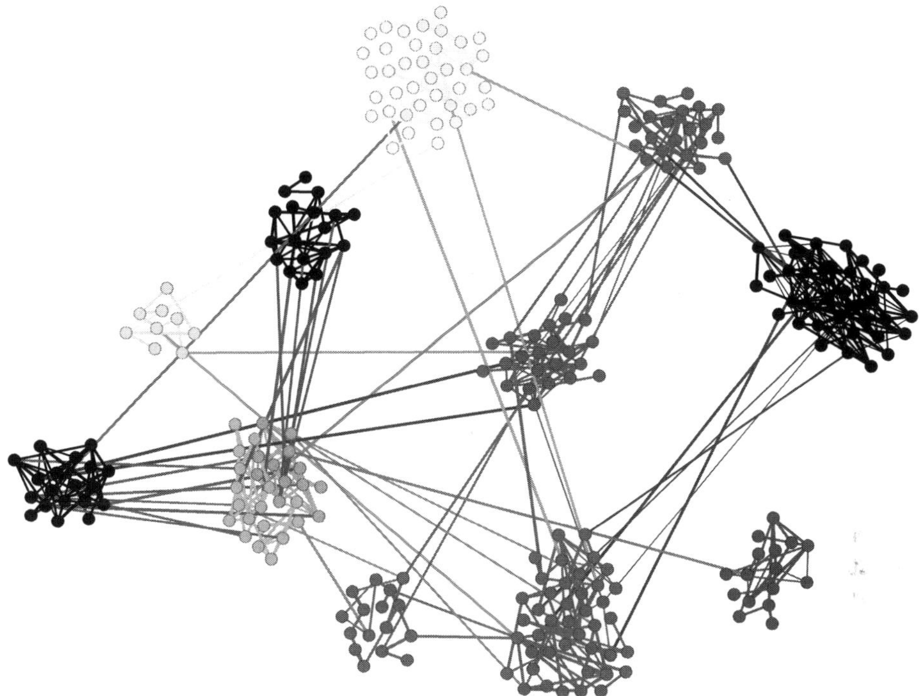

Figure 26: *Communities in the giant component of the A1 phonological network.*

Table 10: Lexical communities of the A1 giant component.

GC communities	*Lexical frequency*		*Phonemic length*		*Neighborhood density*		*Clustering coefficient*	
	Mean	*SD*	*Mean*	*SD*	*Mean*	*SD*	*Mean*	*SD*
Small (<25th percentile)	440.3	74.6	3.7	0.8	3.2	1.6	0.45	0.4
Medium (25th-75th percentile)	441.1	71.7	3.5	0.8	4.2	2.3	0.36	0.3
Large (>75th percentile)	450.3	86.4	3.0	0.8	4.2	2.9	0.33	0.3

Table 11: Lexical communities of the A2 giant component.

GC communities	*Lexical frequency*		*Phonemic length*		*Neighborhood density*		*Clustering coefficient*	
	Mean	*SD*	*Mean*	*SD*	*Mean*	*SD*	*Mean*	*SD*
Medium (25th-75th percentile)	414.9	81.8	3.4	0.8	5.8	3.9	0.33	0.3
Large (>75th percentile)	402.7	75.9	3.8	0.9	5	3.7	0.31	0.3

Table 12: Lexical communities of the B1 giant component.

GC communities	*Lexical frequency*		*Phonemic length*		*Neighborhood density*		*Clustering coefficient*	
	Mean	*SD*	*Mean*	*SD*	*Mean*	*SD*	*Mean*	*SD*
Small (<25th percentile)	391.5	48.8	3.5	0.7	0	0	0	0
Medium (25th-75th percentile)	374.3	78.7	3.8	0.9	5.6	4.3	0.31	0.3
Large (>75th percentile)	380.2	78.3	3.7	1	6.4	5	0.29	0.2

Table 13: Lexical communities of the B2 giant component.

GC communities	Lexical frequency		Phonemic length		Neighborhood density		Clustering coefficient	
	Mean	SD	Mean	SD	Mean	SD	Mean	SD
Small (<25th percentile)	391.5	48.8	3.5	0.7	0	0	0	0
Medium (25th-75th percentile)	357	72.2	4.5	0.8	4.5	3.3	0.31	0.33
Large (>75th percentile)	364.8	76.8	3.9	1	7.1	5.6	0.29	0.26

Table 14: Lexical communities of the C1 giant component.

GC communities	Lexical frequency		Phonemic length		Neighborhood density		Clustering coefficient	
	Mean	SD	Mean	SD	Mean	SD	Mean	SD
Small (<25th percentile)	391.5	48.8	3.5	0.7	0	0	0	0
Medium (25th-75th percentile)	361.7	71.7	4.4	1.1	7.2	6.3	0.38	0.33
Large (>75th percentile)	356.5	77	4.1	1.1	6.7	5.5	0.28	0.26

In the C2 giant component communities, only medium-sized and large communities could be detected, and here, both communities were equal in terms of lexical frequency, phonemic length, node degree, and clustering coefficient (see Table 15).

Table 15: Lexical communities of the C2 giant component.

GC communities	Lexical frequency		Phonemic length		Neighborhood density		Clustering coefficient	
	Mean	SD	Mean	SD	Mean	SD	Mean	SD
Medium (25th-75th percentile)	350.3	76.8	4	1	7.1	6.8	0.29	0.27
Large (>75th percentile)	348.8	77.5	4.2	1.1	7	5.8	0.3	0.3

2.5.2 L1 BRITISH ENGLISH NETWORK

The BNC network showed an unusually small giant component and a number of slightly smaller islands/communities surrounding it.

Table 16: Lexical communities of the BNC giant component.

GC communities	*Lexical frequency*		*Phonemic length*		*Neighborhood density*		*Clustering coefficient*	
	Mean	*SD*	*Mean*	*SD*	*Mean*	*SD*	*Mean*	*SD*
Small (<25th percentile)	3.9	0.5	3.5	0.7	0	0	0	0
Medium (25th-75th percentile)	2.9	1.8	4.9	0.8	2.3	0.9	0.19	0.35
Large (>75th percentile)	3.1	1.7	3.9	0.8	7.3	5.1	0.32	0.24

Similar community dynamics were observed in the BNC network as outlined for the intermediate and advanced ESL networks: high-frequency, short words were primarily found in smaller communities, while denser and more tightly clustered neighborhoods were found in larger communities. The presence of denser neighborhoods in larger communities aligns with Siew's (2013) findings, suggesting the robustness of this measurement concerning phonological community size. The present findings on lexical frequency and phonemic length, however, diverge from Siew's observations. Potential explanations for these differences include the use of different databases for phonological network constructions or variations in word learning dynamics between L1 and L2 users. Further insights into growth patterns within differently sized communities of ESL networks may help elucidate the apparent discrepancies.

In the A1 and A2 learner networks, larger communities contain more words of higher frequency, shorter phonemic length, and denser neighborhoods. As these words are typically learned earlier in language acquisition, the initial build-up of the phonological network and its stratification into (giant component) communities could be geared towards greater robustness and efficiency. Early-acquired words contribute to the formation of robust phonological communities, which may ultimately promote the growth of a cohesive language network necessary for rapid and efficient lexical processing (Siew, 2013). Both L1 and L2 word learning starts with the initial formation of large phonological communities in the giant components of their respective networks. Once a small lexicon has been acquired, the statistics of word learning change so that larger communities receive new neighbors of lower lexical frequency and longer phonemic duration. Simultaneously, these communities become denser and more tightly clustered. Through this dynamic, smaller communities become supplemented with new words which show characteristics of facilitated word learning, such as high frequency and short length. The community structure of the learner networks appears adapted to favor fewer small communities and more medium to large communities, resulting in a multitude of similarly sized communities within the giant component. This effect could be conceptualized as an approach to minimize inequality in network communities, with the aim of establishing comparably sized communities. This network design enhances robustness.

3.
EVOLVING NETWORKS

3.1 THEORETICAL APPROACHES TO NETWORK GROWTH

Phonological networks grow as learners acquire new words. The development of these networks can take diverse paths, and the resulting growth patterns significantly influence network functionality and stability. How new nodes and links are incorporated into a lexical system and which changes are initiated to the overall structure of the network as it grows are fundamental questions for evolving networks.

3.1.1 RANDOM AND SCALE-FREE NETWORK GROWTH

In the early stages of network modeling, the prevalent assumption was the concept of random network design, where node size is fixed and the relationship between two nodes is seen as a random event independent of other links within the network (Janson, Luczak, & Rucinski, 2000; 2001). New nodes entering a system randomly select other nodes to which they can link. This paradigm has its roots in the Erdős–Rényi exponential network model (Erdős & Rényi, 1959), initially designed to represent a static rather than a growing network. The model connects pairs of nodes with a specific probability, leading to a Poisson distribution of degrees. Growth in random networks is predicted to occur in a uniform manner across the network (referred to as "uniform attachment model", see, e.g., Fotouhi & Rabbat, 2013; Lugosi & Pereira, 2019), with the expected degrees of all nodes increasing over time (see Figures 27a and b).

A variety of complex networks do not follow random distributions of growth, with a common observation that some nodes have a large number of links, while many other nodes have only a few or none at all. Networks representing connections of world wide web pages, transportation systems, citation networks of academic works, scientific collaborations, among many other real-life networks, contain few *hubs* (i.e., nodes with a very high number of links) and a majority of minimally connected nodes (Newman, 2001, 2003b). Such scale-free networks are not predicted to add new nodes randomly but according to degree. This process is called "preferential attachment" and it describes the phenomenon that high-degree nodes attract the majority of incoming new nodes (Barabási, 2009; Hébert-Dufresne, Allard, Marceau, Noël, & Dubé, 2011).

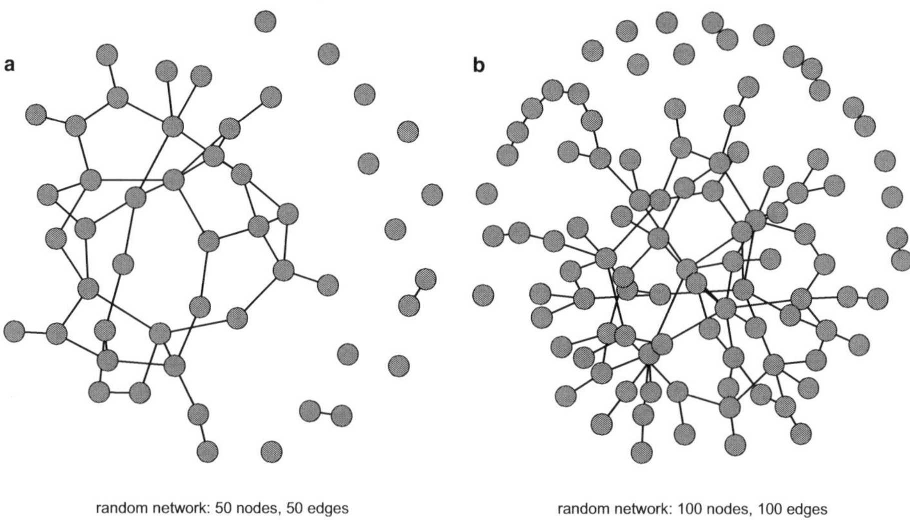

Figures 27a and b: Random network growth (constructed with the R package "igraph", function "erdos.renyi.game").

Conversely, low-degree nodes struggle to grow. Preferential attachment forms the basis of scale-free networks and leads to highly-connected nodes becoming even more highly-connected over time, a "rich-gets-richer" dynamic or the so-called *Matthews effect* (Rigney, 2010). At the same time, nodes with few links become increasingly impoverished ("weak-gets-weaker" phenomenon). Figures 28a and b provide examples illustrating the growth of a non-random scale-free network.

Scale-free networks operate on the premise that not all nodes are created equal (Barabási, 2009; Barabási & Albert, 1999). Certain nodes are more attractive to attach to due to their higher degree: a creator of a new website may choose to hyperlink other popular, high-traffic websites, thereby exercising a bias toward those websites that are already well connected. Some nodes exhibit higher fitness and thus attract the majority of incoming new nodes: for instance, a person's personality can attract more friends in a social network. Preferential attachment gives rise to hubs in networks. As new nodes appear, they tend to attach to highly-connected nodes, driving inequality of degree in the network over time (Bauer & Kaiser, 2017). There is a chronological aspect to growth benefits, with early-acquired nodes being able to increase their connectivity at the expense of late-acquired nodes. In contrast to random networks, in scale-free networks, a small number of edges and hubs become immensely important for overall network connectivity.

Barabási and Albert (1999) proposed that preferential attachment causes networks to become scale-free, characterized by a node distribution following a power law. A non-linear power-law relationship between node size and growth is not the norm, as there can be other mechanisms of preferential attachment (Redner, 2005; Sheridan & Onodera, 2018). Linear preferential attachment can be observed when a new node

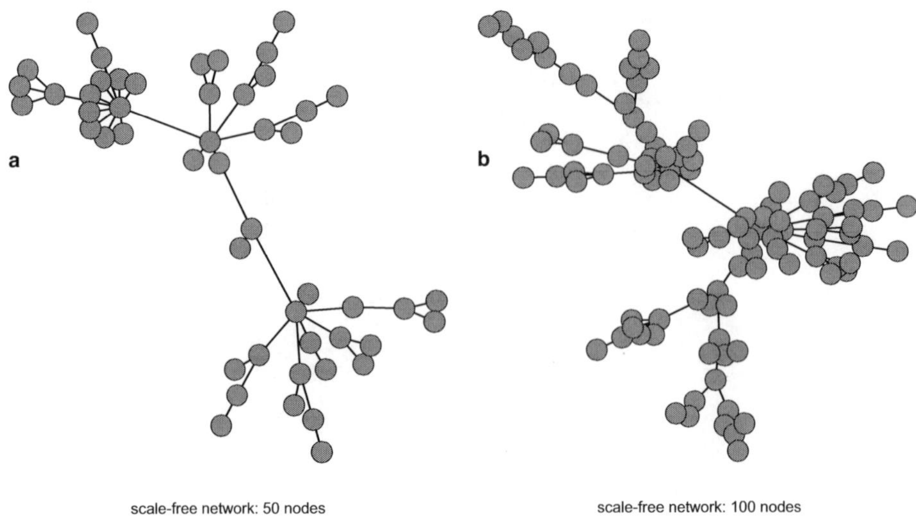

Figures 28a and b: Scale-free network growth (R package "igraph", function "barabasi.game").

is twice as likely to attach to a node with twice as many neighbors compared to a competing node. Non-linear preferential attachment mechanisms, on the other hand, are less predictable and can lead to scenarios where a new node may be ten times as likely to attach to a node with twice as many neighbors. Over time, non-linear growth tends to form a star-shaped network typology (also referred to as "hub-and-spoke" typology), where the "winner-takes-all" mechanism is prevalent and all incoming nodes will primarily attach to the large hub (Vlachos, Parousis-Orthodoxou, & Simos, 2008).

It has been suggested that costs associated with forming new links make a power law distribution less likely to occur (Amaral, Scala, Barthélémy, & Stanley, 2000). If nodes can only accommodate a fixed number of overall neighbors, each new neighbor introduces a cost. Such a restriction is relevant in phonological networks, where factors such as word length, phonemic repertoire, and phonotactic constraints limit the growth potential per node (Vitevitch, 2008). A word cannot indefinitely grow phonological neighbors, as phonotactically legal combinations are limited and the cognitive ability to discriminate words must be upheld by not clustering too many homophones and phonological neighbors together. In fact, power law degree distributions are not commonly found in phonological networks (Vitevitch, 2021; including the ESL network of the present study). Cost-conscious growth can have consequences for assortativity patterns and the presence of lexical isolates (singleton nodes) in a phonological network (Vitevitch, 2008). A striking conclusion from scale-free networks is that many nodes interact with a limited number of other nodes, whereas a small subset of nodes interacts with a high number of other nodes. This places a substantial processing burden on the hub (or hubs). In the case of phonological networks, this interaction pattern attributes high lexical activation influence to a minority of words, whereas the large majority of words have limited ability to diffuse lexical activation to others.

Two crucial concepts in the context of network growth are evolvability and robustness. Evolvability refers to the ability of a network to change and adapt over time (including the incorporation of new nodes), while robustness refers to a network's ability to withstand failures.

3.1.2 EVOLVABILITY AND ROBUSTNESS OF NETWORKS

Per common definition, evolvable networks are able to accommodate changes and adaptations, while robust networks show a topological shape that withstands node and edge disturbances, ensuring a stable connectivity in the face of changes (see, e.g., Payne & Wagner, 2014). There is an intricate relationship between evolvability and robustness: a resilient structure may present challenges to evolvability of a network (Pigliucci, 2008). Robustness and evolvability function as opposing mechanisms – while the former promotes stability, the latter necessitates a certain level of instability (Wagner, 2007). However, robustness must also be recognized as an outcome of the capacity to adapt to changes through evolution (Chen & Lin, 2011). Only an adaptable system can ensure its long-term survival.

3.1.2.1 EVOLVING NETWORKS

One important question in network sciences revolves around identifying the most evolvable node locations within a scale-free network. Hubs, characterized by many neighbors, hold a central position and influence extensive parts of the network. The assumption follows that large hubs should be better insulated against changes, as their numerous links exert conformity pressures within their node neighborhood, suppressing change (Kim, Korbel, & Gerstein, 2007). In the context of phonological networks, the concept of payoff, measured in activation, is central. The more co-activation a phoneme or word receives, the more likely it is to maintain its current (phonological) form and resist changes. In fact, node degree correlates with the rate of change or evolvability (Alvarez-Ponce, Feyertag, & Chakraborty, 2017). Consequently, changes or mutations are frequently expected to manifest in more peripheral nodes. But network dynamics can vary, depending on the type of network under investigation. In some scale-free networks, evolvability is actually facilitated by the existence of "perturbations" or "mutations" in hubs (Helsen, Frickel, Jelier, & Verstrepen, 2019). Genetic networks, for instance, display a higher mutation rate in central and highly connected nodes, offering evolutionary advantages by allowing a fitter phenotype to proliferate through the network (Koubkova-Yu, Chao, & Leu, 2018). Despite the theoretical expectation of slower evolutionary rates in hubs (Alvarez-Ponce et al., 2017; Kim et al., 2007), certain characteristics may predispose hubs to be more evolvable. In a phonological network of L1 German, hubs were more likely to show one type of sound change, while non-hubs were inclined towards another type of sound change (Luef, 2022a). The specific characteristics of these hubs and the nature of the changes (i.e., the type of adaptation) emerge as relevant factors in understanding evolvability in phonological networks. Since hubs are more highly connected and regulate information flow to a greater degree within a network, their behavior has major implications for network connectivity.

3.1.2.2 ROBUSTNESS MEASURES

Network robustness is commonly investigated using the theoretical framework of percolation theory, which stems from statistical physics and mathematics and can be applied to the question of how networks can break up into smaller, non-connected parts (Li, Zhang, Zio, Havlin, & Kang, 2015). It essentially tracks the gradual fragmentation of a network by removing nodes at random, all the while analyzing how their absence influences the integrity of the network (essentially the inverse of a percolation process, Barabási, 2016). The impact of node removal varies. The removal of few nodes has minimal effects, but a larger number can lead to the breakup of the giant component. A critical threshold, defined as the node removal variable f_c, must not be exceeded or the giant component disappears (Barabási, 2016). Random node removal can induce a phase transition from a connected to a fragmented network. Once a finite fraction of nodes (f_c) are removed, network breakup is imminent (Boccaletti, Latora, Moreno, Chavez, & Hwang, 2006). In scale-free networks, however, a large number of nodes can be removed without significantly impacting the network's integrity. This unusual robustness is attributed to the presence of large hubs and giant components (Barabási, 2009; Cohen & Havlin, 2010). Scale-free networks have unusually large fc values, related to their degree distribution (Barabási, 2016), enabling them to withstand a considerable level of node removal without suffering major failures. As random node removal does not consider node degree, the likelihood of a low-degree node being removed in a scale-free network is much higher than the likelihood that one of the very few hubs is affected. Low-degree nodes contribute minimally to network connectedness, and their removal has little impact on the overall network. As seen in Figure 29, a visual representation of a network of 30 nodes, each node has a 1/30th chance of being selected for removal. The probability of selecting one of the 26 small-degree nodes for removal is higher than the chance that one of the three larger-degree or the singular hub node is affected.

Using the "runif" function for uniform distributions in R, 1000 runs of probability simulations of the above network produced the following choices for random node removal (see Table 17): the probability of hub-node 19 failing is not unusually high and the node is selected for random removal only 29 out of 1000 times.

In general, scale-free networks are quite robust against accidental failures or random node/edge removal. However, they may become vulnerable if targeted attacks are directed against the hubs (Albert, Jeong, & Barabási, 2000; Newman, 2002; in phonological/semantic networks: Stella, 2020). Network failures, marked by a loss of connections between nodes, may lead to substantial increases in average path length, signaling compromised network functionality (Albert et al., 2000). Networks become

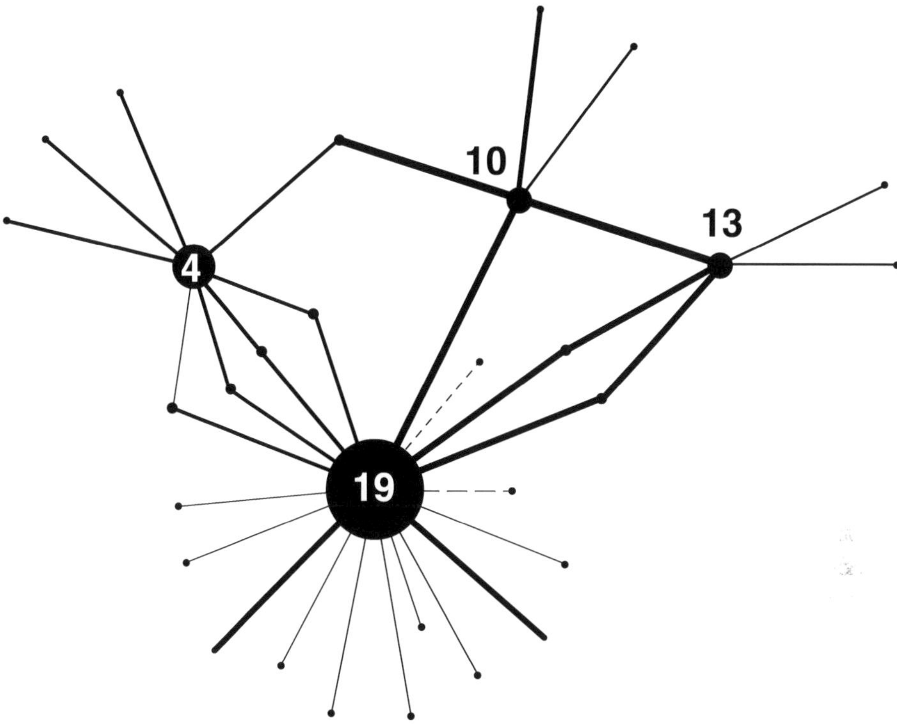

Figure 29: Each node has an equal 0.033 chance of being chosen for removal. This leads to a higher likelihood of one of the numerous small-degree nodes being chosen.

Table 17: Probability of node removal in network of 30 nodes in 1000 simulations.

	Node 19	Node 4	Node 10	Node 13	Average other nodes
Hits	29	24	45	41	33

more robust when node degree is more evenly distributed and less tightly concentrated in one giant component (Hu & Lee, 2020). In both technological and biological networks, the concept of 'cascading failure' describes a chain reaction initiated by an error or failure in one node that leads to failures in connected nodes (Ren, Song, Yang, Baptista, & Grebogi, 2016). Large giant component sizes combined with high clustering coefficients and short average path lengths heighten the risk of cascading failures (Hu & Lee, 2020). In the event of a failure in a highly connected node within the giant component, numerous links may be severed, resulting in an increase in giant component diameter and average path length.

Several network centrality statistics, with degree centrality being a primary one, serve as predictors for robustness, and networks with higher average degrees tend to be more robust (Martin & Niemeyer, 2020). As network centrality statistics are inherently related to network size, robustness predictably varies at different stages of network growth. Zhao and Xu (2009) theoretically explored how to enhance network robustness through growth by comparing three mechanisms of node addition: (1) adding a new neighbor to an isolated node, (2) adding a new neighbor to a low-degree node, and (3) adding a new neighbor to a high-degree node. Results revealed that supplementing low-degree nodes yields the greatest robustness benefits for evolving scale-free networks. This growth strategy significantly reduces the concentration of node clusters in the giant component, leading to the emergence of more numerous but smaller, unconnected clusters. This restructuring acts as a protective measure for the network against failure.

Phonological networks are prone to failure – disease, cognitive decline, or temporary memory loss (e.g., forgetfulness, word-finding difficulties) can diminish phonological neighborhoods, with potential ensuing systemic failures in connectivity of the mental lexicon (Stella, 2020). Non-pathological temporary phonological processing impairments, such as speech errors or perception errors (i.e., 'slips of the ear'), are also indicative of lexical processing failures. Studies on speech errors have shown that phonological neighborhood effects play a role (Harley & Bown, 1998; James & Burke, 2000; Vitevitch, 2002c; Vitevitch & Sommers, 2003). Vitevitch (1997) found that overly dense and overly sparse phonological neighborhoods can both impede lexical processing and lead to more malapropism-type speech errors. This implies that lexical cognition functions optimally when phonological neighborhoods consist of a moderate number of neighbors. Thus, a general mechanism by which word growth in phonological networks is primarily concentrated in low-degree nodes best fits the stability model outlined by Zhao and Xu (2009) and the predictions stemming from Vitevitch (1997). A more equal distribution of (phonological) resources among the giant component, islands, and singleton nodes and a prevalence of more numerous smaller components in a network indicates improved robustness and higher stability and (Estrada, 2006).

3.1.3 GROWING SCALE-FREE NETWORKS

3.1.3.1 BARABÁSI–ALBERT MODEL

Since the inception of preferential attachment, a variety of network growth models have been introduced that aim to supplement the concept, all with the aim to better explain scale-free network growth. In the classical Barabási–Albert model of preferential attachment, each node gets to increase its degree following the equation

$$p_i = k_i / \sum_j k_j$$

where the probability that a new node links to node *i* (p_i) is the degree of the node *i* (k_i), divided by the sum calculated overall pre-existing nodes *j* (i.e., the denominator results in the overall number of edges in the network). Preferential attachment can be seen as highly probabilistic, with the likelihood of node attachment increasing linearly with node degree. For instance, a new node is twice as likely to connect to a six-degree node in the network than it is to a three-degree node. This simple degree-based attachment model exemplifies the rich-gets-richer mechanisms in the network and incorporates a correlation between degree with node age (Barabási, 2009). The fact that older nodes tend to capture the majority of links is referred to as "first mover advantage" (Bianconi & Barabási, 2001).

In their study of phonological network growth in Dutch- and English-speaking children, Siew and Vitevitch (2020a) identified preferential attachment (referred to as 'PATT') as the main growth mechanisms for the early stages of language acquisition (ages 3 to 6 years). However, at more advanced acquisition stages (over 6 years of age), the inverse variant of preferential attachment (referred to as 'iPATT') became the driving force behind phonological neighbor acquisition.[3] Their findings indicated that young children expanded their vocabulary by adding phonological neighbors to high-density neighborhoods. As language acquisition progressed and children developed a more extensive vocabulary, this growth mechanism reversed. At this point, new words became primarily linked to words in lexical islands, which had few neighbors. To further explore these findings, Siew and Vitevitch (2020b) conducted a series of computational simulations of vocabulary growth algorithms, and their results confirmed that an initial phase of PATT followed by iPATT leads to a network typology resembling known phonological networks. Specifically, such a growth dynamic results in a degree distribution that deviates from a power law, and the network exhibits a small network diameter combined with short average path length (Vitevitch, 2008). These growth dynamics were replicated in second language phonological networks of English (see Luef, 2022b). Here, too, PATT dominated growth at lower proficiency levels (up to B2), with iPATT taking over at the C1 level. This trend suggests a potential similarity in lexical growth patterns in first and second language English.

Given that a large giant component makes a network more vulnerable, one strategy to minimize attack risks is to grow in a manner that supplements low-degree nodes. Phonological networks adopt this strategy, underscoring the role of robustness in network construction. Siew and Vitevitch (2020a) and Luef (2022b) identified this dynamic only in the advanced stages of language acquisition. This suggests that the lexicon of adult or advanced language learners is structured to strengthen its resilience and counter vulnerabilities. During the initial stages of network construction, preferential attachment causes a "rich-club" topology where high-degree nodes accumulate most new links. The contrast in vocabulary growth strategies between beginning and advanced language learners provides intriguing perspectives into vocabulary acquisition in beginners and more advanced language learners.

The Barabási-Albert model, originally focused on preferential attachment, has been extended to encompass additional mechanisms, resulting in a family of evolving

---

3 Node degree was used as a proxy variable for preferential attachment probability.

network models. These adaptations aim to provide a more nuanced understanding of the various aspects shaping topologies of real networks (Newman, 2003b). One such extension is the initial attractiveness model (Dorogovtsev, Mendes, & Samukhin, 2000). Barabási (2016) explains this concept using research paper citations: each new research paper has a finite probability of being cited at least once. Similarly, in social networks, a new student arriving at a school is likely to make at least one friend (see, e.g., Ying, 2011). The initial attractiveness principle is effective in capturing real-life scenarios where most unconnected nodes eventually form some initial connections, albeit few and only initially. Networks become more homogeneous if initial attractiveness comes into play. This mechanism reduces the size of hubs, and increases the probability of no-degree or low-degree nodes receiving a small share of new nodes as neighbors. Initial attractiveness weakens preferential attachment, as it favors growth in small-degree nodes. Its effect on high-degree nodes is negligible (Barabási, 2016). By introducing the possibility of small-degree attachment, initial attractiveness leads to a small-degree cutoff in the heavy-tail distribution.

3.1.3.2 FITNESS MODEL

While the preferential attachment model and its inverse variant can explain some phenomena observed in phonological networks, it is essential to recognize that factors beyond degree and node age may influence a word's ability to grow its neighborhood. Several network growth models consider node-intrinsic qualities, exemplified by the internet search engine Google, which, despite entering the scene later, quickly became the dominant hub among search engines (Bell et al., 2017). Here, young age and few previous links did not pose obstacles to Google acquiring the majority of future links. A consideration of node-intrinsic properties that make a node in a network particularly prone to neighbor acquisition can add considerably to growth models. Node fitness, denoting an accumulation of attributes that make a node prone to growth, implies that a fit node attracts more neighbors than a less fit one (Bedogne' & Rodgers, 2006; Caldarelli, Capocci, De Los Rios, & Munoz, 2002). Node fitness can be modeled based on any quantifiable property or properties of individual nodes (Ferretti, Cortelezzi, Yang, Marmorini, & Bianconi, 2012) or depend on the properties of the neighboring nodes (Ferretti et al., 2012; Papadopoulos, Kitsak, Serrano, Boguna, & Krioukov, 2012). The exact fitness qualities depend on the type of network under consideration. In phonological networks, metrics of node fitness can include factors contributing to better retention or retrieval of word forms. Well-known contributors to enhance retention and more efficient word learning include word length, lexical frequency, and phonotactic probability (e.g., Crossley, Skalicky, Kyle, & Monteiro, 2019; Ellis, 2002; Goodman, Dale, & Li, 2008; Storkel et al., 2006; Storkel, 2013).

Fitness-based growth models attribute more growth to fitter nodes and assume that scale-free topologies arise from the unequal distribution of node fitness across networks (Garlaschelli & Loffredo, 2004). This conceptual framework is commonly referred to as the "fit-gets-richer" mechanism (Caldarelli et al., 2002), showing that heavy-tail (or power law) distributions can arise from factors other than degree-driven preferential attachment (Mendes & Da Silva, 2009). While the majority of fitness growth models focus on higher growth in fitter nodes, a related mechanism has been suggested by Bell and colleagues (2017), the "avoidance of the weakest links" dynamic. Such growth occurs in a way that minimizes "maximum exposure to node unfitness" (p. 1), ensuring each node in a network maintains a minimum level of fitness. A bias of new nodes to attach to the least-fit nodes in the system could serve as evidence for this dynamic.

Hybrid models integrate both node fitness and preferential attachment to simulate network growth. A prominent example is the Bianconi-Barabási model, defined by the following equation:

$$p_i = \eta_i k_i / \sum_j \eta_j k_j$$

where the probability of a new neighbor at node *i* can be calculated by taking into account the fitness of the node (η_i) and the fitness of the other nodes in the network (η_j). If two nodes have the same fitness, the one with the higher degree will be more likely selected. If two nodes have the same degree, the one with the higher fitness score will excel (Bell et al., 2017). In the Bianconi-Barabási model, a young node can grow faster than an older one, overcoming the age disadvantage (induced by the first-mover-advantage) through higher fitness.

Measurements of fitness can vary. Node-intrinsic qualities are diverse and depend on the type of network studied. One can also investigate growth rate itself as a fitness metric. Here, neighborhood growth of words is tracked over a period of word learning, and those words that acquire the most links overall are classified as the fittest nodes. This approach captures a network's "collective perception of a node's importance relative to the other nodes" (Barabási, 2016: p. 208) and provides a measure of evolvability by comparing a node's evolution to that of other nodes in the network. The fittest nodes can then be investigated in terms of their intrinsic qualities, and conclusions can be drawn as to what constitutes node fitness in a specific network.

A fitness-related issue in network growth is the Bose-Einstein condensation, a specific behavior of subatomic particles in quantum gas that can be mapped to networks (Bianconi & Barabási, 2001). The original Bose-Einstein condensation (Bose, 1924; Einstein, 1924) pertains to a specific energy state of gas particles, where a group of atoms is cooled close to absolute zero, at which point the atoms begin to clump together and enter the same low energy states. They become incapable of taking on more energy at this point, regardless of how much Bose liquid is added (see Glazer & Wark, 2001). The only particles absorbing the incoming energy are the few ones with high energy levels. This principle finds application in understanding the transitional process from a "fit-gets-richer" to a "winner-takes-all" growth mechanism, a phenomenon in certain networks (Barabási, 2016). By mapping network nodes to energy levels and network links to particles, Bianconi and Barabási (2001) demon-

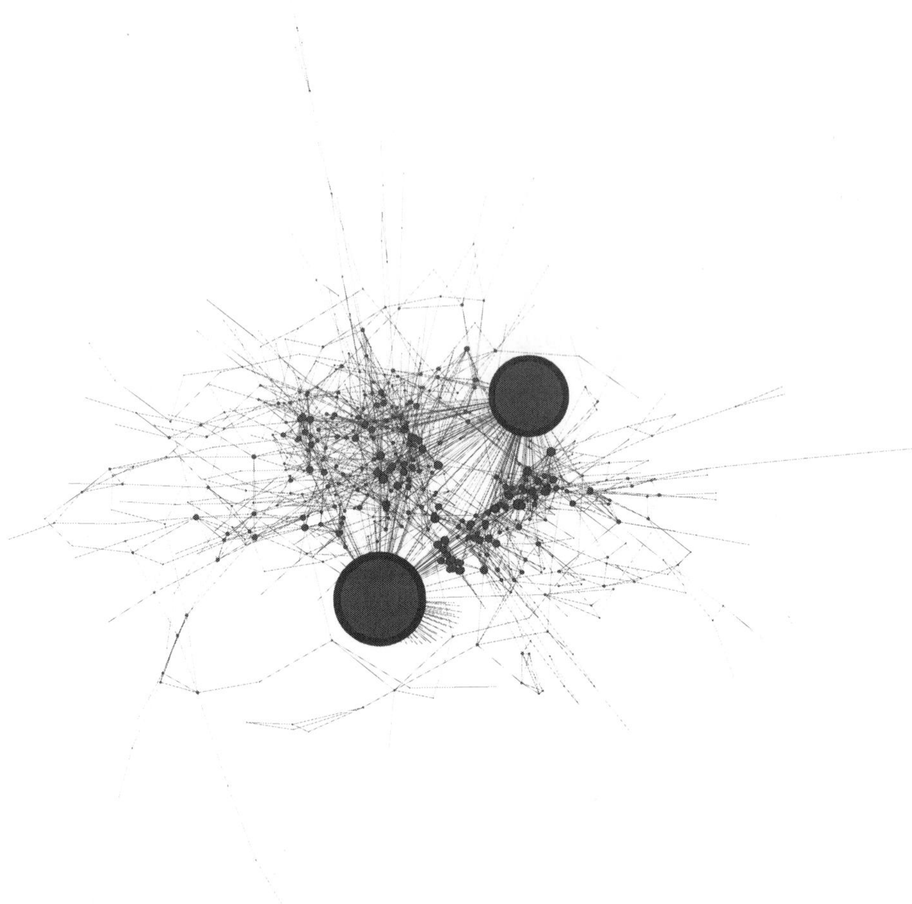

Figure 30: Bose-Einstein condensation in a network with two super-hubs taking all incoming links.

strated that networks can undergo Bose-Einstein condensation. The process unfolds in two distinct phases: an initial scale-free phase of fit-gets-richer dynamic, followed by Bose-Einstein condensation where all network nodes aggregate at the lowest growth level, with a few prolific (fittest) nodes capturing a finite fraction of the new links and turning into super-hubs. Whether a network can undergo a Bose-Einstein condensation depends on the fitness distribution, where a few fittest nodes and a majority of less fit nodes compose the network. Developments of fitness distribution over stages of language learning can inform about a possible Bose-Einstein condensation in phonological networks. Figure 30 depicts a Bose-Einstein condensation in a hypothetical network.

3.1.3.3 INTERNAL LINKING: "DOUBLE PREFERENTIAL ATTACHMENT"

Another distinctive network dynamic can result when new neighbors have the effect of connecting two pre-existing nodes in a network that were previously neighbors. In such a case, two interlinked mechanisms contribute to the establishment of new links: (1) arrival of new nodes and (2) linking of existing nodes. In phonological networks, this is commonly observed during word learning (see Figures 31a and b). In English beginners at the A1 proficiency level, the neighborhoods of "all" and "feel" are not linked. But in slightly advanced learners at the A2 proficiency level, the introduction of the "fall" connects the neighborhoods. This dynamic leads to new predictions regarding the diffusion of lexical activation in the A2 network.

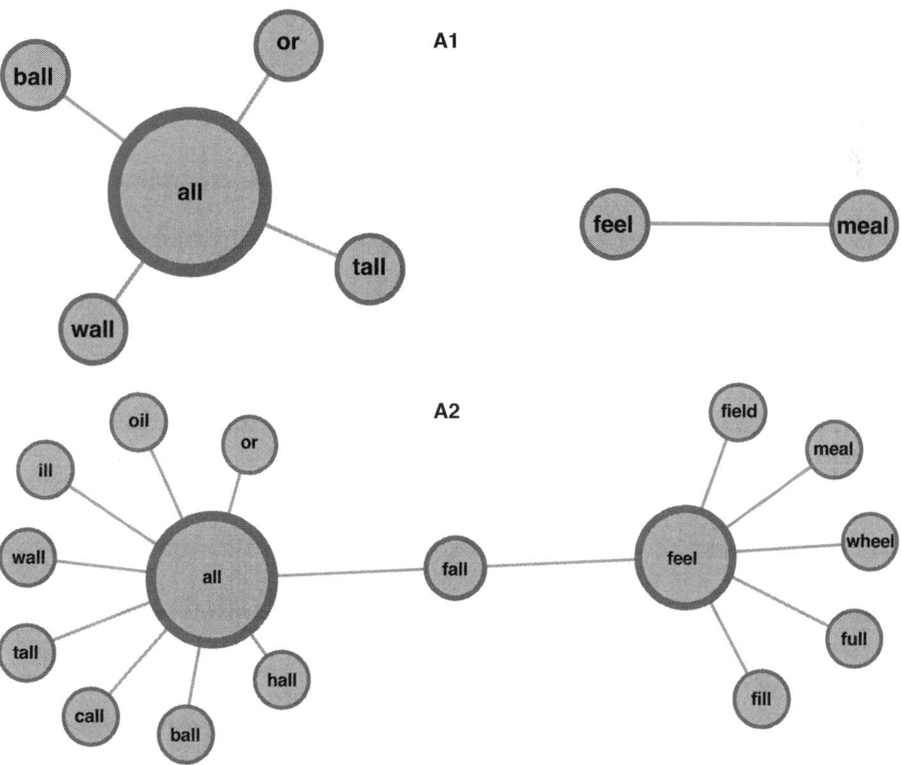

Figures 31a and b: *The introduction of new words can lead to new neighbor formation in pre-existing words in a phonological network (data from the ESL-A1, above, and ESL-A2, below, networks).*

The internal linking mechanism can give rise to what is known as "double preferential attachment" (Ghoshal, Chi, & Barabási, 2013), which is the probability that an internal link connects two high-degree nodes network-internally. In the A2 network, neighborhood density for "all" and "feel" is high, making them more likely to become linked by the introduction of a new word if double preferential attachment is the driving force. Double preferential attachment tends to increase heterogeneity within a network by amplifying the larger hubs through linking. Consequently, small-degree nodes may face limitations in terms of their growth potential (Barabási, 2016). It is also possible that internal links are not governed by preferential attachment but by "random attachment", where internal links are established on a random basis (Ghoshal et al., 2013). In such cases, homogeneity of node degree increases, but this is an unlikely scenario for phonological networks.

3.1.3.4 AGING EFFECTS AND DECLINING NETWORKS

Real networks often undergo node removal, a process akin to forgetting a word in phonological networks due to cognitive decline, temporary memory lapses, or language attrition (Stella, 2020). If node disappearance outpaces node arrival, the network naturally shrinks. This is observable for instance in neurodegenerative disease or when a second language learner stops using a language. Such 'declining networks' experience a higher rate of node loss compared to the rate of new node addition. A mechanism called "preferential survival" has been suggested to account for node loss, with high-degree nodes being better equipped to withstand node deletions (Kong & Roychowdhury, 2008). In some networks, the rate of new node addition may equal the rate of old node removal, potentially leading to the loss of the network's scale-free nature (Saavedra, Reed-Tsochas, & Uzzi, 2008). An essential consideration is whether nodes are removed randomly or if there is a system to node removal. For instance, low-degree nodes may be more susceptible to failure or loss, as observed in lexical networks of aphasics (Stella, 2020). The co-existence of node removal with other network-internal processes can result in complex interactions, as illustrated in a study of the declining network of the garment industry in New York City (Saavedra et al., 2008). Despite the considerable shrinkage of the giant component, the degree distribution remained unaffected. The garment industry network preferentially lost low-degree nodes, demonstrating a 'weak-gets-weaker 'phenomenon. However, the occasional arrival of new nodes followed preferential attachment. This resulted in a tight clustering of the decreasing number of nodes in a giant component, which overall diminished due to node removal exceeding node arrival.

The 'aging effect' (or 'obsolescence effect') in networks refers to the gradual disappearance of nodes with a limited lifespan (Sun, Michaels, & Mahadevan, 2020). This is the case for collaboration networks of scientists, where the professional lifespan of scientists is constrained by the duration of their employment and active publishing period. In these networks, nodes do not vanish abruptly but instead fade away through an aging process. Scientists start collaborations early in their academic career, experience a phase of heightened productivity characterized by a multitude of collaborations, and eventually, towards the end of their career, gradually end collaborations until retirement marks the cessation of collaboration altogether. Various dynamics may influence networks exhibiting aging effects. New nodes may preferentially connect with older ones, potentially accelerating preferential attachment. Alternatively, new nodes may exhibit a tendency to connect with younger nodes, or each new node may attach to the previously introduced one, transforming the network into a chain-like structure (Zhu, Wang, & Zhu, 2003). In phonological networks of second language learners, aging was shown to have an effect on growth potential (Luef, 2023). Growth spurts were most significant in nodes recently added to the network, and the longer a node had been part of the network, the less likely it was to grow a new neighbor. Thus, mainly young nodes were endowed with growth potential. This growth dynamic is a reversal of the first-mover advantage, it could be described as a "late-mover advantage", emphasizing the tendency of young nodes to obtain new neighbors (see Luef, 2023).

3.1.3.5 ACCELERATED GROWTH

Networks may show accelerated growth, even hyper-accelerated growth, in addition to decelerating growth (Gagen & Mattick, 2005; Mendes, 2003). Accelerated growth is defined as a super-linear increase of nodes in a network over time (Liu et al., 2019) and it occurs, for instance, with scientific collaboration networks or the world wide web (Dorogovtsev & Mendes, 2003). Popular network growth theories tend to calculate the probability of a new node attaching to an existing one based on the degree of the existing node (see, e.g., Albert & Barabási, 2002; Barabási & Albert, 1999), defining growth as a linear process. However, many real-world networks deviate from this rule and show growth rates exceeding the linear predictions. Here, the accelerated growth over time eventually leads to the emergence of super-hubs.

3.1.3.6 LOCAL-WORLD NETWORKS

The concept of "local worlds" captures the idea that networks are divided into subgroups, or partitions, where members share more similarity with one another than with other nodes outside the group (Shai, Stanley, Granell, Taylor, & Mucha, 2017). Local-world evolving network models have been developed to account for the fact that in many networks new nodes can only attach to a specific part of the network (Li & Chen, 2003; Li, Jin, & Chen, 2003). Each new node can access a sub-part of the network where the group of existing nodes exhibit similar characteristics. For instance, only certain countries trade with one another. Consequently, a new shipping company can establish routes only between a predefined set of countries, rather than between any two random countries globally that participate in shipping. Local-world models are suited for phonological network investigations: a new word form can only attach to phonologically similar word forms, rather than connect to any random note in the network. There are different ways to conceptualize phonological sub-groups: either through community detection, identifying communities as the natural attachment points for new words (see Cong & Haitao, 2014; Siew, 2013), or by finding all potential neighbors to which a new node can attach, grouping them as "potential attachment points" (the so-called lure-of-the-associates mechanism; Hills et al., 2009b). The first approach defines a larger phonological neighborhood where a new node can find connection points. The second approach zooms in on specific connection points, overlooking the larger phonological neighborhood to which those points belong.

The local-world equation, adapted from Li and Chen (2003), calculates the preferential attachment of node *i*, factoring in the local sub-group of nodes ($_{LOCAL}$) to which an incoming node can potentially attach:

$$p_i = k_i / \sum_{j \in LOCAL} k_j$$

Local-world connectivity has major implications for phonological networks. First, it recognizes that a node has a limited ability to attach in the network, as only a small fraction of the overall nodes is phonologically predisposed for anchoring. Second, the local-world effect generally improves robustness of scale-free networks (Tang & Liu, 2014), an important criterion for cognitive network construction (Walsh & Gluck, 2015), particularly for phonological networks (Siew & Vitevitch, 2016; Stella, 2020). Local-world effects likely occur in combination with other network-relevant mechanisms, including fitness dynamics, internal linking, or accelerated growth, among others. These mechanisms may manifest locally within node communities rather than across the entire network.

3.1.3.7 UNIFORM AND PREFERENTIAL ATTACHMENT

Another group of network growth models, the hybrid random networks (HRN), blends preferential attachment with uniform attachment, a characteristic of random network growth. The probability of new node creation is taken into account when assigning it to the preferential or uniform attachment mode (Wang & Zhang, 2021), along with considering node age, where younger nodes are more likely to attach uniformly (see Pachon, Sacerdote, & Yang, 2018). Classical preferential attachment models predict all nodes in a network to behave in the same way and attach to the highest-degree node. Recent models have relaxed this assumption, allowing new nodes to attach to a network through a combination of uniform and preferential attachment (Cooper & Frieze, 2003; Pachon, Sacerdote, & Yang, 2018). While there are different ways to calculate this combination mathematically (see, e.g., De Ambroggio, Polito, & Sacerdote, 2020), the following equation presents a simple compound variable

$$p_i = UA_i k_i / \sum_j UA_j k_j$$

with uniform attachment "UA" denoting the proportion of a node within its network (for instance, each node in the A1 network has a proportion of $1/606^{th}$). UA and degree of a node (k) are computed proportionally to the sum of all nodes, with their UA values and degree yielding the hybrid uniform/preferential attachment variable. Preferential attachment of node *i* and random attachment probability – the proportion of node *i* in the network – are combined.

The inclusion of uniform attachment leads to lighter tail distributions in the networks compared to what would be expected if preferential attachment was the primary mechanism. An important aspect of node growth in networks is the possibility that a new node does not have to attach to an existing one, as implied by scale-free and most other network models (e.g., Barabási & Albert, 1999). Rather, a new node may enter the network as a singleton node without any immediate neighbors. Phonological networks are characterized by a large proportion of singleton nodes - approximately half of the network (see Gerometta, 2015; Vitevitch, 2008, and the ESL networks) – highlighting the importance of a mechanism to add nodes without attachment as a significant theoretical consideration. Some random network growth models can account for singleton nodes entering the network (Callaway, Hopcroft, Kleinberg, Newman, & Strogatz, 2001). New emerging types of hybrid growth models combine elements from random network growth with preferential attachment and can potentially explain the influx of singleton nodes in a network while considering the role of preferential attachment (e.g., Anwar, Yousuf, & Abid, 2021; Banerjee & Bhamidi, 2021; Callaway et al., 2001; Shao, Zou, Tan, & Jin, 2006; Wang & Zhang, 2021; Weaver, 2015).

Most networks are characterized by a complex combination of growth processes, incorporating elements such as preferential attachment, random attachment, and local-world effects, among others. The prevailing trend in network sciences is to recognize this complexity, leading to the continuous development of new models that amalgamate various growth mechanisms (e.g., Bauer & Kaiser, 2017; Bedogne' & Rodgers, 2006; Bell et al., 2017; Callaway et al., 2001; Dorogovtsev et al., 2000; Ferretti et al., 2012; Pham, Sheridan, & Shimodaira, 2015).

3.2 GROWING PHONOLOGICAL NETWORKS

A growing body of literature is exploring theories related to the growth of lexical networks of first-language users of English and a small range of other languages. Steyvers and Tenenbaum (2005) conducted a pioneering study on semantic network growth, establishing a correlation between word learning probability and the degree centrality of a word in the semantic lexicon. They identified a process akin to preferential attachment, where words were more likely to be learned if they connect to already known words in a child's lexicon, resulting in the scale-free nature of the semantic network (Beckage & Colunga, 2019). The preferential attachment dynamic in semantic growth was also shown in paired-associate-learning tasks, where high-degree words in a semantic network were recognized faster and more accurately (Mak & Twitchell, 2020). Subsequent research on semantic networks by

Hills and colleagues (Hills, Maouene, Riordan, & Smith, 2010; Hills, Maouene, Maouene, Sheya, & Smith, 2009a; Hills et al., 2009b) did not confirm these initial findings. Instead, they identified a growth mechanism called "preferential acquisition" as the main driver for word learning in L1 English-using children. Contrary to preferential attachment, preferential acquisition takes into account the connectivity of a semantic network in the fully-developed adult lexicon (see Hills et al., 2009b). When an evolving network represents an earlier stage of a known, fully-grown network, conclusions can be drawn about the developmental trajectory from the earlier to the final network. In language learning this is naturally the case: a child's growing lexicon can be compared to the adult lexicon. The two linguistic growth algorithms of preferential attachment and preferential acquisition reflect fundamentally different concepts of lexical growth. Preferential attachment suggests that future word knowledge is shaped by the learner's current knowledge, whereas preferential acquisition suggests that it is shaped by the input. In the case of preferential attachment, a new word links to a known word with many neighbors in the learner's current lexicon; in the case of preferential acquisition, a new word links to a highly-connected word in the adult lexicon. As shown by the works of Hills and colleagues, children growing up in an English linguistic environment are more likely to learn words that have more neighbors in the adult L1 English lexicon. Furthermore, Hills et al. (2009b) tested the network growth measure called 'lure-of-the-associates', which predicts that words finding many semantic neighbors in an existing lexicon will be learned more efficiently. This measure essentially counts the number of neighbors a new word can find in the learner's existing lexicon but disregards information about how many neighbors these anchor words themselves have, which is the core feature of preferential attachment. Contrary to Hills et al.'s conclusion, Beckage and Colunga (2019) found that preferential acquisition was not the most influential mechanism for English-speaking children's word learning. Instead, they identified the lure-of-the-associates mechanism as the most influential factor for network growth. The Beckage and Colunga study was focused on individual word learning of children, revealing that children employ all three network growth algorithms (preferential attachment, preferential acquisition, lure-of-the-associates) in idiosyncratic ways.

Siew and Vitevitch (2020a) and Luef (2022b) adapted the three growth measures from Hills et al. (2009) for their study of the growth of the L1 American English phonological network and L2-English networks. They modified their definitions as follows: 'lure of the associates' came to represent the phonological docking words encountered by new words in a network, indicating the potential phonological word forms to which new words could attach. 'Preferential attachment' considered the degree of each potential anchor word, while 'preferential acquisition' counted the degrees of words in the adult English lexicon. Phonological networks were constructed for each vocabulary acquisition stage. Preferential attachment was the dominant mechanism in the early stages of word learning, with the reverse process called "inverse preferential attachment" taking over at later stages. Notably, preferential acquisition and lure-of-the-associates dynamics could not predict the observed growth spurts.

Fourtassi, Bian and Frank (2020) constructed phonological (and semantic) networks of children's language acquisition in ten languages, including English. The study concentrated specifically on nouns and dealt with relatively small networks, ranging from 180 to 339 words. Due to the rarity of one-segment noun neighbors in the networks, the authors opted to include a 2-segment phonological distance score. These significant methodological differences prevent direct comparisons with Siew and Vitevitch (2020b) and Luef (2022b). Fourtassi and colleagues calculated measures of preferential acquisition and preferential attachment similar to Siew and Vitevich (2020a) and Luef (2022b). They observed that preferential acquisition emerged as the primary predictor for word learning across all ten languages studied. Specifically, high-degree words in the adult lexica correlated with enhanced learning in children exposed to the language. Contrary to the findings of Siew and Vitevitch (2020b) and Luef (2022b), preferential attachment had no effect. Fourtassi and colleagues suggest that the ambient learning environment has a larger impact on word learning in children than statistical algorithms based on the children's current vocabulary, a finding in agreement with Hills et al. (2009). An explanation given by Fourtassi and colleagues is that caregivers put more emphasis on words which are connected in their own language, thereby increasing saliency and furthering the learning process in the child (also see Carlson et al., 2014).

An interesting addendum provided by Fourtassi and colleagues (2020) is a cross-linguistic correlation of degree density in the ten languages. For instance, if the word *dog* is highly connected in the English lexicon, is the French word for dog, *chien*, also highly connected in the French lexicon? The answer was clearly 'no', demonstrating that phonological connectivity varies across languages and necessitating that learners acquire knowledge about phonological neighborhood density in each new language. This carries major implications for second language learners who cannot rely on neighborhood statistics from their first language. While it is conceivable that semantic networks show more overlap in node degree across different languages (a question not explored by Fourtassi et al., 2020), phonological networks can differ quite drastically in phonological neighborhood density. Language typology may play a role, since segmental probabilities and frequencies play crucial roles in determining phonological relationships.

In recent studies, researchers have explored the use of multiplex networks, integrating both semantic and phonological dimension of a lexicon (Levy et al., 2021; Stella, 2020; Stella, Beckage, Brede, & de Domenico, 2018). In these networks, two or more layers (i.e., separate networks) are interconnected, and information spreading between the layers can be tracked. While the multiplex approach holds the potential for new insights into word representations in the mental lexicon, it differs from the conventional single-layer networks dedicated solely to either semantic or phonological aspects. Stella et al.'s multiplex networks were designed to address specific questions that involve the combination of phonological and semantic word representations. However, they are constrained by the fact that phonology and semantics are rarely related in English. Cases of polysemy, where one phonological word form can have multiple meanings, such as [nəʊ] (i.e. "no", "know"), represent special instances of activation spreading between phonological and semantic representations (see Castro & Stella, 2018; Castro, Stella, & Siew, 2019). The role of homophones in language learning becomes elevated by these multiplex studies, posing unclear theoretical implications. Current theories of lexical processing can hardly account for a combinatorial effect of semantic and phonological similarity. An intriguing application of multiplex networks to second language learning is the mapping of different languages of a speaker (first and other learned languages) onto distinct layers of either semantic or phonological networks (see Luef, 2025). Such an investigation provides insights into how the first language can prime or facilitate word learning in a second language, without the limitation of having to overcome conceptual differences between semantics and phonology. It is a well-established fact that meaning-based assumptions about words derived from the first language have an impact on another, learned language (e.g., Moreira & Hamilton, 2010). Similarly, phonological similarity between the first and the second language (or third language) influence one another and can predict word learning (Marecka et al., 2021). Examining the interactions between L1 and L2 in a multiplex network provides a platform for uncovering dynamic patterns related to phonological or semantic transfer effects (see Luef, 2025).

3.2.1 GROWING NODES IN THE LEARNER NETWORKS

In the upcoming section, growth in the ESL networks will be explored. The primary emphasis will be on understanding growth patterns and how they impact network components, communities, and individual nodes. In addition, the influence of different growth algorithms on the various proficiency levels of the ESL networks will be examined.[4]

3.2.1.1 NETWORK PARTS

From a macro-level perspective, growth took place primarily in the giant component of all proficiency levels, while singleton nodes displayed the slowest growth rate across all networks (see Figures 32a-c and 33a-b; reported tests are significant *Kruskal-Wallis ANOVAs* at $p<0.05$, with post-hoc *Wilcoxon signed rank tests*).

In the initial stages of language learning, there was a marked expansion in both giant components and islands, which weakened as proficiency increased (see Figures 33a-b). This is a reflection of the overarching macro-analytical pattern to reduce giant component size over the course of language learning.

4 Growth levels will refer to proficiency levels from which growth starts, for instance "A1 growth" references the vocabulary growth taking place to get from the A1 to the A2 lexicon of English as a second language.

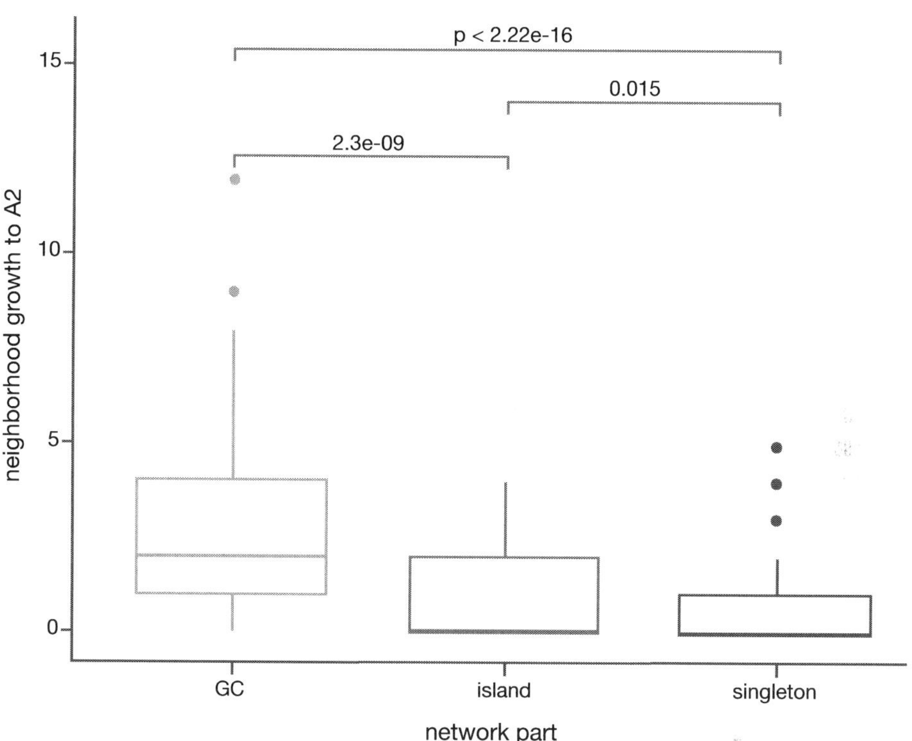

Figure 32a: Growth of network parts in lower-proficiency ESL networks.

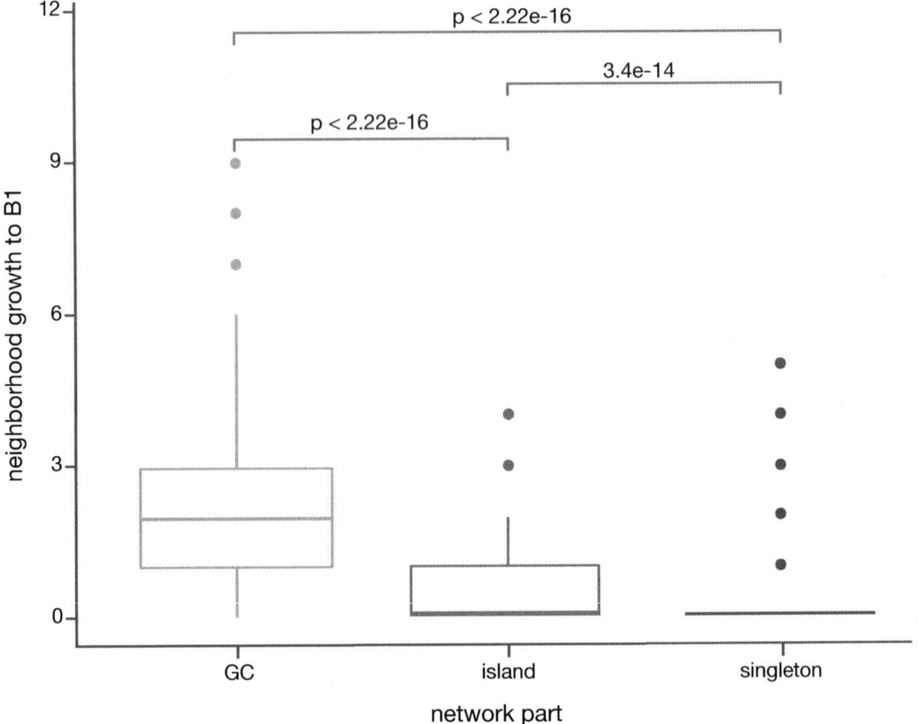

Figure 32b: Growth of network parts in lower-proficiency ESL networks.

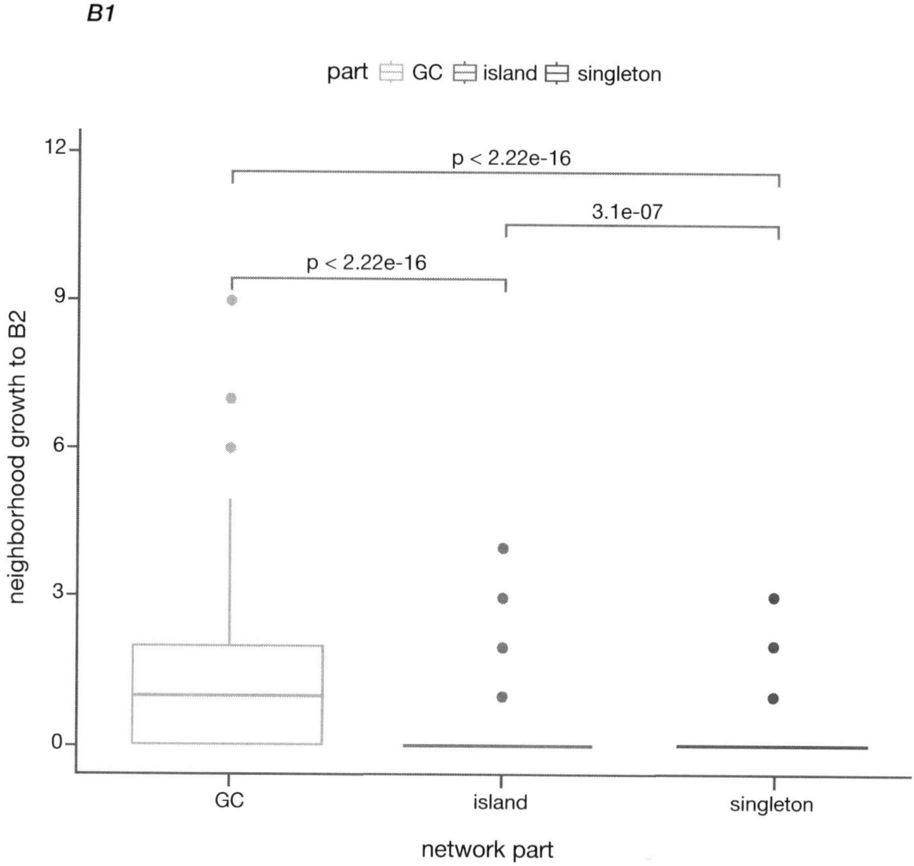

Figure 32b: Growth of network parts in lower-proficiency ESL networks.

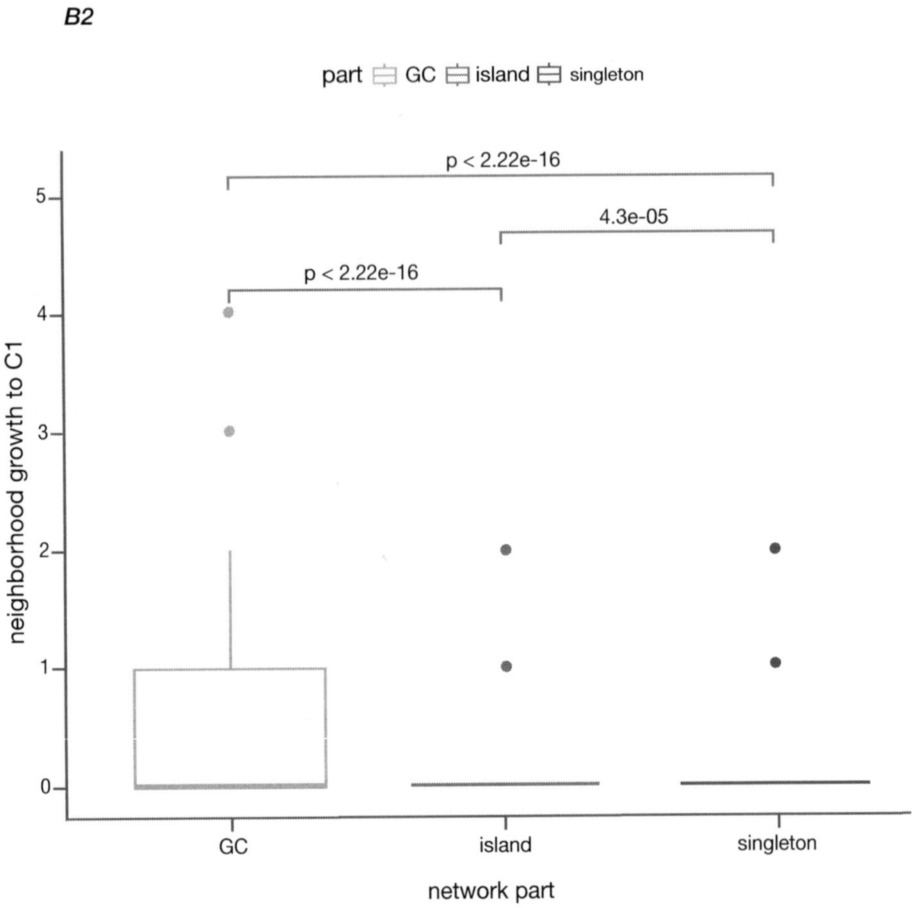

B2

Figures 33a: Growth of network parts in advanced ESL networks.

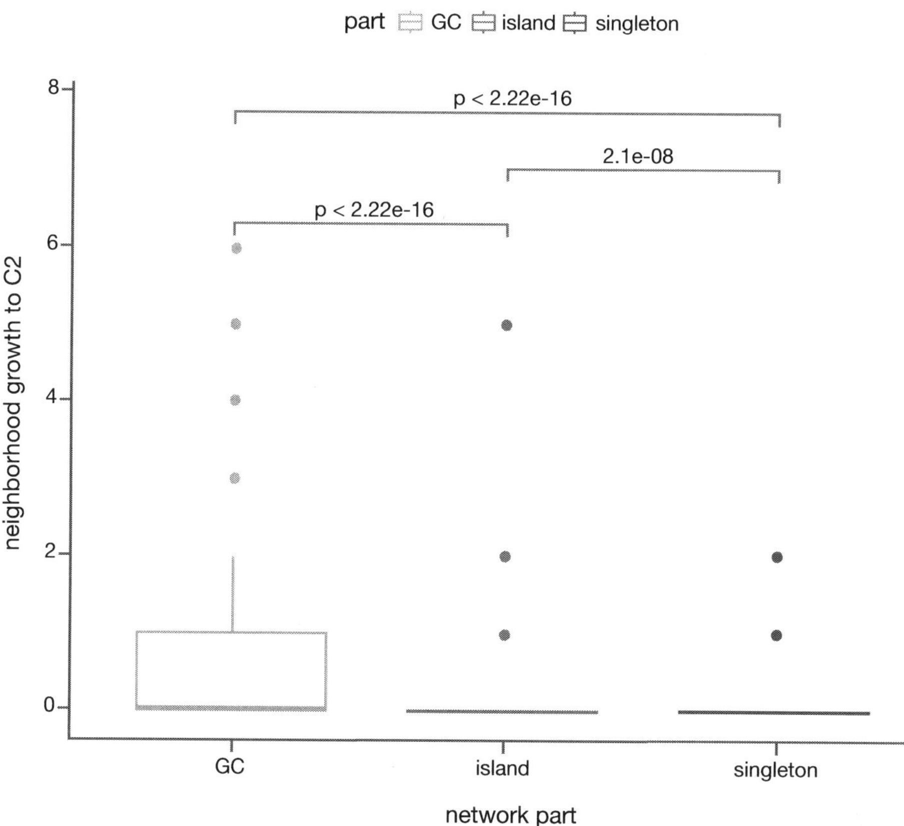

Figures 33b: Growth of network parts in advanced ESL networks.

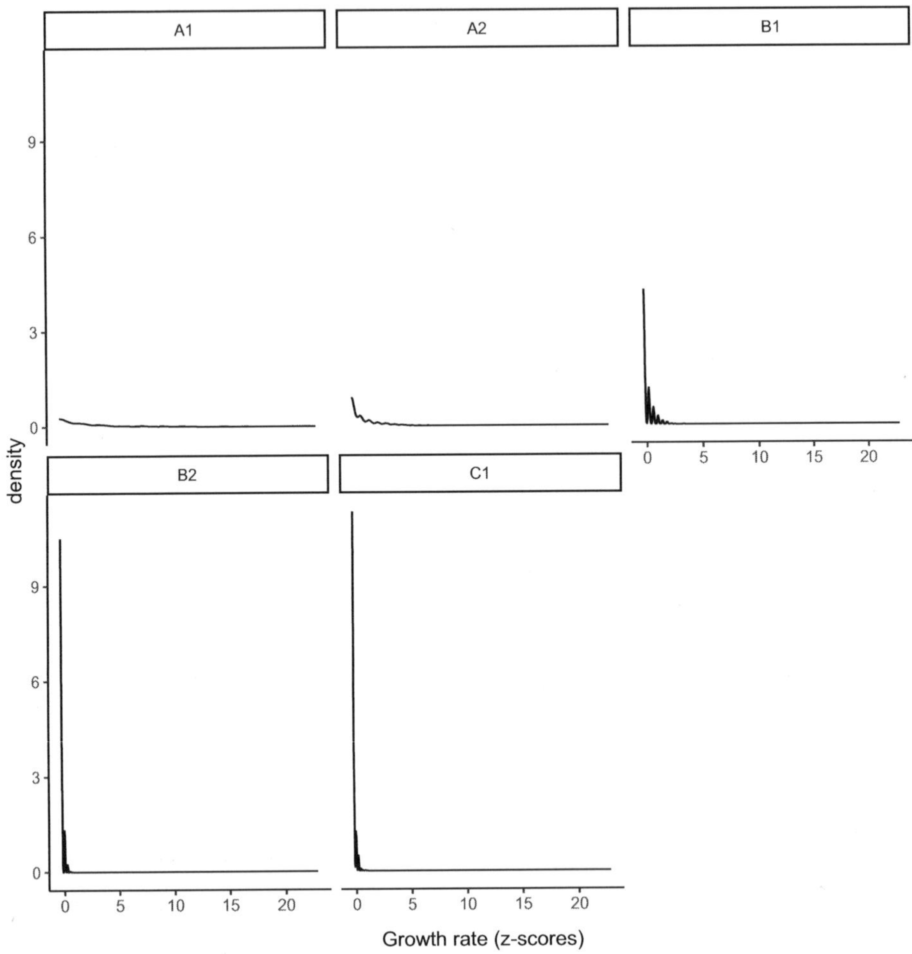

Figure 34: Growth distribution across the proficiency networks. Proficiency levels indicate starting point of growth development, i.e., 'A1' refers to growth occurring between the A1 and A2 level.

In less advanced networks, the distributions of growth rates across proficiency levels displayed more egalitarian tendencies, with numerous nodes being able to grow (see Figure 34). Increasing inequality of growth opportunities became apparent starting at the A2 network, with the advanced learner networks being characterized by a large bias in the growth distribution, where a small number of nodes continued to grow, while the large majority of the nodes did not.

Table 18 presents the best approximations of growth distributions across different ESL proficiency levels.

The multimodal distributions indicate that in each proficiency lexicon, growth is not exclusively focused on specific nodes. Table 19 lists a break-down of the highest-growth nodes identified for each proficiency level, as well as an overall summary.

Table 18: Estimates of growth rate distribution types.

	A1	A2	B1	B2	C1
Best-fitting distribution	Multimodal (dip test p: <0.001)	Multimodal (dip test p: <0.001)	Multimodal (dip test p: <0.001)	Multimodal (dip test p: <0.001)	Multimodal (dip test p: <0.001)

Table 19: Raw node growth rates of the highest-growth nodes per proficiency level (and overall).

A1	A2	B1	B2	C1	Overall (A1-C1)
WILL: 12	SEA/ SEE: 9	SEEM: 9	HOLE/ WHOLE: 4	DEEP: 6	FOR/ FOUR: 23
EIGHT: 9	FALL: 8	SCENE: 7	SIGN: 4	FOUR/ FOR: 6	RAIN: 19
KICK: 9	FOUR/ FOR: 8	SEAT: 7		KEEP: 6	EIGHT: 18
SIT: 9	LOW: 8	SELL: 7		DOOR: 5	WEAR/ WHERE: 18
WHY: 9	BEAN/ BEEN: 7	DEAR: 6		LAW: 5	WILL: 18
HAIR: 8	MIGHT: 7	FACE: 6		LEAD: 5	FAIL: 17
THEIR/ THERE: 8	RIGHT/ WRITE: 7	HEAD: 6		MORE: 5	FEEL: 17
WEAR/ WHERE: 8	SHORT: 7	LIP: 6		NOR: 5	SEA/ SEE: 17
	WAR: 7	RAIL: 6		PAW: 5	WHY: 17
		RAISE: 6		POUR: 5	PAIR: 16
		SALE/ SAIL: 6		RED: 5	PAY: 16
		SET: 6		SHEEP: 5	SIT: 16
		TELL: 6		SHORE: 5	WHITE: 16
				WAR: 5	BEER: 15
				YOUR: 5	BUT: 15

To better understand which node characteristics contribute the most to node growth, a linear mixed effects model using the R package "lme4" and the function "lmer" (Bates, Maechler, Bolker, & Walker, 2014) was calculated to analyze how node growth (relative to network size) is affected by phonemic length, lexical frequency rate, phonotactic probability and network centralities (degree centrality, weighted degree centrality, closeness centrality, betweenness centrality, clustering coefficient, eigenvector centrality), as random effects, "word" and "proficiency level" were entered into the model. Full models were compared with a corresponding null model lacking the fixed effect under investigation using a likelihood ratio test, and the significance of the individual fixed effect was estimated (Dobson, 2002; Forstmeier & Schielzeth, 2011). Prior to analysis, all variables were z-scored.

The variables "degree" and "weighted degree" were correlated at r=-0.9 and combined as an interaction variable. Therefore, the first principal component (PC1) was computed via principal components analysis in order to combine the two variables into one that can account for the majority of the variance (see, e.g., Salem & Hussein, 2019). The first principal component (PC1) of "degree" and "weighted degree" was correlated at -0.71, with PC1 explaining 99% of the variance in the data. The computations were performed with R and the function "prcomp". Due to high correlations with the interaction variable "degree & weighted degree", the two variables "betweenness centrality" (r=0.64) and "eigencentrality" (r=0.73) were removed from the models. The rest of the variables showed variance inflation factors of <1.8 (as calculated with the R package "car" and the function "vif"), and collinearity did not appear to be an issue (Field, 2005; Quinn & Keough, 2002). The following pseudo code was used for the model:

growth rate ~ lexical frequency + phonemic length + phonotactic probability + closeness centrality + clustering coefficient+ degree & weighted degree+(1|word)+(1|proficiency level)

Results of the linear mixed models revealed that node growth was predominantly influenced by phonemic length, lexical frequency rate, phonotactic probability, clustering coefficients, and degree/weighted degree of a node (see Table 20).

Table 20: Results of the linear mixed model analysis.

Predictors	Estimate	Std. error	p
Phonemic length	-0.0055	0.0008	<0.001***
Lexical frequency	0.0034	0.0007	<0.001***
Phonotactic probability	0.0019	0.0006	0.002***
Closeness centrality	-0.0003	0.0006	0.65
Clustering coefficient	0.0075	0.0007	<0.001***
Degree & weighted degree	-0.0051	0.0006	<0.001***

*** p<0.001

To enhance clarity of the results, growth rates were categorized based on how many neighbors each node gained when progressing from one proficiency level to the next. The number of neighbors was standardized to ensure comparability across the networks and different growth rates. Specifically, words which grew a number of phonological neighbors above the 75th percentile were defined as "high" growth rate nodes, words that grew neighbors between the 25th and 75th percentile were defined as "mid" growth rate, and those that grew below the 25th percentile were defined as "low" growth nodes. Nodes that did not acquire any new neighbors were classified as "zero" growth nodes.

Per linear mixed model analysis, the highest-growing nodes were consistently associated with shorter phonemic length across all proficiency levels (see Figure 35). The initial lexica (A1, A2) generally comprised shorter words; thus, the effect of phonemic length on growth was less pronounced. It is important to note that the raw numbers of phonological neighbor acquisition were highest in A1 and A2 (up to 12 neighbors per word, or twice as much as at the C1 level, see Table 19 above).

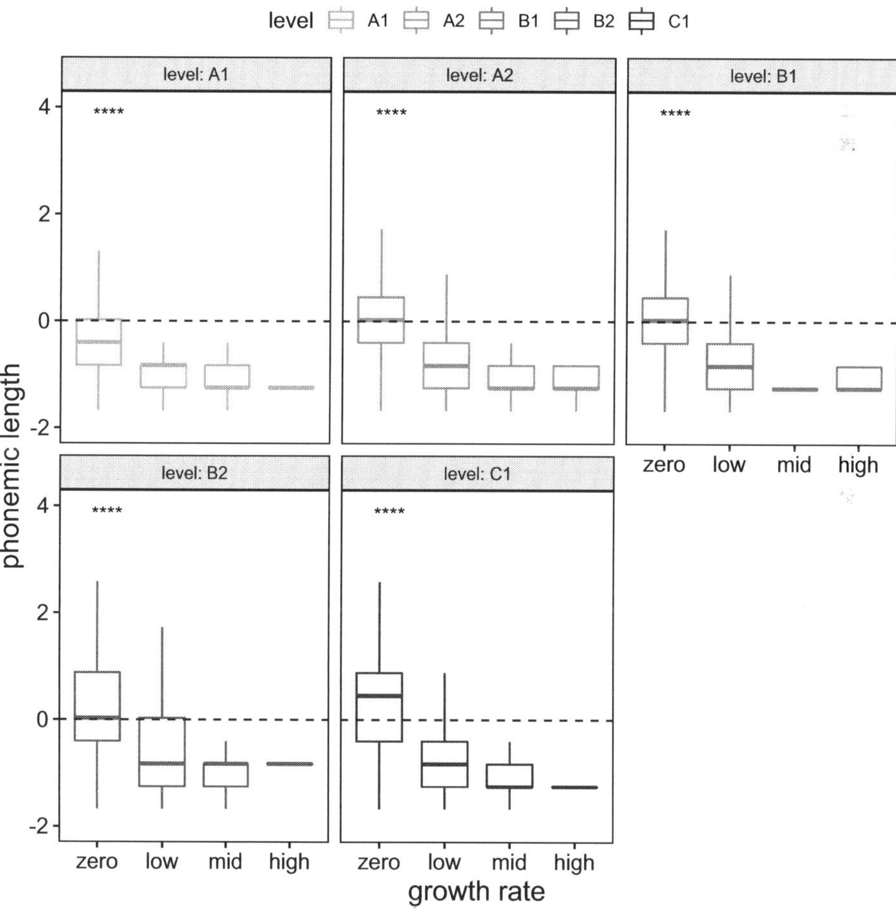

Figure 35: Node growth in relation to (standardized) phonemic length and per proficiency level. Kruskal-Wallis test statistics indicated by asterisks (within-proficiency-group comparisons, *** $p<0.001$).

Concerning lexical frequency rate, prolific node growth was associated with higher lexical frequency rates at each proficiency level (see Figure 36). While the A1 vocabulary showed above-average lexical frequency rates, there was a general proficiency-wise progression towards lower lexical frequency rates for low-growth nodes and higher lexical frequency rates for high-growth nodes, which was most pronounced at the C1 level.

The impact of phonotactic probability on node growth varied across proficiency levels, as illustrated in Figure 37. High phonotactic probability aided phonological neighbor acquisition at the initial A1 level but had the opposite effect in later proficiency stages. The relationship between node growth and phonotactic probability was statistically significant only in the A2 and C1 levels, where increased growth was

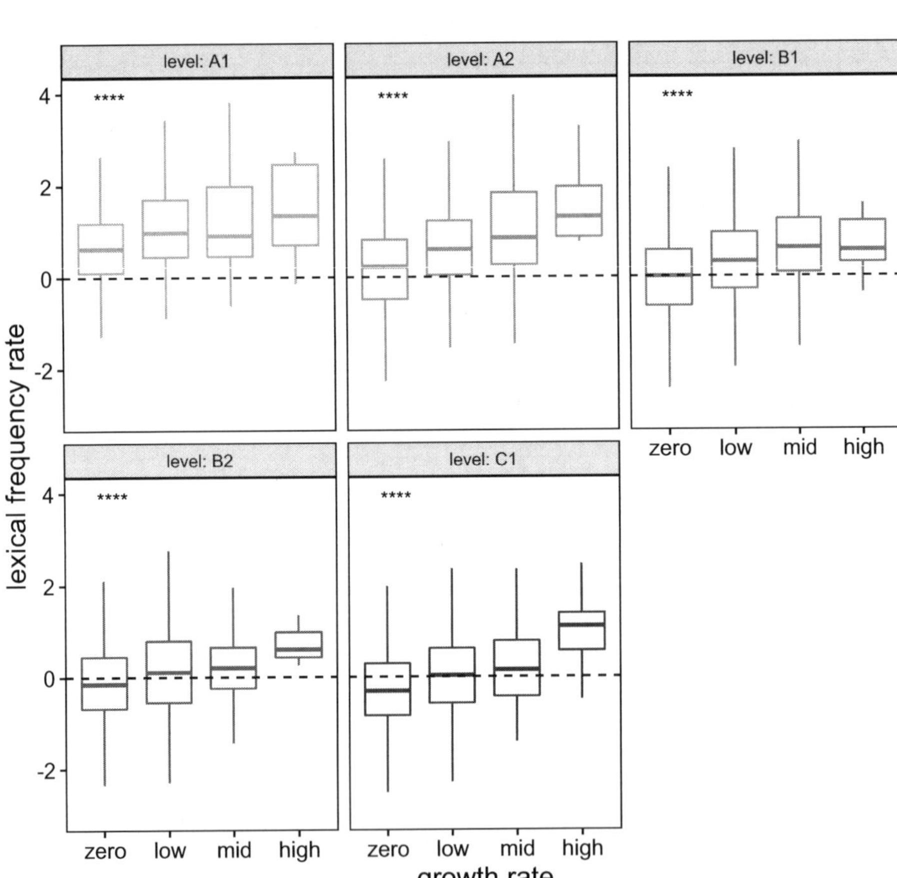

Figure 36: Node growth and (standardized) lexical frequency rates of words. Kruskal-Wallis test statistics indicated for each proficiency level (*** p<0.001).

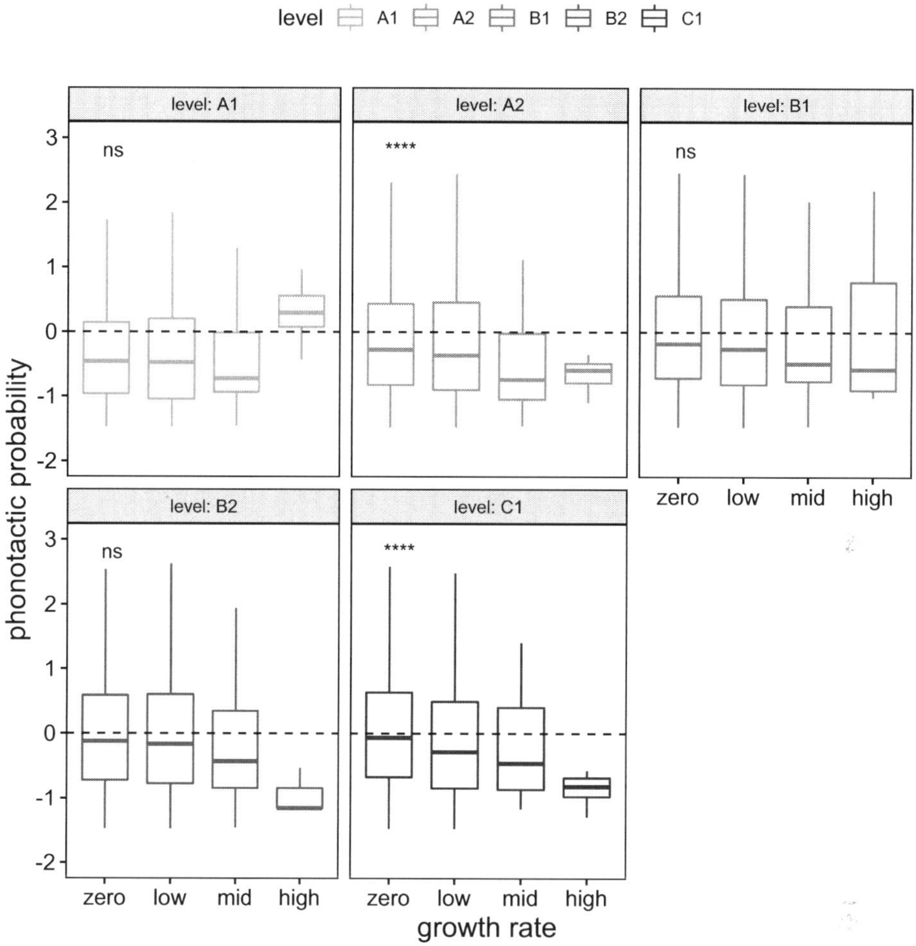

Figure 37: Node growth and (standardized) phonotactic probability of words. Kruskal-Wallis test statistics indicated for each proficiency level ('ns'=non-significant, *** p<0.001).

associated with lower phonotactic probability. In a limited lexicon, highly probable phonotactic combinations can accumulate without impairing word discriminability. However, as word learning progresses and the lexicon expands, the "high probability disadvantage" (as discussed by Storkel et al., 2006, for L1 English child language acquisition) sets in and increases confusability of similar word forms. It appears there may be a saturation effect where the lexicon exhausts high-probability segments to such an extent that discriminability is compromised. Consequently, low-probability phonotactics develop an advantage, aiding in the discrimination of word forms.

Growing nodes were consistently characterized by high clustering coefficients across all proficiency levels (see Figure 38), suggesting a tendency to densely interconnect phonological neighborhoods through growth, where phonological neighbors of tar-

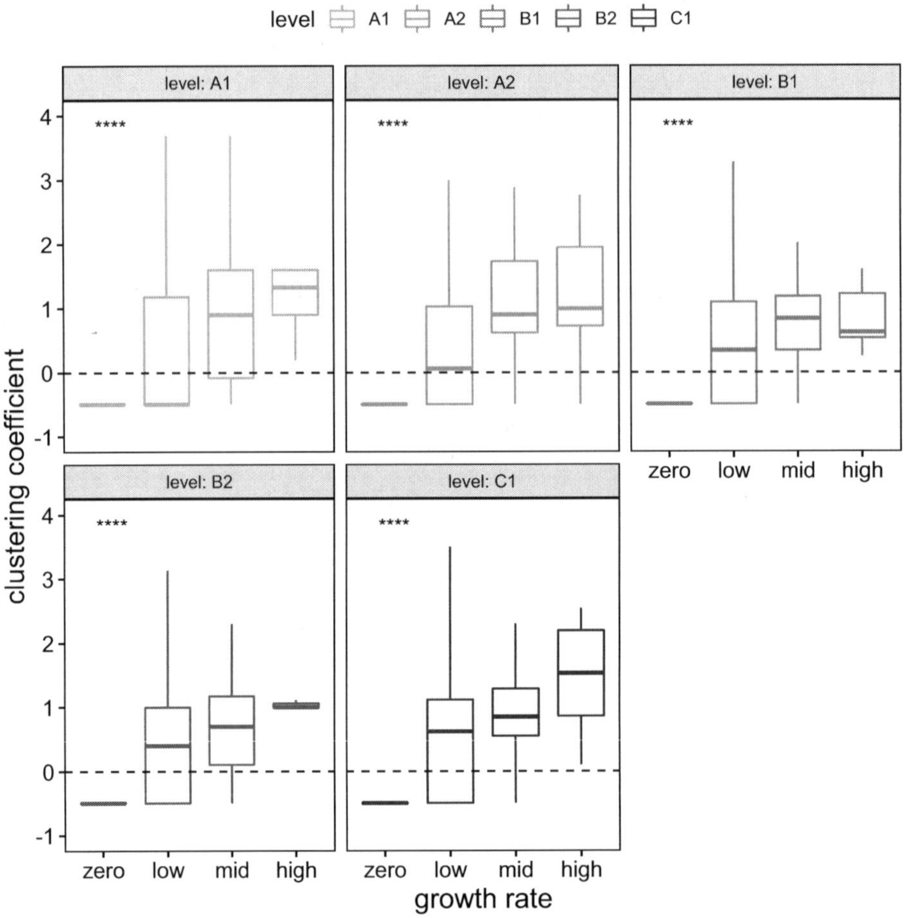

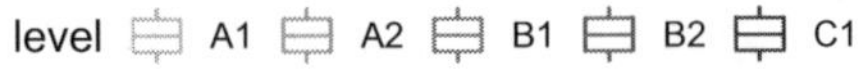

Figure 38: Node growth and (standardized) clustering coefficients of words. Kruskal-Wallis test statistics indicated for each proficiency level (*** p<0.001).

get words also become neighbors of one another. This finding supports previous studies indicating a word learning advantage when a new word integrates into a densely populated phonological neighborhood (see Gaskell & Dumay, 2003; Storkel et al., 2006).

The interaction between node degree and weighted degree significantly influenced node growth, with growing nodes being consistently characterized by a combination of high degree and weighted degree (see Figures 39a and b).

The outcomes of the regression model align closely with the key factors identified in the literature that contribute to word learning efficiency: high lexical frequency, low phonotactic probability, high neighborhood density, and tightly clustered word neighborhoods are reliable indicators of learning probability.

By virtue of their well-connectedness, nodes experiencing the highest growth typically reside in the giant component. Notably, nearly 100% of high-growth nodes

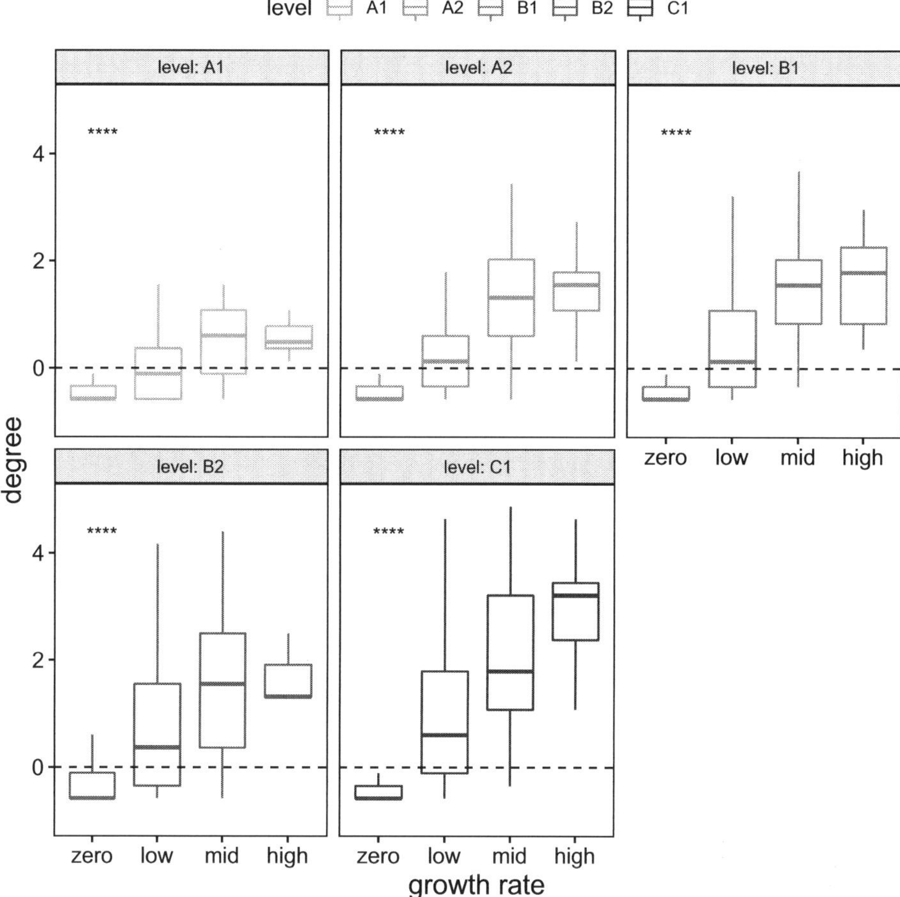

Figures 39a: Node growth and (standardized) degree and weighted degree. Kruskal-Wallis test statistics indicated per proficiency level (*** p<0.001).

are part of the giant component across all proficiency levels (see Figures 40a-e). In general, the giant component encompasses nodes of all growth classes (high, mid, low, zero), whereas the islands and singletons mainly contain nodes of mid, low, and zero growth.

Although high growth rates are exclusively concentrated in the giant component in the initial proficiency levels, high growth rates can also be observed in the C1 islands (see Figure 40e).

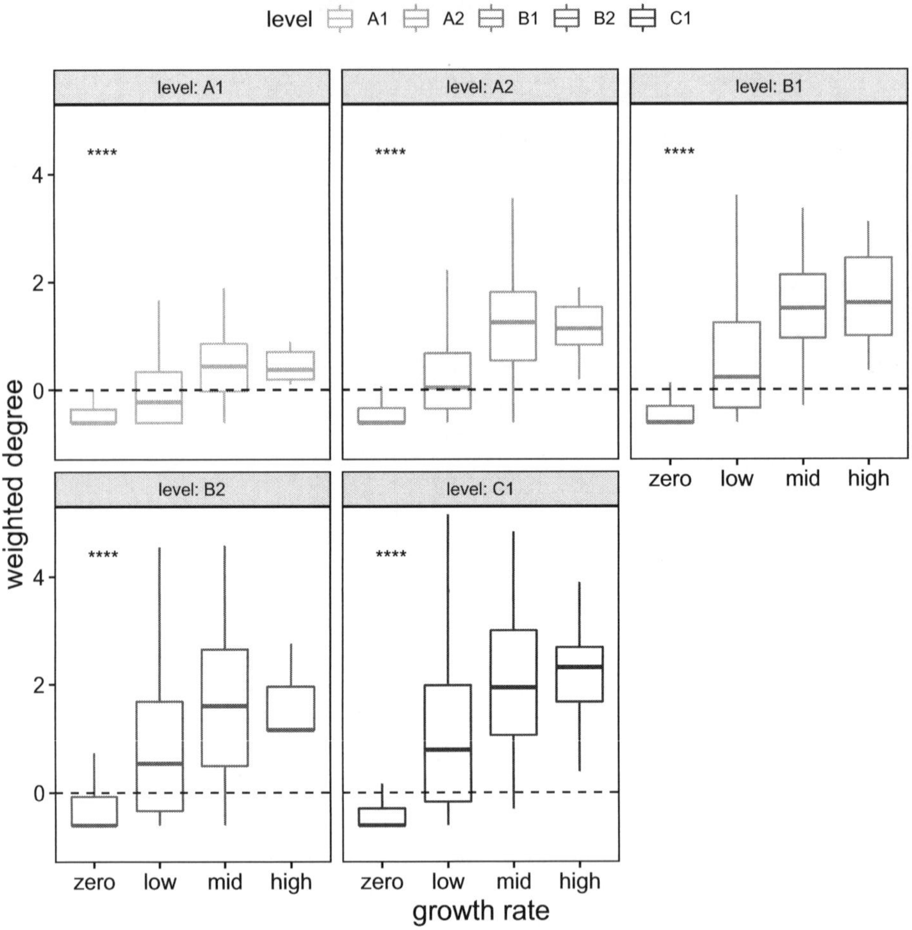

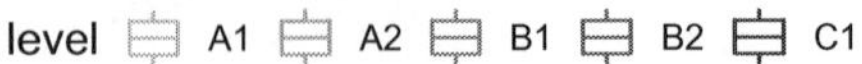

Figures 39b: Node growth and (standardized) degree and weighted degree. Kruskal-Wallis test statistics indicated per proficiency level (*** p<0.001).

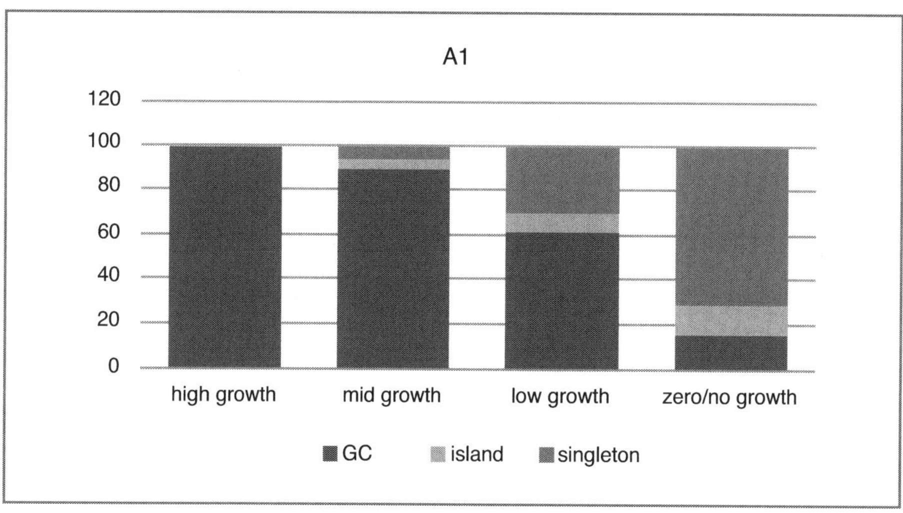

Figures 40a: Node growth and network parts (giant component, islands, singletons).

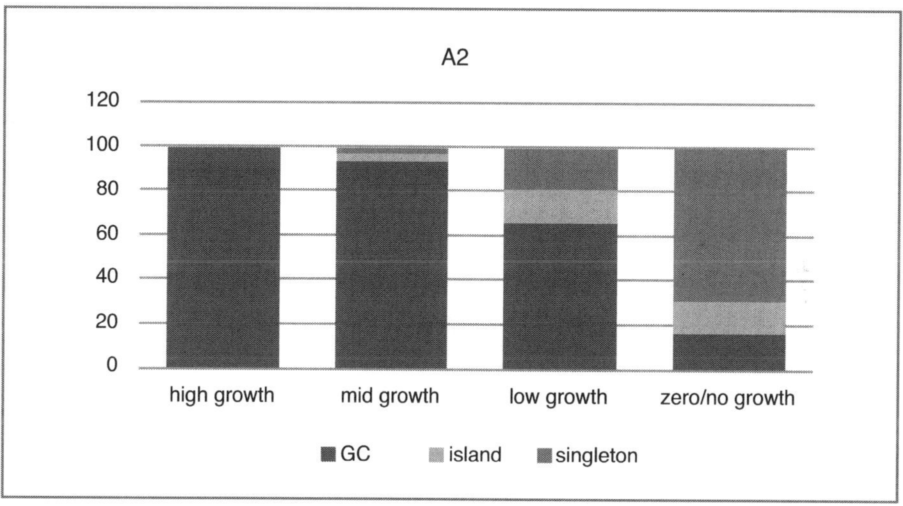

Figures 40b: Node growth and network parts (giant component, islands, singletons).

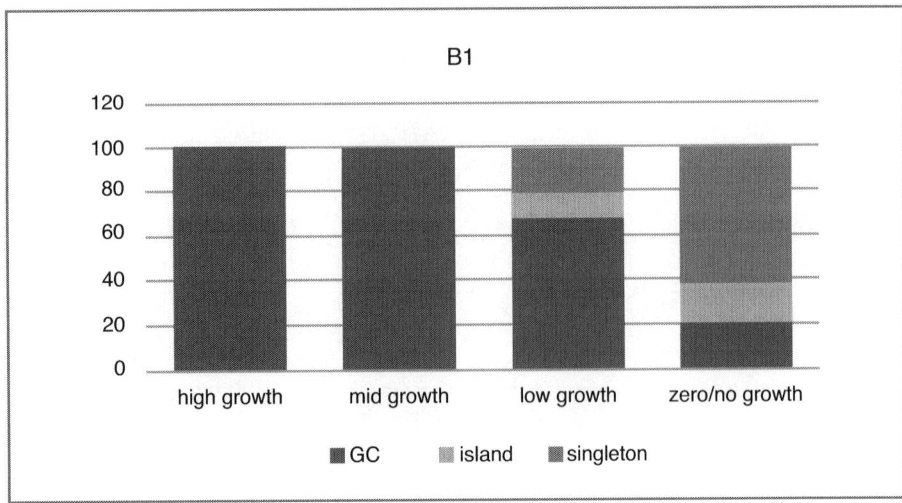

Figures 40c: Node growth and network parts (giant component, islands, singletons).

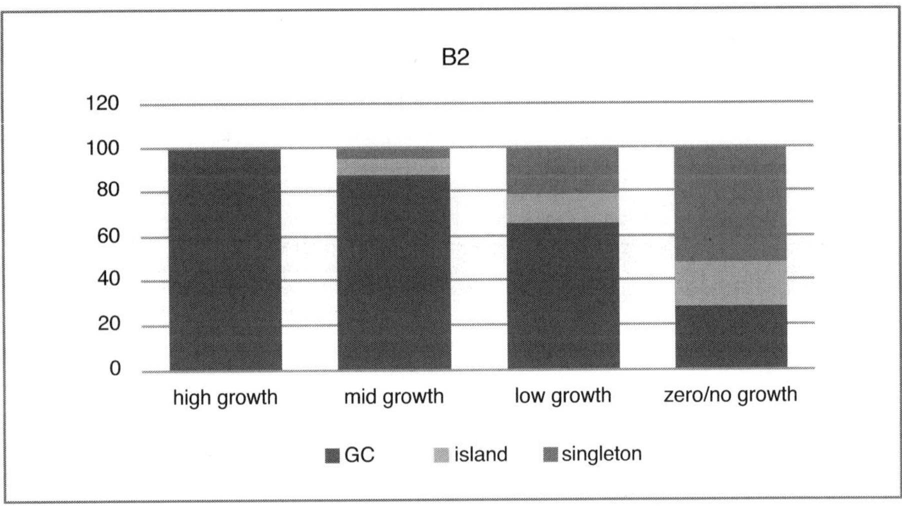

Figures 40d: Node growth and network parts (giant component, islands, singletons).

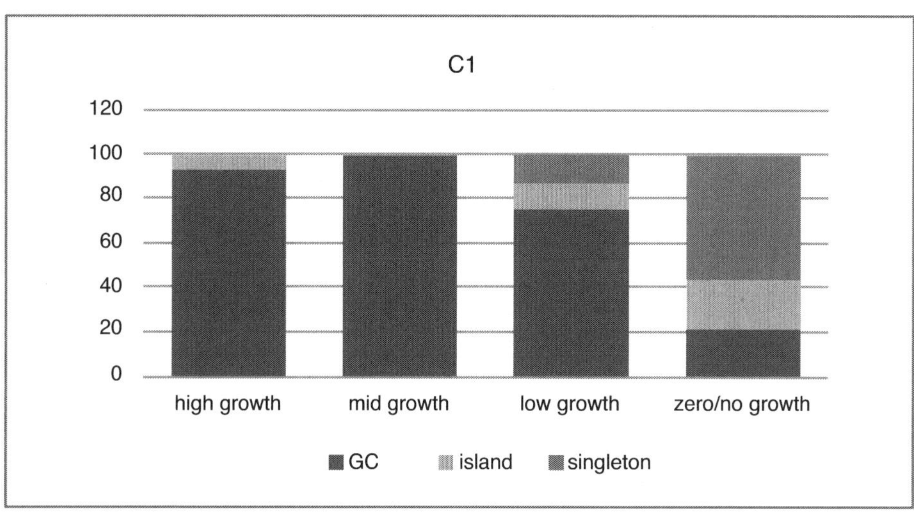

Figures 40e: Node growth and network parts (giant component, islands, singletons).

3.2.1.2 COMMUNITY GROWTH

In the early stages of ESL learning, the majority of growth takes place in the mid-sized communities, as depicted in Figure 41. Contrastingly, during the advanced stages of language learning, growth is most prolific in the larger communities. Smaller communities, relatively speaking, exhibit less growth. This phenomenon may stem from larger communities' tendency to house words with diverse lexical characteristics. The A1 network tends to accumulate words of higher lexical frequency rate and shorter phonemic length in larger clusters, similar to what Siew (2013) found in a phonological network of American English. As learning progresses, the larger communities gradually receive fewer high-frequency, short words. Instead, they become enriched with longer, lower-frequency words. This shift in lexical development alters the trajectory of community growth. As illustrated in Figure 41, growth initially supports mid-sized and larger communities, but becomes more equally distributed across communities of various sizes in the more advanced proficiency stages, starting with the B2 lexicon.

The growth patterns observed in the early proficiency stages may lay the groundwork for mid-sized and larger community formation. This finding is in line with the idea put forth by Siew (2013) that larger communities are established earlier in language learning and are a prerequisite for robust language development.

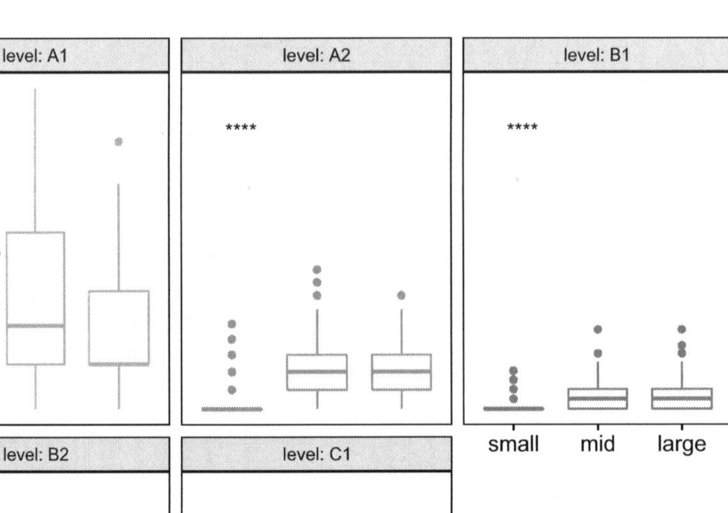

Figure 41: Growth rate and community sizes across the proficiency levels. Kruskal-Wallis test statistics indicated per proficiency level (*** p<0.001).

3.2.2 GROWTH PROBABILITY ALGORITHMS

3.2.2.1 PREFERENTIAL ATTACHMENT PROBABILITY

The probability of a node gaining a new neighbor per growth cycle is proportional to the sum and degree of all nodes in the network. When applied to the ESL networks, this resulted in different distributions of the preferential attachment ('PA') value across proficiency levels (see Figure 42). Preferential attachment probability is spread more widely in the beginner networks (A1, A2), but develops into a highly competitive resource over time. By the C1 level, only few prolific nodes have high preferential attachment probabilities. As ESL proficiency advances, a select few nodes emerge that accu-

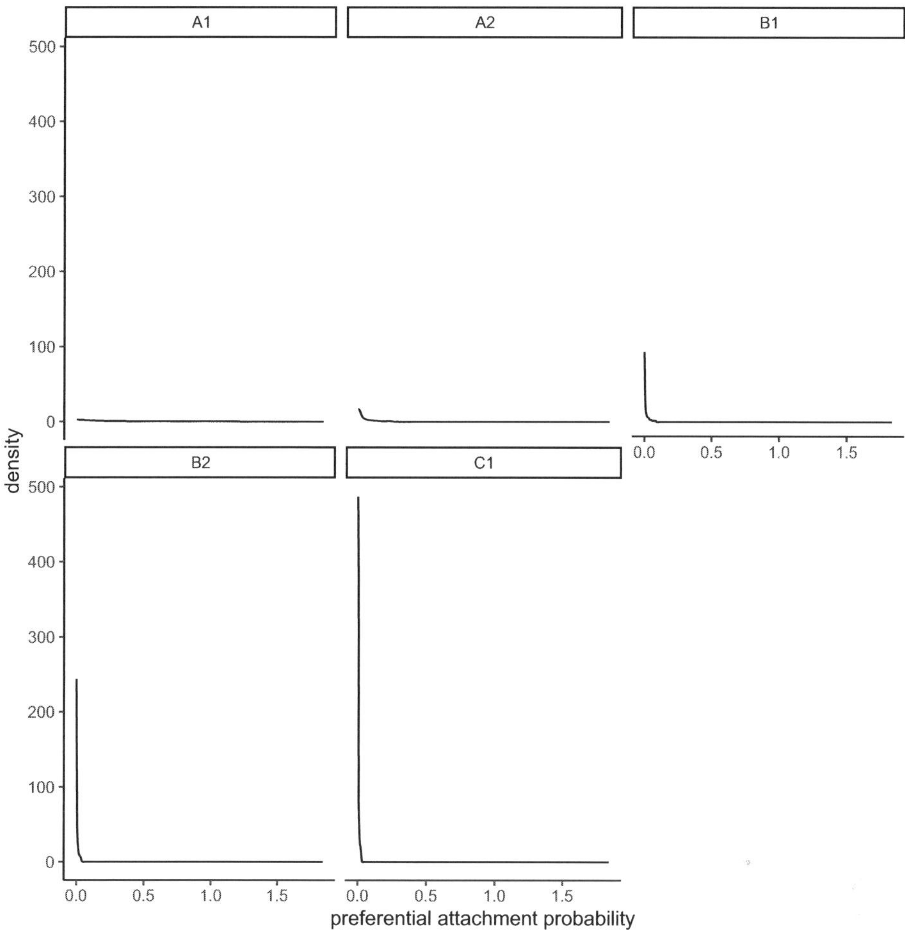

Figure 42: Probability of preferential node attachment in the different learner networks.

mulate growth opportunities, while the vast majority of nodes experiences a decrease in their competitive edge.

Estimations of the distributions of preferential attachment probability across the ESL proficiency networks are presented in Table 21.

Table 21: Distributions of preferential attachment probabilities in the ESL networks.

	A1	*A2*	*B1*	*B2*	*C1*
Best-fitting distribution	Bimodal (dip test p: <0.001)	Multimodal (dip test p: <0.001)	Multimodal (dip test p: <0.001)	Multimodal (dip test p: <0.001)	Multimodal (dip test p: <0.001)

Preferential attachment probabilities narrow as the ESL networks grow. Starting at the B1 level, the rich-gets-richer dynamic accelerates, resulting in few nodes being endowed the majority of growth opportunities via preferential attachment at the C1 level. The bi- and multimodal distribution types indicate that PA-driven growth exhibits multiple – even if skewed – peaks.

3.2.2.2 FITNESS PROBABILITY

Node fitness refers to the "inherent competitive ability (or the 'attractiveness') that a node has, which influences the rate at which it acquires links from other nodes as the network evolves over time" (Bell et al., 2017, p. 1). This measure of growth-related fitness stems from node attributes that raise the likelihood of neighbor attachment. In the context of phonological networks, the learnability of a word is synonymous with its fitness. Drawing from previous psycholinguistic literature, attributes that make a word more likely to be acquired and retained by adult learners include

- high lexical frequency (e.g., Chen & Truscott, 2010)
- high phonotactic probability (e.g., Benitez & Saffran, 2021; Storkel et al., 2013; but see Storkel et al., 2006)
- high neighborhood density or high node degree in network terms (e.g., Stamer & Vitevitch, 2012; Storkel et al., 2006)
- high clustering coefficient (Goldstein & Vitevitch, 2014)

Several well-established factors influencing word learning, including proximity to L1 (Poltrock, Chen, Kwok, Cheung, & Nazzi, 2018), the context of word learning (Elgort, Beliaeva, & Boers, 2020), instructional setting (Luef, Ghebru, & Ilon, 2018), and phonological familiarity (Kaushanskaya, Yoo, & Van Hecke, 2013), among others, could not be explored in the current ESL dataset due to the unavailability of information on these variables. To assess node fitness in this study, the variables 'lexical frequency rate', 'phonotactic probability', 'node degree', and 'clustering coefficient' were combined into an interaction variable termed 'fitness' through principal components analysis for dimensionality reduction (Salem & Hussein, 2019). Composite z-scored principal components of the four variables were computed, with the first principal component (PC1) designated as the "fitness" variable. The results revealed a correlation of 0.64 between the first principal component and node degree, while lexical frequency rate and clustering coefficient exhibited a correlation coefficient of 0.42 and 0.62, respectively. Phonotactic probability showed a correlation coefficient of -0.17, indicating a negative relationship with the other variables, as predicted by Storkel et al. (2006). The first principal component accounted for 44% of the variance in the data. Figure 43 shows its distributional pattern at each proficiency level.

The distributions of node fitness in the learner networks are presented in Table 22. To facilitate calculations of these distributions, a constant value of "10" was added to

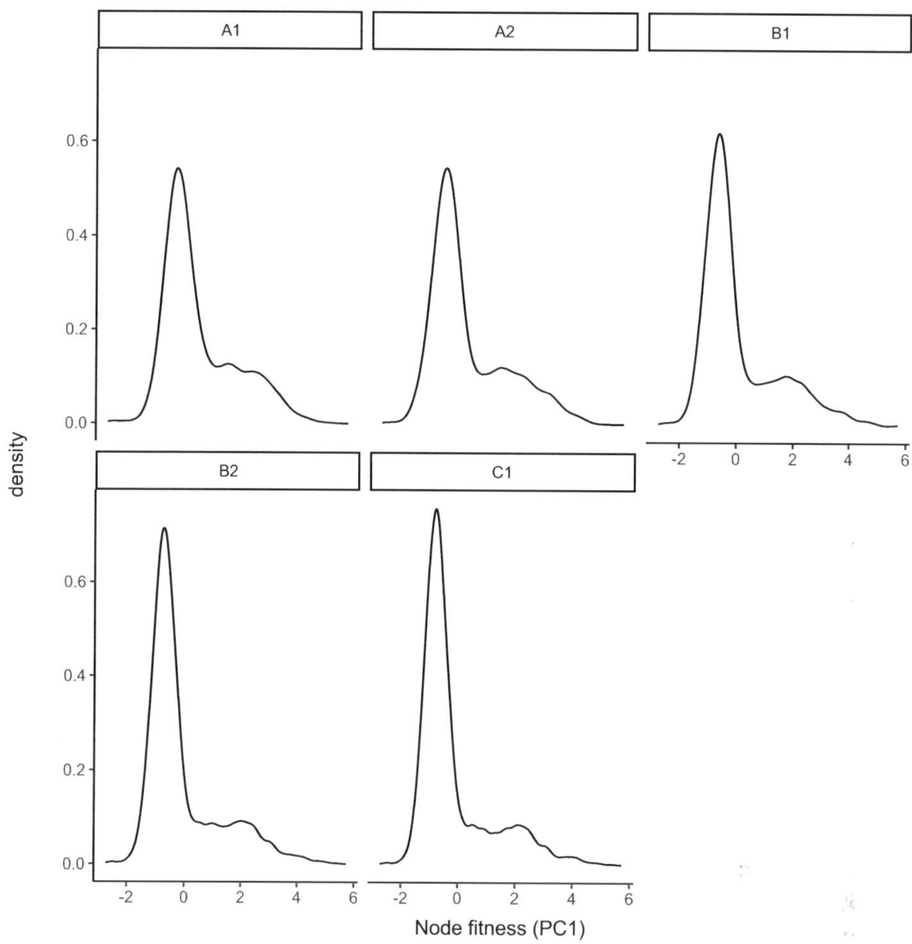

Figure 43: Distributions of node fitness across ESL networks (PC 1).

each data point, ensuring a shift to positive numbers. Hartigan's dip test yielded p>0.9, excluding the possibility that a distribution may be bimodal.

Table 22: Distribution types of node fitness of ESL learner network growth.

	A1	*A2*	*B1*	*B2*	*C1*
Best-fitting distribution	Power law	Power law	Power law	Power law	Power law

The distribution of fitness across all networks reflects the fact that few words possess all characteristics of improved word learning. At the beginning stages of language learning, a larger percentage of words are of high fitness, and while their fitness is higher than that of the other words, the difference between high- and low-fitness words is less extreme. During the course of word learning, fewer high-fitness words gain higher fitness scores.

3.2.2.3 PREFERENTIAL ATTACHMENT AND FITNESS: PAFit

PAFit was calculated using the following equation:

$$p_i = \eta_i k_i / \Sigma_j \eta_j k_j$$

where the probability of node *i* to grow new links is the proportion of *i*'s fitness and degree of the overall sum of nodes per network multiplied by those nodes' fitness values and degrees. The distribution of PAFit in the networks is exclusively focused on few nodes, which gain scores over the course of learning (see Figure 44).

The distributions of PAFit in the learner networks are presented in Table 23. A value of "1" was added to each data point in order to shift the data to positive numbers for distribution fitting.

Table 23: Distribution types of PAFit in the learner networks.

	A1	A2	B1	B2	C1
Best-fitting distribution	Burr	Log-logistic	Log-logistic	Weibull	Weibull

PAFit values are visibly concentrated on specific nodes across the proficiency levels. The advantage of few prolific nodes increases substantially over the course of word learning, so that PAFit values increase exclusively in the nodes already showing high PAFit values to begin with.

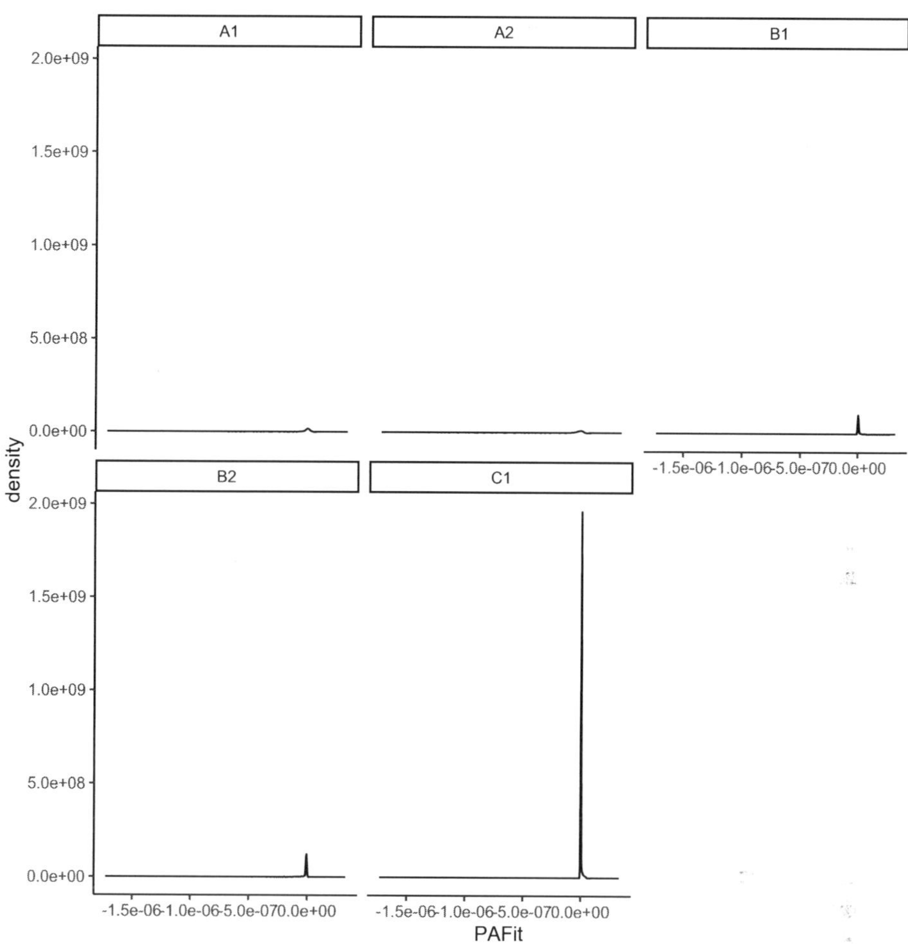

Figure 44: PAFit distributions across the learner networks.

3.2.2.4 HYBRID MODEL OF UNIFORM AND PREFERENTIAL ATTACHMENT

The probability of random attachment in conjunction with preferential attachment involves integrating preferential attachment values for each node with the node's representational proportion in the network, denoted as the uniform attachment probability ('UA'):

$$p_i = UA_i k_i / \sum_j UA_j k_j$$

The distribution of this hybrid variable is shown in Figure 45 (and table 24).

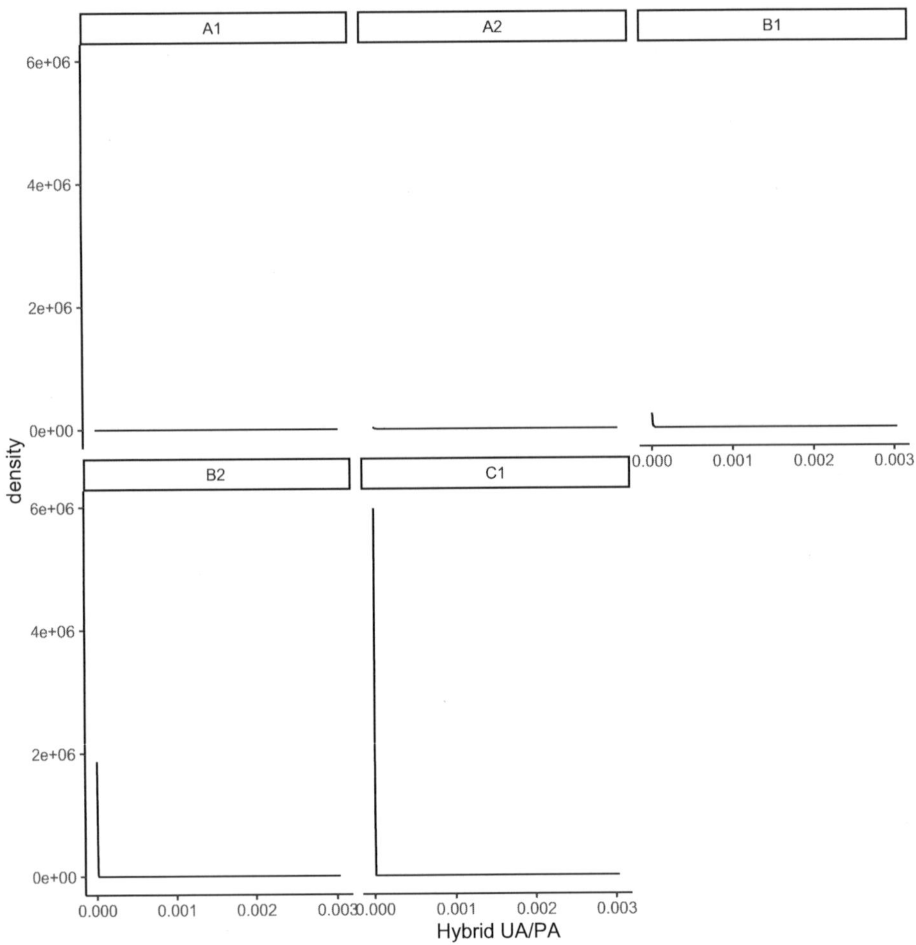

Figure 45: Distributions of the hybrid uniform/preferential attachment variable.

Table 24: Distributions of the hybrid uniform/preferential attachment variable.

	A1	*A2*	*B1*	*B2*	*C1*
Best-fitting distribution	Power law	Power law	Power law	Power law	Power law

Similar to PAFit, hybrid UA/PA values develop into an exclusive asset across all ESL networks. This is due to their calculations, where the effect of one attachment mechanism is not considered independently but only their interaction (i.e., only non-zero values can be multiplied). Although initially modest, the hybrid UA/PA scores progressively reach significant magnitudes during the advanced proficiency stages.

3.2.2.5 STATISTICAL ASSESSMENT

Rarely do singular explanations suffice to explain complex phenomena, and this certainly applies to word learning and network science. Many network measures are conceptually or mathematically related (consider eigenvector and betweenness centrality or preferential attachment and PAFit), with changes in one often affecting changes in the other. It becomes reasonable to consider that multiple network growth algorithms might be relevant determiners for network growth dynamics, and that these algorithms collectively influence a network. Previous research has suggested this possibility (Fourtassi et al., 2020; Siew & Vitevitch, 2020a). Additionally, idiosyncratic principles of language learning can contribute, with different learners relying on different strategies for lexical network growth (Beckage & Colunga, 2019). Psycholinguistic investigations into lexical processing and word learning reveal that a myriad of factors and their interactions are responsible for observed effects. To account for the word learning effect in the context of the present study, statistical analyses were conducted to identify the most influential factors on growth from the numerous network-related and lexical variables measured.

Previously, various network centrality statistics influencing phonological networks were discussed, including degree centrality, weighted degree centrality, closeness centrality, betweenness centrality, and eigenvector centrality. Some, like degree and weighted degree, have been documented to play a role in network growth or word learning, being able to account for neighborhood effects. Denser neighborhoods and those characterized by phonologically closer word forms are known to expand during word learning in both first and second languages (Stamer & Vitevitch, 2012; Storkel, 2001, 2002; Storkel et al., 2006). The high clustering coefficient, indicating the interconnectedness of the phonological neighborhood, has been associated with facilitated word learning (Goldstein & Vitevitch, 2014). Words with high degree and weighted degree centralities, along with high clustering coefficients are expected to possess higher growth potential in all networks. Closeness centrality, signifying the phonological proximity of a target word to all others in the network (a fact known to incur a recognition advantage, see Goldstein & Vitevitch, 2014), can convey information about the extended phonological neighborhood beyond the one-segment metric. Words with high closeness centrality can be conceptualized as having numerous extended neighbors, leading to the assumption that word learning is facilitated by the dynamic of a "denser extended neighborhood", similar to the effect of degree centrality but extending beyond one degree of separation. In a similar vein, words of high eigenvector centrality may attract new neighbors by virtue of their denser extended neighborhoods. Degree (and weighted degree), closeness, and eigenvector centralities may all be contributing to a rich-gets-richer dynamic in a network, where higher centrality statistics predict more growth. If only the closest (one-segment) neighbors matter, degree and weighted degree play an outsized role. If the two-hop neighbors are influential, eigenvector centrality could be influencing growth. If the larger three-and-more hop neighborhood plays a role, this should become evident through the effect of closeness centrality on growth.

Betweenness centrality is conceptually tied to internal linking of nodes and the key question here is whether "bridge words", which connect different neighborhoods, tend to solidify their outstanding position by acquiring more neighbors. As indicated by previous research (Vitevitch & Goldstein, 2014), such strategically positioned key words in phonological networks enjoy activation benefits leading to lexical retrieval advantages. It is conceivable that through their strengthened representations, words of high betweenness centrality are able to attract new neighbors.

In a first step, Pearson's correlation coefficients (r) were calculated to assess the predictive relationship between network growth algorithms, network centrality measures, and well-known word learning variables (lexical frequency, phonemic length, phonotactic probability), with actual network growth. They are listed in Table 25. As preferential attachment and the hybrid variable UA/PA were highly correlated at each proficiency level (r>0.9), the hybrid variable was excluded from further analysis.

Table 25: Pearson's correlation coefficients of variables with growth rate per proficiency level (dark gray cells r>0.6; light gray cells r>0.5).

	A1	A2	B1	B2	C1
PA	0.49	0.69	0.56	0.36	0.51
PAFit	-0.21	-0.52	0.39	-0.24	0.39
Fitness	0.41	0.63	0.51	0.32	0.46
Lexical frequency	0.23	0.3	0.22	0.11	0.16
Phonotactic probability	0.06	-0.08	-0.02	-0.003	-0.06
Phonemic length	-0.43	-0.51	-0.44	-0.26	-0.37
Degree	0.49	0.69	0.56	0.36	0.51
Weighted degree	0.51	0.68	0.55	0.37	0.5
Closeness centrality	0.07	0.06	0.03	0.01	-0.01
Betweenness centrality	0.43	0.42	0.32	0.32	0.34
Clustering coefficient	0.32	0.48	0.39	0.22	0.31
Eigenvector centrality	0.19	0.5	0.42	0.2	0.34

The most robust correlations with growth rates were found for preferential attachment, degree, and weighted degree. This suggests that rich nodes get richer in phonological neighborhood growth. Almost all correlations are positive, except for phonemic length, where shorter words tend to acquire more neighbors, and PAFit, which is associated with lower growth values in the A1, A2, and B2 lexica but with higher growth values in the B1 and C1 lexica.

Correlations vary by proficiency level. The A2 level leads in terms of the magnitude of the correlations involving the majority of the variables, while the B2 level lags on many of them. Specific learning dynamics at various proficiency levels might be responsible for these correlation patterns (such as lower PAFit scores in lower proficiency levels). Moreover, the utility of certain network growth statistics may be contingent on vocabulary size in a given lexicon. The available pool of words to be learned shrinks as the networks grow, necessitating different word acquisition strategies (see Luef, 2022b).

To determine the network variable exerting the most impact on node growth at each proficiency level, a series of linear mixed effects regression models were conducted, with separate models for each proficiency level lexicon. These models used growth rate as the outcome variable, representing the number of new words that each lexical entry acquires in moving to the next proficiency level. All variables were z-scored. The following independent variables (fixed effects) were included:

- preferential attachment probability
- node fitness (first principal component)
- PAFit
- phonemic length
- lexical frequency
- phonotactic probability
- degree*weighted degree centrality (i.e., interaction variable due to high correlation)
- closeness centrality
- betweenness centrality
- eigenvector centrality
- clustering coefficient

As a random effect, the variable 'network part' was included to accommodate possible influences associated with the part of the network to which a word belongs (i.e., giant component, islands, singletons). The inclusion of random slopes was not feasible due to resulting convergence issues. The following pseudo code was used for all models:

*growth ~ PA+fitness+PAFit+phonemic length+lexical frequency+phonotactic probability+degree*weighted degree+closeness+betweenness+eigenvector+clustering coefficient +(1|network part)*

The R package "lme4", with the function "lmer" (Bates et al., 2014), was used to perform linear mixed effects analysis of the relationship between the fixed effects and the growth rate per word from one proficiency level to the next. P values were obtained by likelihood ratio tests, comparing the full model with the effect in question against a model without the specific effect (Dobson, 2002; Forstmeier & Schielzeth, 2011). Multicollinearity testing was performed with the function "vif" of the

R package "car" to ensure low variance inflation factors (Field, 2005; Quinn & Keough, 2002). In case of variables exhibiting correlations of >0.6, one of them was removed from the model. Due to its high correlation with preferential attachment across all lexica, the variable hybrid UA/PA was removed from each model. Results of the mixed model analyses are presented separately for each ESL proficiency level network.

In the A1 network, lexical frequency rate and clustering coefficient were removed due to their substantial correlation with one another (r=0.8), along with their high correlation with node fitness (r=–0.9). In addition, phonotactic probability was correlated with fitness (r=–0.72) and thus removed. Among the remaining variables, preferential attachment, phonemic length, and closeness and betweenness centralities emerged as significant contributors to network growth (see Table 26). Specifically, high preferential attachment probability and high betweenness centrality, as well as short phonemic length and low eigenvector centrality, led to higher growth rates in A1 nodes.

Table 26: Results of the linear mixed effects regression model of the A1 network growth variables.

	Estimate	Std. Error	p
PA probability	1.40931	0.54620	<0.001***
PAFit	0.42792	0.23253	0.07
Fitness	0.24336	0.14270	0.09
Phonemic length	–0.36294	0.11568	0.002**
Degree*weighted degree	0.05806	0.28030	0.81
Closeness centrality	–0.08952	0.08098	0.27
Betweenness centrality	1.06728	0.33410	0.001**
Eigenvector centrality	–0.34313	0.14608	0.02*

*** p<0.001, ** p<0.01, * p<0.05

A comparison of standardized regression coefficients showed that preferential attachment and eigenvector centrality were most influential for A1 growth (see Figure 46).

In the A2 network, both phonotactic probability and lexical frequency rate were removed, as they correlated with one another (r=0.6) and with fitness (r=–0.8). PAFit correlated with preferential attachment (r=0.73) and the interaction degree*weighted degree (r=0.88), thus PAFit was removed from the model. In the A2 network, the majority of network growth variables were highly significant predictors for lexical growth (see Table 27).

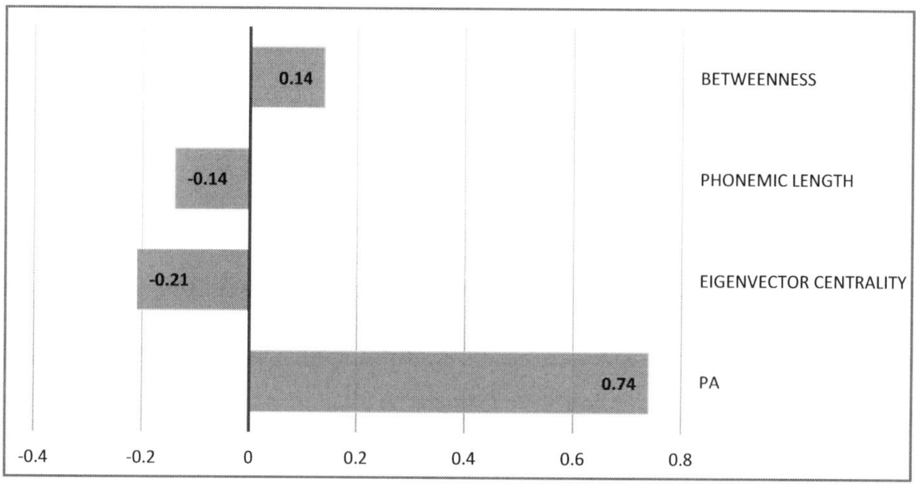

Figure 46: Standardized regression coefficients of significant network growth variables in the A1 network.

Table 27: Results of the linear mixed effects regression model of the A2 network growth variables.

	Estimate	Std. Error	p
PA probability	18.937	0.25134	0.001***
Fitness	0.01024	0.07902	0.89
Phonemic length	−0.21353	0.04652	<0.001***
Degree*weighted degree	−0.18185	0.05562	0.001**
Closeness centrality	−0.10529	0.03412	0.002**
Betweenness centrality	−0.21632	0.09911	0.03*
Eigenvector centrality	−0.15096	0.06423	0.018*
Clustering coefficient	0.01503	0.04285	0.73

*** p<0.001, ** p<0.01, * p<0.05

As shown in Figure 47, preferential attachment and eigenvector centrality proved most influential for growth.

Variables removed from the B1 network included phonotactic probability and lexical frequency rate, given their correlation of r=−0.8 with fitness. Again, preferential attachment emerged as a highly significant predictor for lexical growth, along with many other variables (see Table 28 and Figure 48).

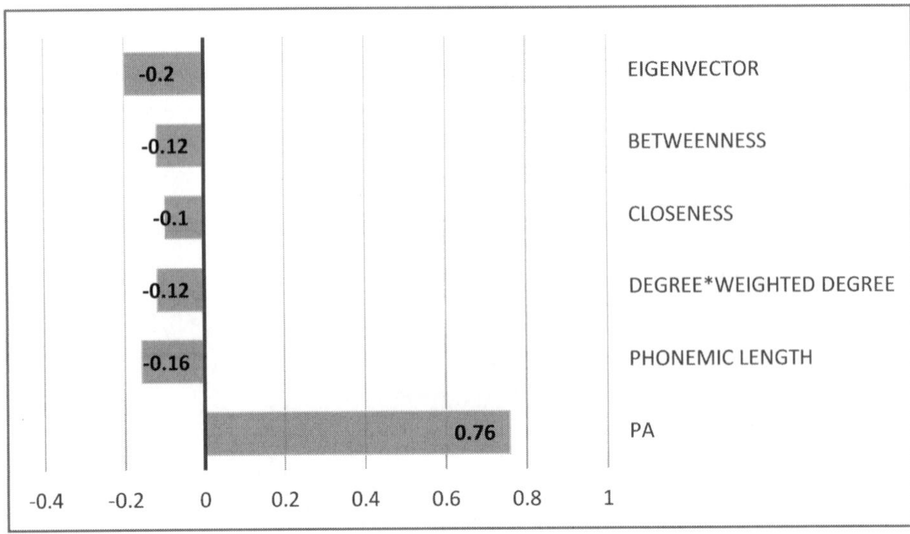

Figure 47: Standardized regression coefficients of significant network growth variables in the A2 network.

Table 28: Results of the linear mixed effects regression model of the B1 network growth variables.

	Estimate	Std. Error	p
PA probability	1.05182	0.19826	<0.001***
PAFit	−0.34913	0.07729	0.001***
Fitness	0.19270	0.04657	0.001***
Phonemic length	−0.08894	0.02470	<0.001
Degree*weighted degree	−0.16823	0.02888	<0.001***
Closeness centrality	−0.10242	0.01859	0.014*
Betweenness centrality	−0.02920	0.03033	0.34
Eigenvector centrality	0.25415	0.04492	<0.001***
Clustering coefficient	−0.09076	0.02568	<0.001***

*** p<0.001, * p<0.05

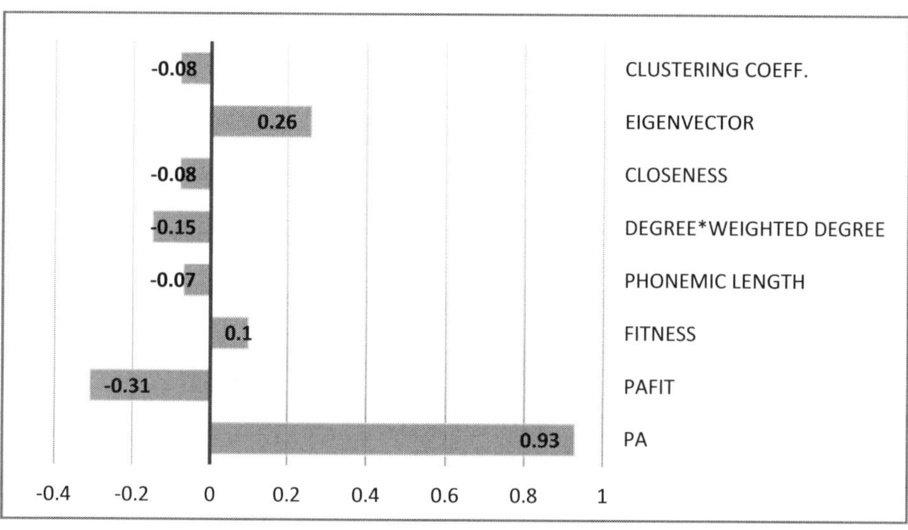

Figure 48: Standardized regression coefficients of significant network growth variables in the B1 network.

In the B2 network, the interaction variable degree*weighted degree was correlated with PAFit (r=0.72), and phonotactic probability and lexical frequency with fitness (r>0.7). Consequently, degree*weighted degree, phonotactic probability, and lexical frequency were removed (see Table 29).

Table 29: Results of the linear mixed effects regression model of the B2 network growth variables.

	Estimate	Std. Error	p
PA probability	0.2661017	0.0216774	<0.001***
PAFit	0.0783564	0.0227093	<0.001***
Fitness	0.0320535	0.0178999	0.07
Phonemic length	-0.0067843	0.0080066	0.4
Closeness centrality	-0.0156975	0.0061455	0.02*
Betweenness centrality	0.0236926	0.0086342	0.006**
Eigenvector centrality	-0.0837386	0.0168937	<0.001***
Clustering coefficient	0.0009425	0.0090544	0.9

*** p<0.001, ** p<0.01, * p<0.05

Preferential attachment had the largest impact on growth in the B2 network, followed by PAFit and eigenvector centrality (see Figure 49).

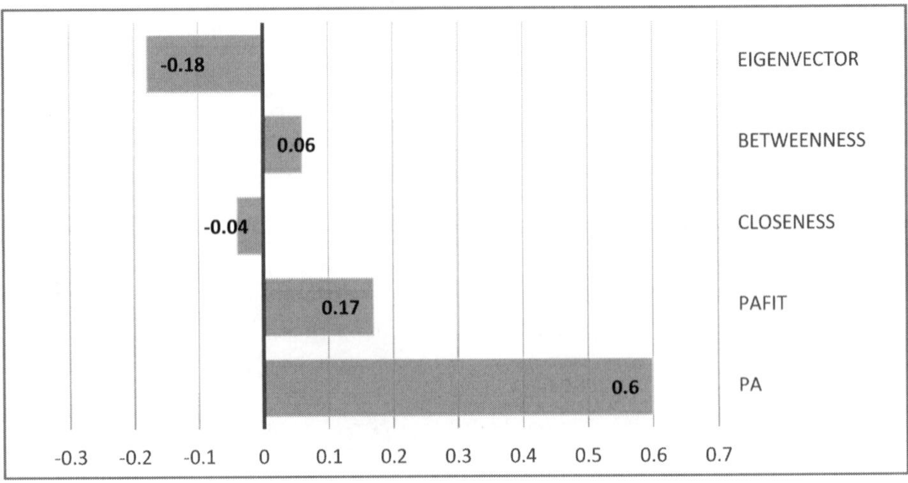

Figure 49: Standardized regression coefficients of significant network growth variables in the B2 network.

In the C1 analysis, removed variables included lexical frequency rate and phonotactic probability (both correlated with fitness at r>0.72), as well as degree, which correlated with PAFit at r=0.72 (see Table 30).

Table 30: Results of the linear mixed effects regression model of the C1 network growth variables.

	Estimate	Std. Error	p
PA probability	8.213e+06	4.241e+05	<0.001***
PAFit	8.817e-03	2.580e-02	0.73
Fitness	8.768e-03	2.052e-02	0.67
Phonemic length	-4.124e-02	8.651e-03	<0.001***
Closeness	-3.774e-02	6.787e-03	0.009**
Betweenness	-4.327e-02	8.867e-03	<0.001***
Eigenvector centrality	-1.873e-01	2.074e-02	<0.001***
Clustering coefficient	-6.781e-03	1.043e-02	0.52

*** p<0.001, ** p<0.01

Preferential attachment and eigenvector centrality were the dominant mechanisms influencing growth in the C1 lexicon (see Figure 50).

Across all networks, the effect of preferential attachment was ubiquitous and overwhelming. Eigenvector centrality was also significant at all proficiency levels, whereas the effects of the other variables were more specifically linked to certain proficiency

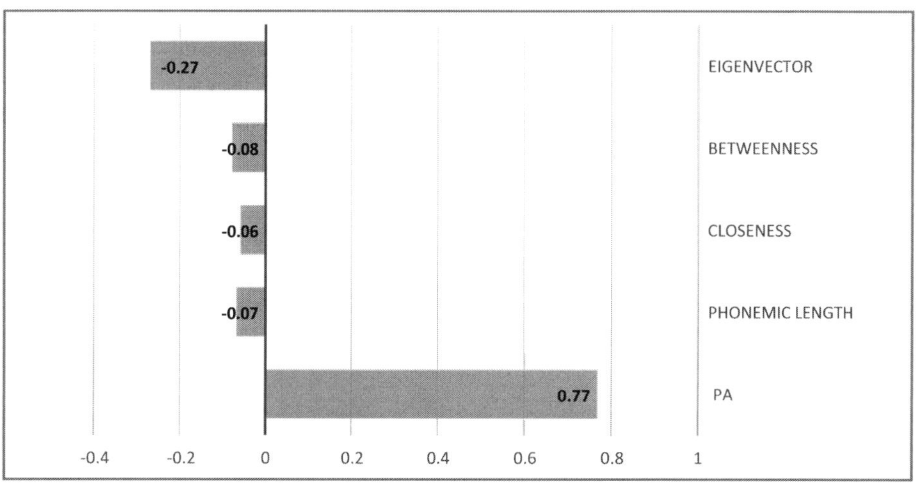

Figure 50: Standardized regression coefficients of significant network growth variables in the C1 network.

levels (see Figure 51 for an overview). Overall, the results clearly indicate the involvement of multiple network growth dynamics in the development of ESL phonological networks.

For each significant network growth variable, the direction of its influence on the growth rate is depicted in Figure 51. High preferential attachment scores consistently predicted high growth at all proficiency levels, displaying the tendency of rich words

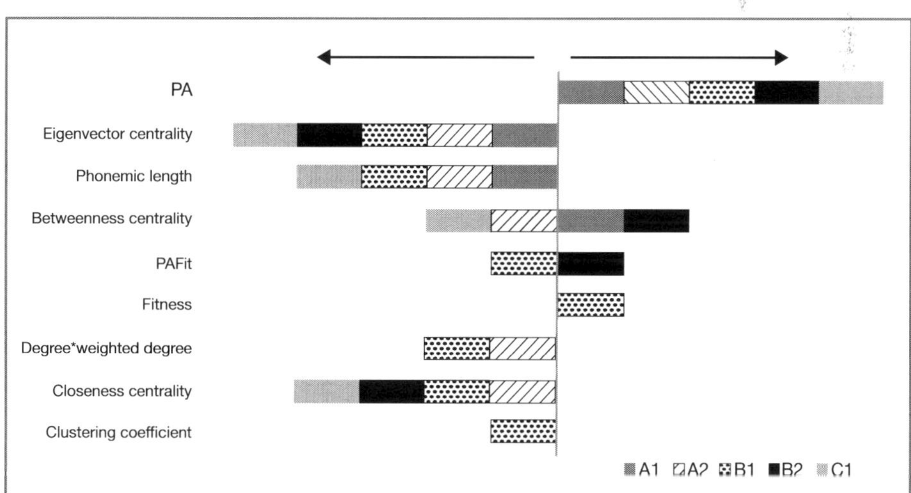

Figure 51: *Significant network growth variables in the learner networks and their characteristics (positive, negative values) in the promotion of growth.*

getting richer. Eigenvector centrality had the inverse effect and low values furthered growth in all networks. Closeness centrality mirrored this trend and low values were predictive for growth. The implication here is that network growth occurs primarily by adding new words to those with sparser extended neighborhoods (i.e., low eigenvector and closeness centralities) across all proficiency networks. Over time, one-degree neighborhoods tend to become denser through learning, while extended neighborhoods (a few hops removed) preferentially remain sparse. This growth dynamic (schematized in Figure 52) results in a network structure where large hubs are surrounded by sparse neighborhoods (similar to a "hub-and-spoke" typology).

When betweenness centrality was significant (A1, A2, B2, C1), the direction of influence varied depending on the proficiency level: high betweenness centrality facilitated growth at the A1 level but hindered it at the C1 level. Nodes with high betweenness centrality in the initial A1 lexicon have limited opportunities to benefit

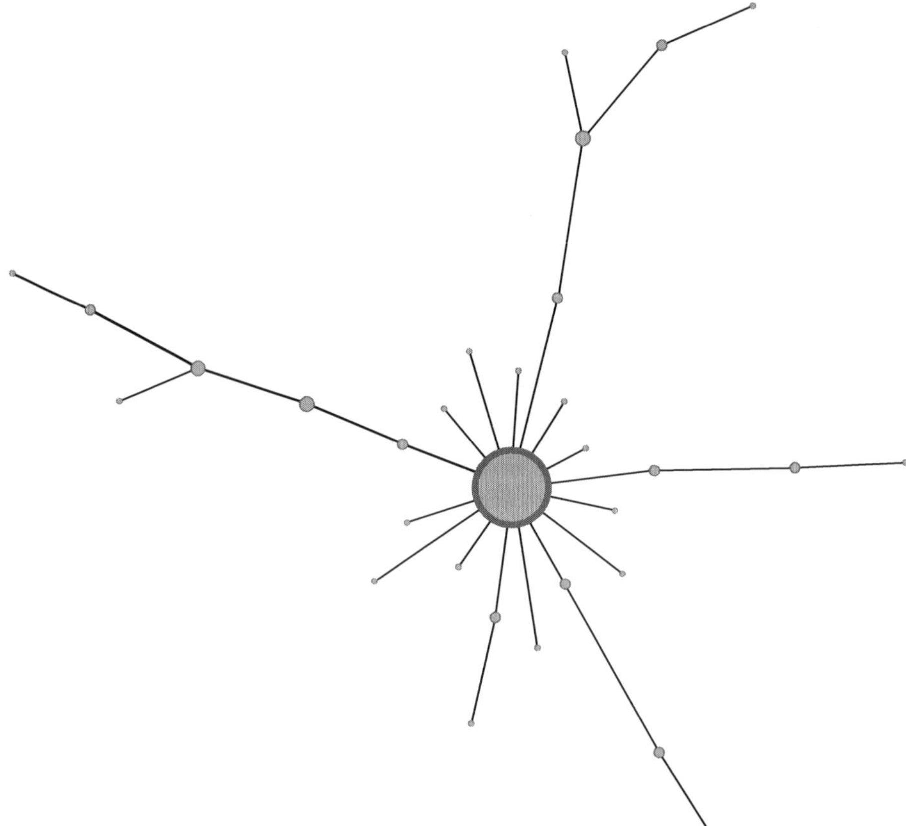

Figure 52: Network structure favored by growth according to preferential attachment in combination with low closeness and eigenvector centralities: denser phonological neighborhoods (i.e., larger hubs) surrounded by sparser extended neighborhoods.

from co-activation compared to their counterparts in the C1 network, as activation is assumed to accrue over time (Chan & Vitevitch, 2009; Goldstein & Vitevitch, 2014). During the early stages of network development, there might be a tendency to avoid words with high betweenness centrality, as they represent a particular vulnerability of networks due to their central positions. Such frail linking points in a network can be strengthened through growth. In larger networks, more numerous links exist between all nodes, relieving some of the burden placed on nodes with high betweenness centralities. Growth at key betweenness centrality positions may become less prevalent in such scenarios.

The limited impact of node fitness and PAFit on growth rules out the possibility that phonological networks adhere to fitness models of network growth. While these models offer intriguing hypotheses for lexical learning by focusing on word characteristics, such as lexical frequency and phonotactic probability, the results of the present study unequivocally demonstrate the superiority of preferential attachment in guiding phonological network growth.

3.2.3 DEVELOPMENTAL GROWTH TRENDS

3.2.3.1 GROWTH FLUCTUATIONS: AGING EFFECTS

Within a lexicon, some nodes undergo growth only once in their lifespan, while others exhibit more consistent growth patterns. Of the latter group, a question arises concerning the developmental trajectory of growth. Specifically, at which point of their tenure in a lexical system do words show their largest growth potential? Such questions were explored in a sub-analysis examining the growth development of continuously growing nodes. These nodes consistently accumulate neighbors from their introduction to the system until reaching the most advanced ESL proficiency level. As visible in Figure 53, there is a declining trend in growth rate in relation to word age. Continuously growing words experience their most substantial growth upon initial introduction to the lexicon, after which their growth gradually declines. A word's growth rate is thus highly predictable based on its entry point into the lexical system. Initial growth lags cannot be overcome by later growth spurts (also see Luef, 2023).

This developmental growth dynamic indicates a preference for new words to initially attach to dense neighborhoods (a known tendency in word learning), thereby gaining the maximum number of neighbors upon entry in the system. However, this largest initial growth potential declines as proficiency increases. Over time in the lexicon, words experience a reduction in their growth potential, indicating an aging effect in the phonological networks of ESL learners. This pattern could reflect a tendency to learn phonologically similar words in a minimal number of growth spurts (see Luef, 2023). Human cognition underlying lexical learning might maximally leverage phonological similarity and acquire similarity neighborhoods in lexical bursts.

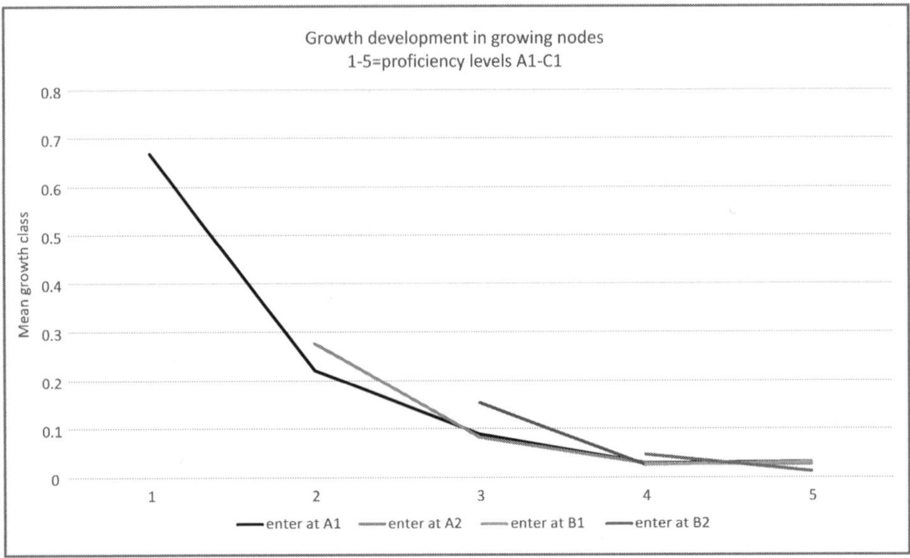

Figure 53: Growth patterns of consistently growing nodes from their entry points in the lexicon until the C1 proficiency level.

3.2.3.2 INITIAL ATTRACTIVENESS

The likelihood of a word to acquire at least one neighbor in the learning process from A1 to C1 is generally low. The majority of singleton words never grow any neighbors and remain singletons throughout all proficiency levels. Of the 161 singleton nodes that first appear in the A1 network, only 24 will eventually grow a neighbor by the C1 level; 85% will remain unconnected. Of the 532 singletons that appear in the A2 network, 390 (=74%) never grow a neighbor; and of the 1017 singletons in the B1 network, 854 (=84%) will never grow a neighbor. The B2 network houses 1529 singletons of which 1357 (=89%) will remain singletons in the C1 network. Several lexical characteristics contribute to the initial attractiveness of a word, increasing the probability of gaining a neighbor. Phonemically shorter words tend to have more opportunities to grow at least one neighbor, as depicted in Figure 54.

Phonotactic probability serves as another effective indicator of growth opportunities, and words containing lower phonotactic probability biphones are more likely to eventually acquire at least one neighbor (see Figure 55).

Moreover, high lexical frequency raises the probability of acquiring at least one neighbor throughout the ESL learning stages (see Figure 56).

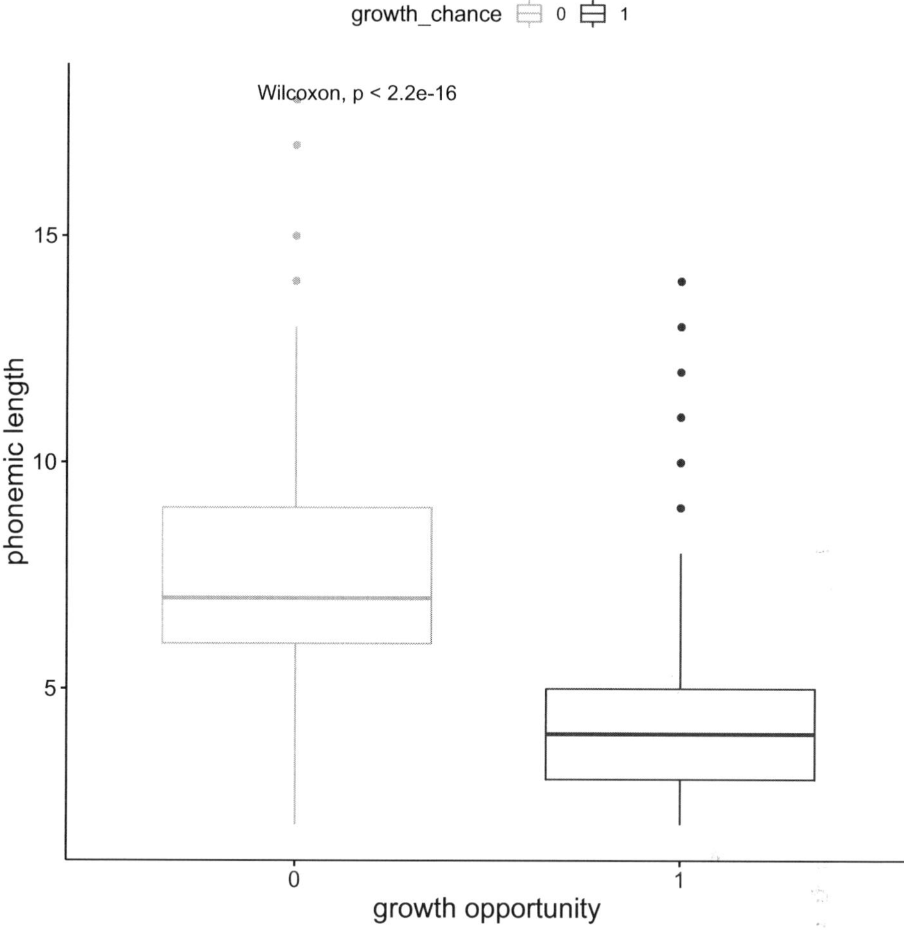

Figure 54: Short words are more likely to acquire at least one neighbor (0=never grow a neighbor, 1=grow at least one neighbor at any proficiency level).

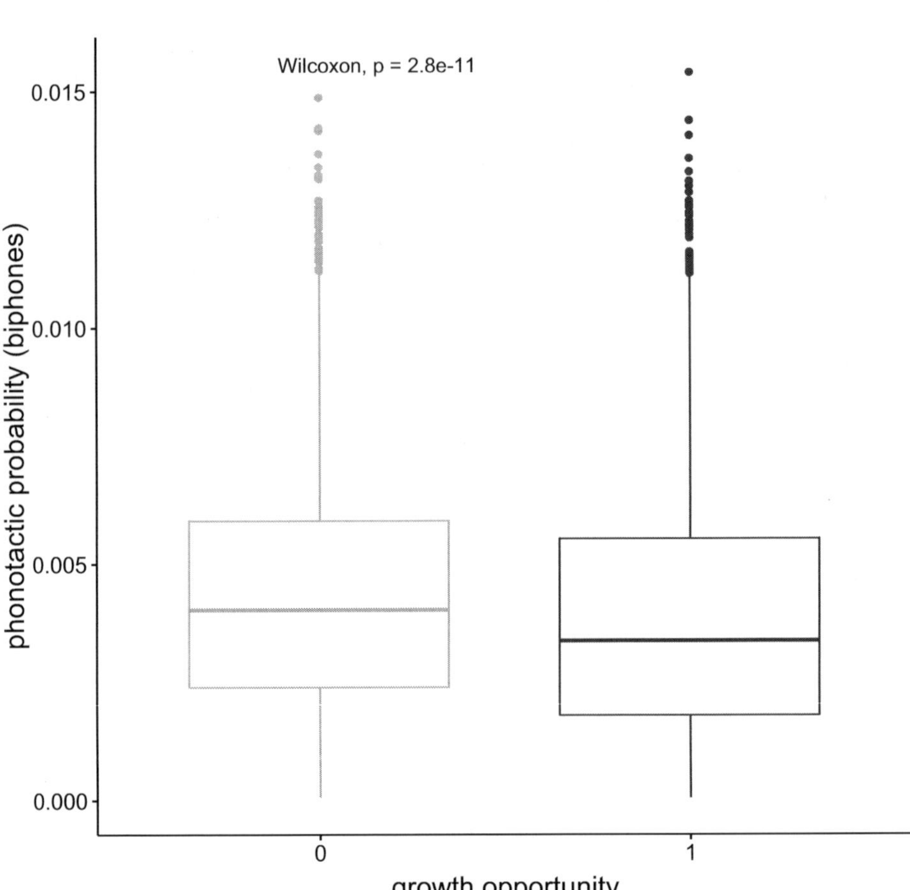

Figure 55: Low phonotactic probability raises the likelihood of a word growing at least one neighbor neighbor (0=never grow a neighbor, 1=grow at least one neighbor at any proficiency level).

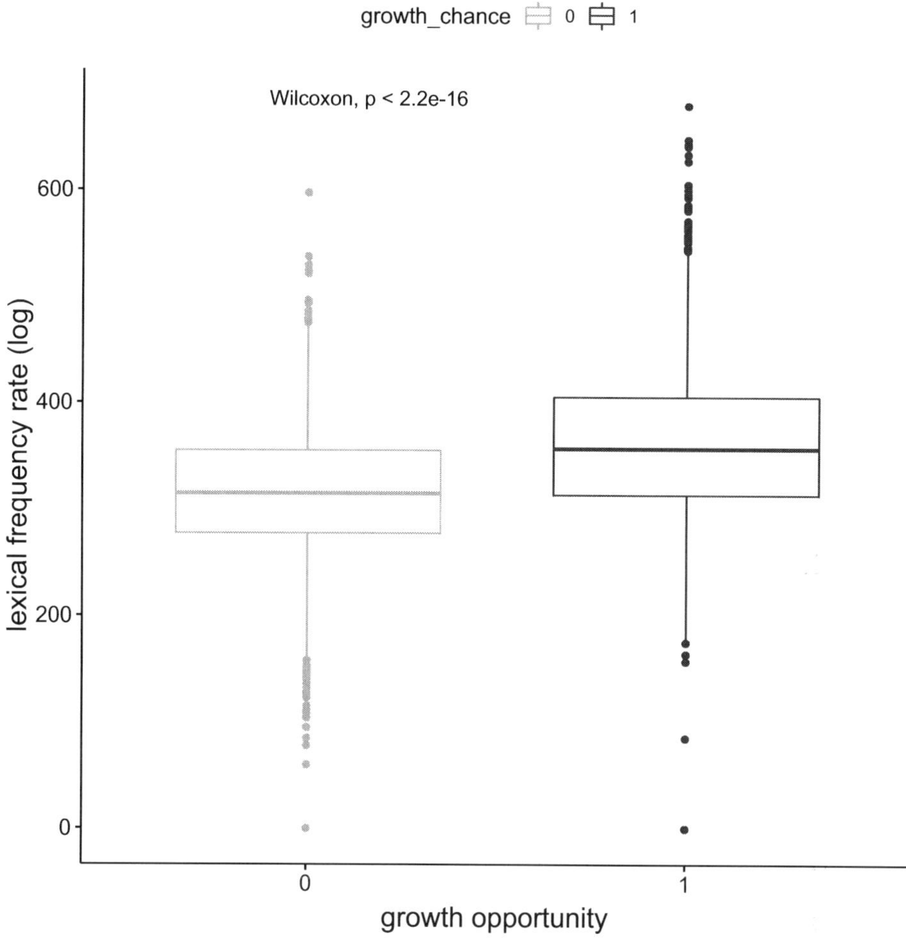

Figure 56: High lexical frequency rate raises the likelihood of a word growing at least one neighbor neighbor (0=never grow a neighbor, 1=grow at least one neighbor at any proficiency level).

A generalized linear regression model (using the R function "glm") with the dependent variable of "growth opportunity" (0=never grow a neighbor, 1=grow at least one neighbor at any proficiency level) was computed to assess the influence of phonotactic probability, phonemic length, and lexical frequency rates. The following model code was used:

Growth (yes/no)~phonotactic probability+phonemic length+lexical frequency(log), family=binomial

Results show that all three factors play a role in a node's ability to acquire at least one neighbor (see Table 31 for the results).

Table 31: Initial attractiveness is influenced by phonotactic probability, phonemic length, and lexical frequency rate.

	Estimate	Std. Error	z value	p
Phonotactic probability	56.25	13.3	4.24	$<0.001^{***}$
Phonemic length	-0.68	0.02	-31.3	$<0.001^{***}$
Lexical frequency	0.007	0.0005	12.67	$<0.001^{***}$

*** $p<0.001$

Initial attractiveness can be calculated with a modified preferential attachment equation, following Dorogovtsev, Mendes, and Samukhin (2000), where the probability of the acquisition of at least one neighboring node is defined as *k+A*, with A being the 'initial attractiveness constant' inferred from the preferential attachment rule incorporating initial attractiveness

$$p(k_i) = (A+k_i) / \sum_j (A+k_j)$$

Thus, it can be calculated that p(0)~*A*, where even non-connected nodes are awarded growth opportunities (Barabási, 2016). In the learner networks, *A* decreases from the beginning to more advanced stages (see Table 32), mirroring the findings displayed in Figure 53.

Table 32: Initial attractiveness constants for each ESL network.

	A1	A2	B1	B2	C1
A	0.39	0.21	0.16	0.06	0.05

The values of A in Table 32 indicate that initial attractiveness is much higher in early acquired words of the A1 lexicon but decreases substantially over the course of learning. By the B2 and C1 levels, it becomes highly unlikely for a singleton node to grow an initial and exclusive neighbor. According to Barabási (2016), the presence of initial attractiveness in a network has two consequences: it makes the network more homogenous by decreasing hub sizes, and it causes the degree distribution to deviate from a power law. Node growth not only occurs in highly connected nodes but may also extend to some unconnected nodes, thereby introducing a random component to the attachment probability.

3.2.3.3 FIRST-MOVER-ADVANTAGE

Words acquired early during vocabulary build-up typically enjoy an advantage in terms of overall neighbor acquisition, a concept called "first-mover-advantage" (Barabási, 2016). Preferential attachment incapsulates the first-mover-advantage, as well-connected nodes exclusively gain links from the outset of the growth process. This results in a substantial link advantage for nodes initially present in a network. In some networks, a chronological preference for growth exists where, for instance, new words tend to attach to young nodes that have only recently been added to the network. This has been shown for phonological networks of second language American English (Luef, 2023). Alternatively, a tendency to attach to old nodes in a network could indicate a stronger foothold of those older nodes in the network, where new nodes preferentially attach to them. A recent study on phonological neighborhood density (though not from the network viewpoint) showed that, in child first language acquisition, early-learned words play a more important role for lexical competition than late-acquired words (Karimi & Diaz, 2020). Specifically, the age of acquisition affected how strongly or weakly a word was activated in its phonological neighborhood. It is generally assumed that the earlier the acquisition age of a word, the stronger its lexical activation (also see Alario et al., 2004; Belke, Brysbaert, Meyer, & Ghyselinck, 2005; Gilhooly & Watson, 1981; Navarrete, Pastore, Valentini, & Preressotti, 2015, for similar findings). This has implications for word age and its role in lexical networks. The Barabási-Albert network model predicts that older nodes accumulate more growth over time, expressed as $k(t)=t^{1/2}$, with t representing a specific time step (Barabási, 2016).

To investigate the first-mover-advantage in the ESL networks, the number of overall neighbors of early-acquired words (A1, A2 levels) was compared to those of late-acquired words (B2, C1). Given the impact of preferential attachment on network growth, early acquisition is expected to lead to a larger accumulation of neighbors across the learning period (up to C1). An overview of node growth classes and age of acquisition of words demonstrates an advantage for early-learned words, while late-learned words exhibit slow growth. In fact, early-learned words by far exceed all other proficiency levels in terms of neighbor accumulation, as indicated by mean growth across proficiency level lexica: A1=2.6 words, A2=1.3 words, B1=0.6 words, B2=0.3 words, C1=0.1 words). This indicates a tendency for older nodes acquired early in language learning to gain more neighbors, underscoring the significance of word age for lexical processing (also see Karimi & Diaz, 2020).

3.2.4 GROWTH PRINCIPLES IN COMMUNITIES

Given that communities of different sizes show a heterogenous makeup in terms of lexical characteristics (Siew, 2013), a closer examination of community growth in the learner networks was conducted, focusing on prevalent network growth algorithms.

Growth algorithms were calculated for each proficiency level in small, medium-sized, and large communities (see Table 33) and results showed a tendency for preferential attachment probability to be higher in mid-sized and larger communities. Node fitness and PAFit were also generally higher in the medium and larger communities, indicating a potential growth advantage for larger communities. Small communities seem to be awarded fewer opportunities to grow neighbors via the investigated growth algorithms. Here, rich (=large) communities become richer through growth.

Table 33: Growth algorithms in network communities of different sizes.

Level	*Community size*	*Growth rate*		*PA (normalized)*		*Fitness*		*PAFit (normalized)*	
		Mean	*SD*	*Mean*	*SD*	*Mean*	*SD*	*Mean*	*SD*
A1	Small (<25th percentile)	1.6	1.4	0.5	0.2	1.6	1.1	−0.04	0.05
	Medium (<25th>75th percentile)	3.4	2.5	0.6	0.3	1.5	0.9	−0.07	0.09
	Large (>75th percentile)	1.9	1.8	0.6	0.4	1.4	1.3	−0.1	0.2
A2	Small (<25th percentile)	0.3	0.6	0.004	0.009	−0.56	0.5	−0.04	0.03
	Medium (<25th>75th percentile)	2.3	1.9	0.1	0.07	1.4	1.4	−0.22	0.3
	Large (>75th percentile)	2	1.8	0.1	0.06	1.22	1.3	−0.18	0.3
B1	Small (<25th percentile)	0.18	0.4	0.001	0.002	−0.7	0.5	0.006	0.004
	Medium (<25th>75th percentile)	1.15	1.5	0.024	0.02	1.1	1.4	0.028	0.04
	Large (>75th percentile)	1.4	1.4	0.03	0.02	1.3	1.4	0.04	0.06
B2	Small (<25th percentile)	0.07	0.27	0.0006	0.001	−0.72	0.5	1.07e-06	8.29e-06
	Medium (<25th>75th percentile)	0.33	0.67	0.007	0.005	0.75	1.3	−7.65e-05	1.32e-04
	Large (>75th percentile)	0.36	0.6	0.013	0.01	1.29	1.4	−2.06e-04	2.99e-04
C1	Small (<25th percentile)	0.05	0.23	0.0004	0.0007	−0.78	0.5	1.84e-07	1.06e-06
	Medium (<25th>75th percentile)	0.36	0.6	0.007	0.007	1.1	1.6	−2.21e-05	4.1e-05
	Large (>75th percentile)	0.63	0.9	0.009	0.007	1.12	1.4	−2.34e-05	3.6e-05

As can be seen in Figures 57a-c, preferential attachment, fitness, and PAFit differ between differently-sized communities across all learner networks.

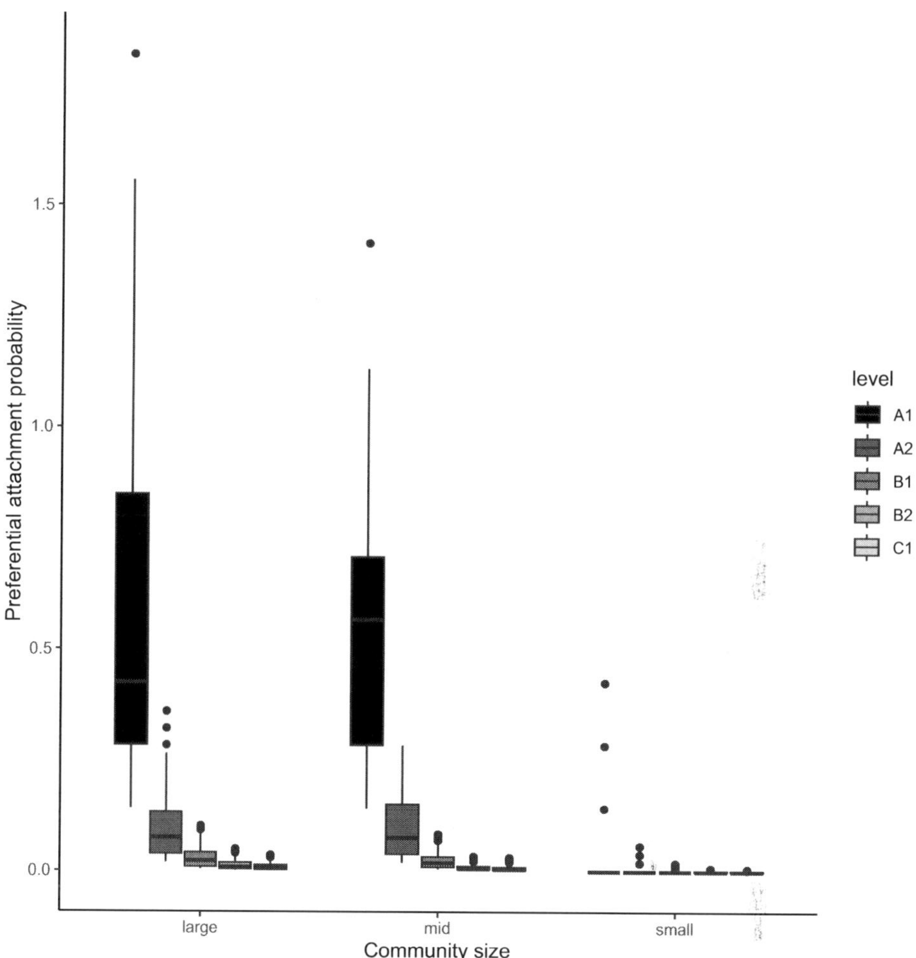

Figures 57a: Preferential attachment probability, node fitness, and PAFit differ between proficiency levels and community sizes.

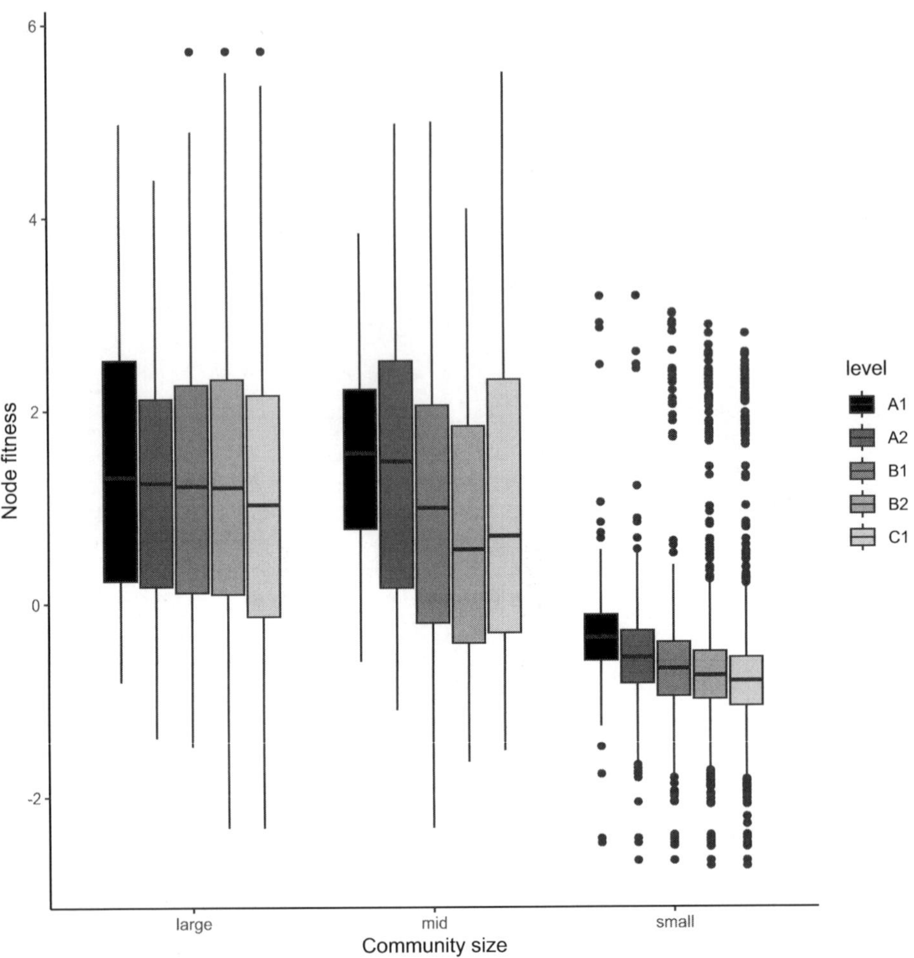

Figures 57b: Preferential attachment probability, node fitness, and PAFit differ between proficiency levels and community sizes.

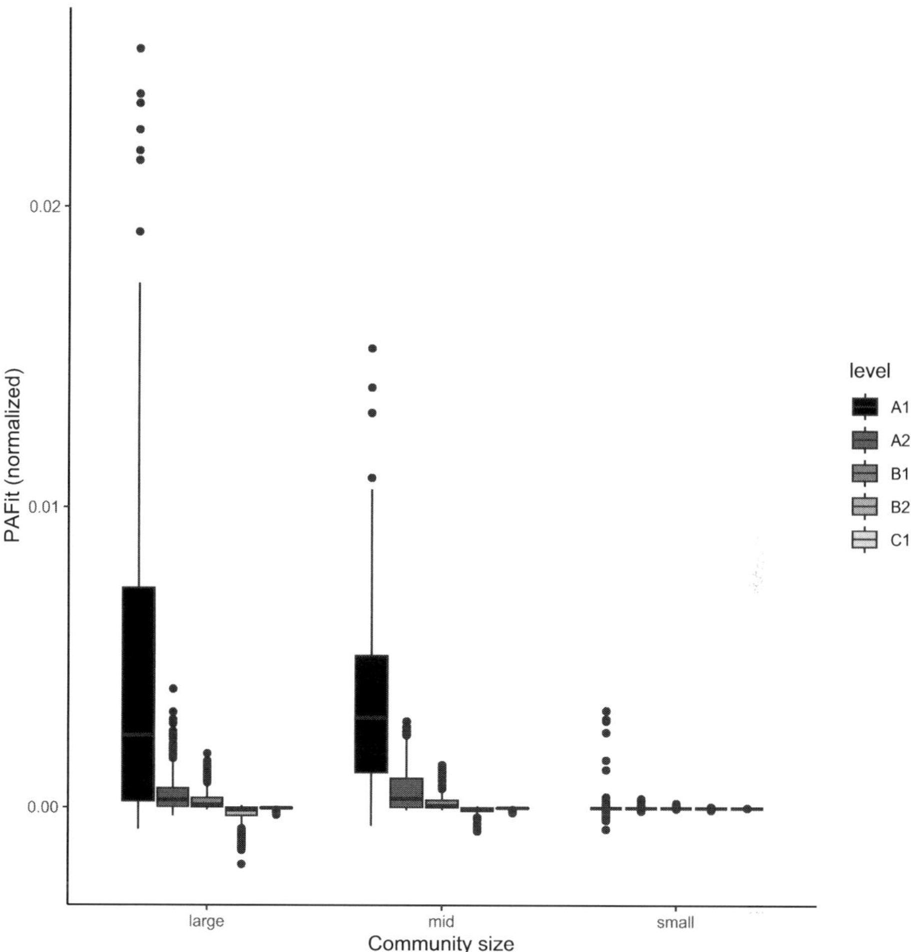

Figures 57c: Preferential attachment probability, node fitness, and PAFit differ between proficiency levels and community sizes.

The observation that preferential attachment and PAFit values are the highest in mid-sized and large communities of the A1 network implies that these factors can have a more substantial influence on growth in these specific communities. Node fitness was relatively low in small communities, which shows that any advantage gained from high fitness is primarily bestowed upon words in mid-sized and larger communities.

The results in Figures 57a-c reveal a clear trend: the patterns of actual community growth (see Figure 41) do not perfectly align with the patterns suggested by preferential attachment (57a), fitness (57b), and PAFit (57c). While preferential attachment seems to be the best match based on visual inspection, it is evident that community growth must be additionally governed by other growth principles. Communities of medium and larger size record the highest growth rates, supporting findings by Siew (2013) who suggested that large communities are constructed first in child language acquisition to form the basis for rapid and efficient lexical processing (also see Luef, 2024). This trend is particularly relevant for earlier language proficiency stages (A1, A2) where growth rates are the highest of all networks. Here, preferential attachment and PAFit might be the primary mechanisms to support the development of robust and larger communities.

3.2.5 SUMMARY

In this chapter, four main strands of growth perspectives were discussed. First, growth rates of individual nodes and their placements in the larger structures of the ESL networks were analyzed to gain insights into which network-mathematical and psycholinguistic factors predispose a word to higher growth. Results demonstrated differences between proficiency levels, lexical characteristics, as well as network components. Second, the impact of growth algorithms and network centrality statistics on growth were examined, with findings indicating that phonological ESL networks are best described as Barabási-Albert growth models, with preferential attachment as the dominant mode. Eigenvector and closeness centralities also affected growth, and the network structure supported by the observed growth patterns of the phonological ESL networks indicate a preference for hub formation, with denser closer neighborhoods (one phonological segment distance) but sparser distant neighborhoods (more than one phonological segment distance). Third, extensions of the Barabási-Albert model, including initial attractiveness and aging mechanisms were also shown to influence growth in the ESL networks. Their contributing effect weakens preferential attachment and allows for random attachment, making their presence crucial in explaining growth in singleton nodes. Fourth, community growth patterns highlighted unequal growth opportunities for differently-sized communities, with medium-sized and larger communities displaying clear advantages over small communities in terms of growth probabilities resulting from the investigated growth algorithms.

The overall picture emerging from the growth analyses of the ESL phonological networks presented here is one of unequal growth distributions: the rich get richer on all levels of the network. On the micro level, dense phonological neighborhoods tend to grow denser over time; on the meso level, mid-sized and larger communities receive the majority of growth opportunities; and on the macro level, giant components tend to expand at the expense of smaller, less connected parts of the network. Such extreme imbalances are commonly observed in social, technological, and biological networks, and it comes as no surprise that "rich words" in the network-theoretical and psycholinguistic sense would gain growth advantages in lexical networks. The findings presented here have direct implications for spoken word recognition and production at different levels of language proficiency. Future research may focus on developmental trajectories concerning the ease and/or difficulty of lexical access for specific words during various stages of vocabulary development.

4. CONCLUSION

4.1 UTILITY OF NETWORK SCIENCE FOR LEXICAL RESEARCH

This book has highlighted the advantages of network science for studying the mental lexicon of (second) language learners. It is clear that network-theoretical concepts can contribute to our understanding of word learning and lexical access. Underpinning the methodology of network theory are the assumptions that a system is governed by both local and global rules, which work in tandem to influence the behaviors of the individual constituents. In contrast, a reductionist view utilizes only a fraction of the available information within a lexical system and tends to underestimate its complexity by failing to account for global properties that may impose unexpected constraints. Until recently, the mental lexicon was studied exclusively from the "bottom-up" perspective of local rules governing small groups of interrelated words in functional neighborhoods. The introduction of network science has ushered in a "top-down" approach to studying the mental lexicon, following the rationale of complex systems. Rather than conceiving of the mental lexicon as an accumulation of independent, co-existing local word neighborhoods, lexical networks posit a complex lexical storage system characterized by far-reaching interconnections spanning a large number of words. According to this view, lexical learning is seen as a process of network growth, emphasizing the idea that network changes are dependent on network structure – encapsulating Steven Strogatz' rule that "structure always affects function". This interplay between the grander layout of the lexical network and the possibilities it offers for investigating word learning is significant to acknowledge, especially in light of long-known evidence that not all words share equal learning probabilities. Network science provides a lens through which we can understand how individual words become integrated into learners' pre-existing lexical knowledge, enabling us to derive new predictions about learning. The theoretical framework offered by this book has the potential to contribute to theories on second language word memory and learning, and may serve as a methodological foundation for future studies investigating lexical processes in second languages.

Understanding phonological networks within the context of evolving network theories enhances our understanding of scale-free growth by detailing growth algorithms governing the different proficiency stages of a lexicon. Preferential attachment has an overwhelming influence on growth at all stages of network development, supporting a dominant theory of evolving networks. In contrast, fitness growth models, which seem intuitive for lexical growth, appear to be less applicable to phonological networks. It seems that cumulative advantages in phonological networks excel over quality of those neighbors, with profound implications for the growing architecture of a phonological network over time. Principles such as rich-get-richer, initial attractiveness, aging effects, and the first-mover-advantage in phonological networks align well with traditional views of scale-free networks. This underscores the utility and relevance of network-theoretical growth algorithms when applied to phono-lexical data.

A number of pertinent issues have emerged from the findings presented here, extending beyond the scope of this book but warranting exploration in future studies adopting a network approach to second language vocabulary. A select few will be briefly highlighted below.

First, the developmental trend of hub formation during network growth carries potential consequences for the learning of phonetic and phonological detail in a second language. In initial learning stages, not all phonological contrasts may be successfully mastered, with challenges such as the difficulty of dental fricatives for learners whose first language lacks the sound. This frequently leads to substitutions, for instance, using sibilants or labio-dental fricatives, resulting in phonological word forms such as "sink" instead of "think" in the vocabulary of many ESL learners. As learning progresses, phonological learning generally improves, leading to the acquisition of the correct dental fricative [θ]. A question arises regarding the diffusion of this phonological 'innovation' as the second language lexicon grows. Do hub-words impede the introduction of the new feature due to their many neighbors exerting pressure to maintain a conservative phonological standard (i.e., 'more traditional' /s/)? Or, conversely, are hubs the primary facilitators of this phonological change, efficiently disseminating the new feature throughout their linked neighbors and the wider network? A similar question could be explored in the context of sound change in general. The roles of hubs and peripheral nodes in the dissemination of phonological changes are potentially interesting, as they may have far-reaching consequences for the phonology of a lexical network.

Another intriguing research question pertains to language loss or network decline. Second language learners may forget a language over time, leading to a reduction in their vocabulary. Analyzing which network parts begin to disintegrate first and which parts are able to maintain their structure the longest, whether build-up and decline tend to concentrate on similar nodes, and what constitutes the most robust core of a network (its 'backbone', see Vitevitch & Sale, 2023) can yield valuable insights for developing strategies to understand language attrition. Learners as well as language educators stand to benefit from such an analysis.

The network-theoretical approach to the mental lexicon has yet to be broadly evaluated by psycholinguistics and tested under different experimental conditions. However, there can be no doubt that it has the potential to complement current methods of studying word memory and learning. The most promising possibility is that lexical network science will be understood as a natural extension of the traditional lexical neighborhood analysis, offering a valuable tool to examine the inner workings and developmental functions of the mental lexicon from a new perspective.

REFERENCES

Aitchison, J. (2012). Words in the mind: An introduction to the mental lexicon. London: John Wiley & Sons.

Alario, F.-X., Ferrand, L., Laganaro, M., New, B., Frauenfelder, U. H., & Segui, J. (2004). Predictors of picture naming speed. *Behavior Research Methods, Instruments, and Computers, 36*(1), 140–155.

Albert, R., & Barabási, A. (2002). Statistical mechanics of complex networks. *Reviews of Modern Physics, 74*, 47–97.

Albert, R., Jeong, H., & Barabási, A. L. (2000). Error and attack tolerance of complex networks. *Nature, 406*, 378–382.

Alexy, O., George, G., & Salter, A. J. (2013). Cui bono? The selective revealing of knowledge and its implications for innovative activity. *Academy of Management Review, 38*(2).

Alvarez-Ponce, D., Feyertag, F., & Chakraborty, S. (2017). Position matters: Network centrality considerably impacts rates of protein evolution in the human protein-protein interaction network. *Genome Biology and Evolution, 9*(6), 1742–1756.

Amaral, L. A. N., Scala, A., Barthélémy, M., & Stanley, H. E. (2000). Classes of small-world networks. *Proceedings of the National Academy of Sciences of the United States of America, 97*, 11149–11152.

Anwar, R., Yousuf, M. I., & Abid, M. (2021). Uniform preferential selection model for generating scale-free networks. *Methodology and Computing in Applied Probability*, *24*, 449–470.

Arbesman, S., Strogatz, S. H., & Vitevitch, M. S. (2010). The structure of phonological networks across multiple languages. *International Journal of Bifurcation and Chaos, 20*(3), 679–685.

Arutiunian, V., & Lopukhina, A. (2020). The effects of phonological neighborhood density in childhood word production and recognition in Russian are opposite to English. *Journal of Child Language, 47*(6), 1244–1262.

Bailey, T. M., & Hahn, U. (2001). Determinants of wordlikeness: Phonotactics of lexical neighborhoods?. *Journal of Memory and Language, 44*, 568–591.

Banerjee, S., & Bhamidi, S. (2021). Persistence of hubs in growing random networks. *Probability Theory and Related Fields, 180*, 891–953.

Barabási, A. L. (2009). Scale-free networks: A decade and beyond. *Science, 325*, 412–413.

Barabási, A. L. (2016). *Network science*. Cambridge, UK: Cambridge University Press.

Barabási, A. L., & Albert, R. (1999). Emergence of scaling in random networks. *Science, 286*, 509–512.

Bard, E. G., & Shillcock, R. C. (1993). Competitor effects during lexical access: Chasing Zipf's tail. In G. E. Altmann & R. C. Shillcock (Eds.), *Cognitive models of speech processing: The second Sperlonga meeting* (pp. 235–275). Hillsdale, NJ: Lawrence Erlbaum Associates.

Bard, E. G., Shillcock, R. C., & Altmann, G. E. (1988). The recognition of words after their acoustic offsets in spontaneous speech: Evidence of subsequent context. *Perception and Psychophysics, 44*, 395–408.

Baronchelli, R., Ferrer-i-Cancho, R. F., Pastor-Satorras, R., Chater, N., & Christiansen, M. H. (2013). Networks in cognitive science. *Trends in Cognitive Science, 17*, 348–360.

Bastian, M., Heymann, S., & Jacomy, M. (2009). *Gephi: An open source software for exploring and manipulating networks.* Paper presented at the International AAAI Conference on Weblogs and Social Media.

Bates, D., Maechler, M., Bolker, B., & Walker, S. (2014). {lme4}: Linear mixed-effects models using Eigen and S4. *R Package version 1,* 1–7.

Bauer, R., & Kaiser, M. (2017). Nonlinear growth: An origin of hub organization in complex networks. *Royal Society Open Science, 4*(3), 160691.

Beckage, N. M., Aguilar, A., & Colunga, E. (2015). *Modeling lexical acquisition through networks.* Paper presented at the Proceedings of the 37th Annual Conference of the Cognitive Science Society, Austin, TX.

Beckage, N. M., & Colunga, E. (2016). Language networks as models of cognition: Understanding cognition through language. In A. Mehler, A. Lücking, S. Banisch, P. Blanchard, & B. Job (Eds.), *Towards a theoretical framework for analyzing complex linguistic networks: Understanding complex systems* (pp. 2–20). Berlin, Heidelberg: Springer.

Beckage, N. M., & Colunga, E. (2019). Network growth modeling to capture individual lexical learning. *Complexity, 2019,* 7690869.

Beckage, N. M., Smith, L., & Hills, T. T. (2011). Small worlds and semantic network growth in typical and late talkers. *PLoS ONE, 6*(5), e19348.

Bedogne', C., & Rodgers, G. (2006). Complex growing networks with intrinsic vertex fitness. *Physical Review E, 74*(4), 046115.

Belke, E., Brysbaert, M., Meyer, A. S., & Ghyselinck, M. (2005). Age of acquisition effects in picture naming: Evidence for a lexical-semantic competition hypothesis. *Cognition, 96*(2), B45–54.

Bell, M., Perera, S., Piraveenan, M., Bliemer, M., Latty, T., & Reid, C. (2017). Network growth models: A behavioural basis for attachment proportional to fitness. *Scientific Reports, 7,* 42431.

Benham, S., Goffman, L., & Schweickert, R. (2018). An application of network science to phonological sequence learning in children with developmental language disorder. *Journal of Speech, Language, and Hearing Research, 61*(9), 2275–2291.

Benitez, V. L., & Saffran, J. R. (2018). Two for the price of one: Concurrent learning of words and phonotactic regularities from continuous speech. *PLoS ONE, 16*(6), e0253039.

Berg, T., & Schade, U. (1992a). The role of inhibition in a spreading-activation model of language production. I. The psycholinguistic perspective. *Journal of Psycholinguistic Research, 21,* 405–434.

Berg, T., & Schade, U. (1992b). The role of inhibition in a spreading-activation model of language production. II. The simulation perspective. *Journal of Psycholinguistic Research, 21*(6), 435–462.

Bialystok, E. (2010). Bilingualism. *Wiley Interdisciplinary Reviews: Cognitive Science, 1,* 559–572.

Bianconi, G., & Barabási, A. L. (2001). Bose-Einstein condensation in complex networks. *Physical Review Letters, 86*(24), 5632–5635.

Blondel, V. D., Guillaume, J.-L., Lambiotte, R., & Lefebvre, E. (2008). Fast unfolding of communities in large networks. *Journal of Statistical Mechanics: Theory and Experiment, P10008*(10). https://doi.org/10.1088/1742-5468/2008/10/P10008

Boccaletti, S., Latora, V., Moreno, Y., Chavez, M., & Hwang, D. U. (2006). Complex networks: Structure and dynamics. *Physical Reports, 424,* 175–308.

Boccara, N. (2010). *Modeling complex systems.* Berlin et al.: Springer.

Bock, K., & Levelt, W. J. M. (1994). Language production: Grammatical encoding. In M. A. Gernsbacher (Ed.), *Handbook of psycholinguistics* (pp. 945–984). San Diego, CA: Academic Press.

Bonacich, P. (1972). Technique for analyzing overlapping memberships. *Sociological Methodology, 4,* 176–185.

Bonacich, P. (2007). Some unique properties of eigenvector centrality. *Social Networks, 29*(4), 555–564.

Bonacich, P., & Lloyd, P. (2015). Eigenvector centrality and structural zeroes and ones: When is a neighbor not a neighbor? *Social Networks, 43,* 86–90.

Bose, S. (1924). Planck's law and the light quantum hypothesis. *Zeitschrift für Physik, 26,* 178.

Broersma, M., & Cutler, A. (2008). Phantom word activation in L2. *System: An International Journal of Educational Technology and Applied Linguistics, 36,* 22–34.

Broido, A. D., & Clauset, A. (2019). Scale-free networks are rare. *Nature Communications, 10,* 1017.

Brown, G. D. A., Neath, I., & Chater, N. (2007). A temporal ratio model of memory. *Psychologial Review, 114*, 539–576.

Bryla, B. (2015). *Oracle Database 12c handbook: Manage a scalable, secure Oracle enterprise database environment*. New York et al.: McGraw Hill.

Brysbaert, M., Mandera, P., & Keuleers, E. (2017). The word frequency effect in word processing: An updated review. *Current Directions in Psychological Science, 27*(1), 45–50.

Brysbaert, M., Stevens, M., De Deyne, S., Voorspoels, W., & Storms, G. (2014). Norms of age of acquisition and concreteness for 30,000 Dutch words. *Acta Psychologica, 150*, 80–84.

Buchwald, A. (2011). Neighborhood effects. In M. van Oostendorp, C. J. Ewen, E. Hume, & K. Rice (Eds.), *The Blackwell companion to phonology: Volume IV Phonological interfaces* (pp. 2070–2088). Chichester, UK: Wiley-Blackwell.

Caldarelli, A., Capocci, A., De Los Rios, P., & Munoz, M. A. (2002). Scale-free networks from varying vertex intrinsic fitness. *Physical Review Letters, 89*, 258702.

Callaway, D. S., Hopcroft, J. E., Kleinberg, J. M., Newman, M. E. J., & Strogatz, S. H. (2001). Are randomly grown graphs really random? *Physical Review E: Statistical, Nonlinear, and Soft Matter Physics, 64*(4), 041902.

Caramazza, A., Costa, A., Miozzo, M., & Bi, Y. (2001). The specific-word frequency effect: Implication for the representation of homophones in speech production. *Journal of Experimental Psychology: Learning, Memory, and Cognition, 27*, 1430–1450.

Carlson, M. T., Sonderegger, M., & Bane, M. (2014). How children explore the phonological network in child-directed speech: A survival analysis of children's first word productions. *Journal of Memory and Language, 75*, 159–180.

Carrasco-Ortiz, H., Midgley, K. J., & Frenck-Mestre, C. (2012). Are phonological representations in bilinguals language specific? An ERP study on interlingual homophones. *Psychophysiology, 49*(4), 531–543.

Carreras, I., Miorandi, D., Canright, G. S., & Engo-Monsen, K. (2007). Eigenvector centrality in highly partitioned mobile networks: Principles and applications. *Studies in Computational Intelligence, 69*, 123–145.

Castro, N., & Siew, C. S. Q. (2020). Contributions of modern network science to the cognitive sciences: Revisiting research spirals of representation and process. *Proceedings of the Royal Society A: Mathematical, Physical and Engineering Sciences, 476*, 20190825.

Castro, N., & Stella, M. (2018). The multiplex interplay between phonological and semantic networks impacts word production across different types of aphasia. *Frontiers in Human Neuroscience, 12*.

Castro, N., Stella, M., & Siew, C. S. Q. (2019). Quantifying the interplay of semantics and phonology during failures of word retrieval by people with aphasia using a multiplex lexical network. *Cognitive Science, 44*(9), e12881.

Castro, N., Vitevitch, M. S. (2023). Using network science and psycholinguistic megastudies to examine the dimensions of phonological similarity. *Language and Speech, 66*(1), 143–174.

Chan, K. Y., & Vitevitch, M. S. (2009). The influence of the phonological neighborhood clustering coefficient on spoken word recognition. *Journal of Experimental Psychology: Human Perception and Performance, 35*(6), 1934–1949.

Chan, K. Y., & Vitevitch, M. S. (2010). Network structure influences speech production. *Cognitive Science, 34*, 685–697.

Charles-Luce, J., & Luce, P. A. (1990). Similarity neighbourhoods of words in young children's lexicon. *Journal of Child Language, 17*(1), 205–215.

Chen, B.-S., & Lin, Y.-P. (2011). On the interplay between evolvability and network robustness in an evolutionary biological network: A systems biology approach. *Evolutionary Bioinformatics*, EBO. S8123.

Chen, C., & Truscott, J. (2010). The effects of repetition and L1 lexicalization on incidental vocabulary acquisition. *Applied Linguistics, 31*(5), 693–713.

Chen, Q., & Mirman, D. (2012). Competition and cooperation among similar representations: Toward a unified account of facilitative and inhibitory effects of lexical neighbors. *Psychological Review, 119*(2), 417–430.

Chen, Q., & Mirman, D. (2014). Interaction between phonological and semantic representations: Time matters. *Cognitive Science, 39*(3), 538–558.

Clauset, A., Shalizi, C. R., & Newman, M. E. J. (2009). Power-law distributions in empirical data. *SIAM Review, 51*(4), 661–703.

Cohen, R., & Havlin, S. (2010). *Complex networks: Structure, robustness and function*. New York: Cambridge University Press.

Collins, A., & Loftus, E. (1975). A spreading-activation theory of semantic processing. *Psychological Review, 82*, 407–428.

Cong, J., & Haitao, L. (2014). Approaching human language with complex networks. *Physics of Life Reviews, 11*(4), 598–618.

Cooper, C., & Frieze, A. (2003). A general model of web graphs. *Random Structures and Algorithms, 22*(3), 311–335.

Crossley, S. A., Skalicky, S., Kyle, K., & Monteiro, K. (2019). Absolute frequency effects in second language lexical acquisition. *Studies in Second Language Acquisition, 41*, 721–744.

Csardi, G., & Nepusz, T. (2006). The igraph software package for complex network research. *InterJournal: Complex Systems, 1695*.

D'Agostino, R. B., & Stephens, M. A. (1986). *Goodness-of-fit techniques*. New York, Basel: Marcel Dekker, Inc.

Dale, P. S., & Fenson, L. (1996). Lexical development norms for young children. *Behavior Research Methods, 28*, 125–127.

De Ambroggio, U., Polito, F., & Sacerdote, L. (2020). On dynamic random graphs with degree homogenization via anti-preferential attachment probabilities. *Physica D: Nonlinear Phenomena, 414*, 132689.

de Boysson-Bardies, B., & Vihman, M. M. (1991). Adaptation to language: Evidence from babbling and first words in four languages. *Language, 67*, 297–319.

De Deyne, S., Kenett, Y. N., Anaki, D., Faust, M., & Navarro, D. (2017). Large-scale network representations of semantics in the mental lexicon. In M. N. Jones (Ed.), *Frontiers of cognitive psychology: Big data in cognitive science* (pp. 174–202). New York: Routledge/ Taylor & Francis Group.

De Deyne, S., Navarro, D., Perfors, A., Brysbaert, M., & Storms, G. (2019). "The small world of words": English word association norms for over 12,000 cue words. *Behavior Research Methods, 51*, 987–1006.

Dearing, J. W. (2008). Evolution of diffusion and dissemination theory. *Journal of Public Health Management & Practice, 14*(2), 99–108.

Delignette-Muller, M. L., & Dutang, C. (2015). fitdistrplus: An R package for fitting distributions. *Journal of Statistical Software, 64*(4), 1–34.

Dell, G. S. (1986). A spreading-activation theory of retrieval in sentence production. *Psychological Review, 93*(3), 283–321.

Dell, G. S., & Gordon, J. (2003). Neighbors in the lexicon: Friends or foes? In N. O. Schiller & A. S. Meyer (Eds.), *Phonetics and phonology in language comprehension and production: Differences and similarities* (pp. 9–38). London: De Gruyter Mouton.

Dell, G. S., Martin, N., & Schwartz, M. F. (2007). A case-series test of the interactive two-step model of lexical access: Predicting word repetition from picture naming. *Journal of Memory and Language, 56*, 490–520.

Dell, G. S., Schwartz, M. F., Martin, N., Saffran, E. G., & Gagnon, D. A. (1997). Lexical access in aphasic and nonaphasic speakers. *Psychologial Review, 104*(4), 801–838.

Desroches, A. S., Newman, R. L., & Joanisse, M. F. (2009). Investigating the time course of spoken word recognition: Electrophysiological evidence for the influences of phonological similarity. *Journal of Cognitive Neuroscience, 21*, 1893–1906.

Dijkstra, T., Miwa, K., Brummelhuis, B., Sappelli, M., & Baayen, R. H. (2010). How cross-language similarity and task demands affect cognate recognition. *Journal of Memory and Language, 62*, 284–301.

Dijkstra, T., Timmermans, M., & Schriefers, H. (2000). On being blinded by your other language: Effects of task demands on interlingual homograph recognition. *Journal of Memory and Language, 42*(4), 445–464.

Dobson, A. J. (2002). *An introduction to generalized linear models*. Boca Raton: Chapman & Hall/ CRC.
Dóczi, B. (2019). An overview of conceptual models and theories of lexical representation in the mental lexicon. In S. Webb (Ed.), *The Routledge handbook of vocabulary studies* (pp. 46–65). New York: Routledge.
Donnelly, S., & Kidd, E. (2020). Individual differences in lexical processing efficiency and vocabulary in toddlers: A longitudinal investigation. *Journal of Experimental Child Psychology, 192*, 104781.
Dorogovtsev, S. N., & Mendes, J. F. F. (2003). Accelerated growth of networks. In S. Bornholdt & H. G. Schuster (Eds.), *Handbook of graphs and networks* (pp. 318–341). Berlin: Wiley-VCH.
Dorogovtsev, S. N., Mendes, J. F. F., & Samukhin, A. N. (2000). Structure of growing networks with preferential linking. *Physical Review Letters, 85*(21), 4633–4636.
Downey, B., Hallmark, B., Cox, M. P., Norquest, P., & Lansing, J. S. (2008). Computational feature-sensitive reconstruction of language relationships: Developing the ALINE distance for comparative historical linguistic reconstruction. *Journal of Quantitative Linguistics, 15*(4), 340–369.
Downey, S. S., Sun, G., & Norquest, P. (2017). alineR: An R package for optimizing feature-weighted alignments and linguistic distances. *The R Journal, 9*(1), 138–152.
Einstein, A. (1924). Quantentheorie des einatomigen idealen Gases. *Sitzungsberichte der Preussischen Akademie der Wissenschaften, Physikalisch-mathematische Klasse*, 261–267.
Elgort, I., Beliaeva, N., & Boers, F. (2020). Contextual word learning in the first and second language. *Studies in Second Language Acquisition, 42*, 7–32.
Ellis, N. C. (2002). Frequency effects in language processing: A review with implications for theories of implicit and explicit language acquisition. *Studies in Second Language Acquisition, 24*, 143–188.
English Vocabulary Profile (n. d.). Retrieved September 3, 2022, from https://www.englishprofile.org/wordlists
Epskamp, S., Cramer, A. O. J., Waldorp, L., Schmittmann, V. D., & Borsboom, D. (2012). qgraph: Network visualizations of relationships in psychometric data. *Journal of Statistical Software, 48*(4), 1–18.
Erdős, P., & Rényi, A. (1959). On random graphs I. *Publ. Math. Debrecen, 6*, 290–297.
Estes, W. K. (1975). Some targets for mathematical psychology. *Journal of Mathematical Psychology, 12*, 263–282.
Estrada, E. (2006). Network robustness to targeted attacks: The interplay of expansibility and degree distribution. *The European Physical Journal B - Condensed Matter and Complex Systems, 52*, 563–574.
Estrada, E. (2016). When local and global clustering of networks diverge. *Linear Algebra and its Applications, 488*, 249–263.
Fay, D., & Cutler, A. (1977). Malapropisms and the structure of the mental lexicon. *Linguistic Inquiry, 8*(3), 505–520.
Feather, N. (1971). Organization and discrepancy in cognitive structures. *Psychological Review, 78*, 355–379.
Ferretti, L., Cortelezzi, M., Yang, B., Marmorini, G., & Bianconi, G. (2012). Features and heterogeneities in growing network models. *Physical Review E, 85*, 066110.
Field, A. (2005). *Discovering statistics using SPSS*. London: Sage Publications.
Forstmeier, W., & Schielzeth, H. (2011). Cryptic multiple hypotheses testing in linear models: Overestimated effect sizes and the winner's curse. *Behavioral Ecology and Sociobiology, 65*, 47–55.
Fotouhi, B., & Rabbat, M. G. (2013). Network growth with arbitrary initial conditions: Degree dynamics for uniform and preferential attachment. *Physical Review E, 88*(6), 062801.
Fourtassi, A., Bian, Y., & Frank, M. C. (2020). The growth of children's semantic and phonological networks: Insights from 10 languages. *Cognitive Science, 44*(7), e12847.
Foygel, D., & Dell, G. S. (2000). Models of impaired lexical access in speech production. *Journal of Memory and Language, 43*, 182–216.
Freeman, L. C. (1979). Centrality in social networks: Conceptual clarification. *Social Networks, 1*, 215–239.
Fricke, M., Baese-Berk, M., & Goldrick, M. (2016). Dimensions of similarity in the mental lexicon. *Language, Cognition and Neuroscience, 31*(5), 639–645.
Friedrich, C. K., Felder, V., Lahiri, A., & Eulitz, C. (2013). Activation of words with phonological overlap. *Frontiers in Psychology, 4*, 48815. https://doi.org/10.3389/fpsyg.2013.00556

Frisch, S. A. (2011). Frequency effects. In M. van Oostendorp, C. J. Ewen, E. Hume, & K. Rice (Eds.), *The Blackwell companion to phonology: Phonological interfaces* (pp. 2137–2163). Chichester, UK: Blackwell Publishing Ltd.

Gagen, M. J., & Mattick, J. S. (2005). Accelerating, hyperaccelerating, and decelerating networks. *Physical Review Letters, 72*, 016123.

Gahl, S., Yao, Y., & Johnson, K. (2012). Why reduce? Phonological neighborhood density and phonetic reduction in spontaneous speech. *Journal of Memory and Language, 66*(4), 789–806.

Garlaschelli, D., & Loffredo, M. (2004). Fitness-dependent topological properties of the word trade web. *Physical Review Letters, 93*, 188701.

Gaskell, M. G., & Dumay, N. (2003). Lexical competition and the acquisition of novel words. *Cognition, 89*, 105–132.

Gass, S., & Selinker, L. (2008). *Second language acquisition: An introductory course*. New York: Routledge.

Gerometta, J. A. (2015). *Network modeling of the developing mental lexicon: Phonological links within and between lexical communities*. The City University of New York.

Ghoshal, G., Chi, L., & Barabási, A. L. (2013). Uncovering the role of elementary processes in network evolution. *Scientific Reports, 3*, 2920.

Gilhooly, K. J., & Watson, F. L. (1981). Word age-of-acquisition effects: A review. *Current Psychological Reviews, 1*(3), 269–286.

Gillespie, C. S. (2014). Fitting heavy tailed distributions: The poweRlaw package. *arXiv*. http://doi.org/10.48550/arXiv.1407.3492

Glazer, A. M., & Wark, J. S. (2001). *Statistical mechanics*. Oxford, UK: Oxford University Press.

Goh, W. D., Suarez, L., Yap, M. J., & Tan, S. H. (2009). Distributional analyses in auditory lexical decision: Neighborhood density and word frequency effects. *Psychonomic Bulletin and Review, 16*, 882–887.

Goldbeck, J. (2015). *Introduction to social media investigation*. Amsterdam: Elsevier.

Goldinger, S. D., Luce, P. A., & Pisoni, D. B. (1989). Priming lexical neighbors of spoken words: Effects of competition and inhibition. *Journal of Memory and Language, 28*(5), 501–518.

Goldrick, M., Folk, J. R., & Rapp, B. (2010). Mrs. Malaprop's neighborhood: Using word errors to reveal neighborhood structure. *Journal of Memory and Language, 62*(2), 113–134.

Goldstein, R., & Vitevitch, M. S. (2014). The influence of clustering coefficient on word-learning: How groups of similar sounding words facilitate acquisition. *Frontiers in Psychology, 5*, 1307.

Goldstein, R., & Vitevitch, M. S. (2017). The influence of closeness centrality on lexical processing. *Frontiers in Psychology, 8*, 1683.

Gomez-Rodriguez, M., Leskovec, J., & Krause, A. (2012). Inferring networks of diffusion and influence. *ACM Transactions on Knowledge Discovery from Data, 5*(4), 1–37.

Goodman, J. C., Dale, P. S., & Li, P. (2008). Does frequency count? Parental input and the acquisition of vocabulary. *Journal of Child Language, 35*(3), 515–531.

Gordon, J. K. (2002). Phonological neighborhood effects in aphasic speech errors: Spontaneous and structured contexts. *Brain and Language, 82*(2), 113–145.

Gráf, T. (2017). The story of the learner corpus LINDSEI_CZ. *Studies in Applied Linguistics, 8*(2), 22–35.

Gravino, P., Servedio, V. D. P., Barrat, A., & Loreto, V. (2012). Complex structures and semantics in free word association. *Advances in Complex Systems, 15*(3–4), 1250054–1250075.

Greenberg, J. H. (1966). *Language universals: With special reference to feature hierarchies*. Berlin: Mouton de Gruyter.

Griffiths, T., Steyvers, M., & Firl, A. (2007). Google and the mind: Predicting fluency with PageRank. *Psychological Science, 18*, 1069–1076.

Gruenenfelder, T. M., & Pisoni, D. B. (2009). The lexical restructuring hypothesis and graph theoretic analyses of networks based on random lexicons. *Journal of Speech, Language, and Hearing Research, 52*(3), 596–609.

Haggett, P., & Chorley, R. J. (1972). *Network analysis in geography*. London: Edward Arnold.

Haigh, C. A., & Jared, D. (2007). The activation of phonological representations by bilinguals while reading silently: Evidence from interlingual homophones. *Journal of Experimental Psychology: Learning, Memory, and Cognition, 33*(4), 623–644.

Harley, T. A., & Bown, H. E. (1998). What causes a tip-of-the-tongue state? Evidence for lexical neighbourhood effects in speech production. *British Journal of Psychology, 89*, 151–174.

Hartigan, J. A., & Hartigan, P. M. (1985). The dip test of unimodality. *Annals of Statistics, 13*(1), 70–84.

Havas, B., Taylor, J. S. H., Vaquero, L., de Diego-Balaguer, R., Rodriguez-Fornells, A., & Davis, M. H. (2018). Semantic and phonological schema influence spoken word learning and overnight consolidation. *Quarterly Journal of Experimental Psychology, 71*(6), 1469–1481.

He, H., & Deng, Y. (2015). The mental lexicon and English vocabulary teaching. *English Language Teaching, 8*(7), 40–45.

Hébert-Dufresne, L., Allard, A., Marceau, V., Noël, P.-A., & Dubé, L. J. (2011). Structural preferential attachment: Network organization beyond the link. *Physical Review Letters, 107*(15), 158702.

Helsen, J., Frickel, J., Jelier, R., & Verstrepen, K. J. (2019). Network hubs affect evolvability. *PloS Biology, 17*(1), e3000111.

Hills, T. T., Maouene, J., Riordan, B., & Smith, L. (2010). The associative structure of language: Contextual diversity in early word learning. *Journal of Memory and Language, 63*(3), 259–273.

Hills, T. T., Maouene, M., Maouene, J., Sheya, A., & Smith, L. (2009a). Categorical structure among shared features in networks of early-learned nouns. *Cognition, 112*(3), 381–396.

Hills, T. T., Maouene, M., Maouene, J., Sheya, A., & Smith, L. (2009b). Longitudinal analysis of early semantic networks. *Psychological Science, 20*(6), 729–739.

Hoffmann, T., Peel, L., Lambiotte, R., & Jones, N. S. (2020). Community detection in networks without observing edges. *Science Advances, 6*(4).

Hohenberger, A., & Peltzer-Karpf, A. (2009). Language learning from the perspective of nonlinear dynamic systems. *Linguistics, 47*(2), 481–511.

Hoover, J. R., Storkel, H. L., & Hogan, T. P. (2010). A cross-sectional comparison of the effects of phonotactic probability and neighborhood density on word learning by preschool children. *Journal of Memory and Language, 63*(1), 100–116.

Hu, P., & Lee, L. (2020). Community-based link-addition strategies for mitigating casading failures in modern power systems. *Processes, 8*(2).

Huang, S., Bian, X., Wu, G., & McLemore, C. (1997). CALLHOME Mandarine Chinese Lexicon. *Linguistic Data Consortium, University of Pennsylvania.*

Humphries, M. D., & Gurney, K. (2008). Network 'small-world-ness': A quantitative method for determining canonical network equivalence. *PLoS ONE, 3*(4), e0002051.

Humphries, M. D., Gurney, K., & Prescott, T. J. (2006). The brainstem reticular formation is a small-world, not scale-free, network. *Proceedings of the Royal Society B: Biological Sciences, 273*(1585), 503–511.

Ferrer-i-Cancho, R. F., & Solé, R. V. (2001). The small world of human language. *Proceedings of the Royal Society B: Biological Sciences, 268*, 2261–2265.

Iyengar, S. R., Veni Madhavan, C. E., Zweig, K. A., & Natarajan, A. (2012). Understanding human navigation using network analysis. *Topics in Cognitive Science, 4*, 121–134.

Jakobson, R. (1941/68). *Child language, aphasia and phonological universals*. The Hague: Mouton.

James, L. E., & Burke, D. M. (2000). Phonological priming effects on word retrieval and tip-of-the-tongue experiences in young and older adults. *Journal of Experimental Psychology: Learning, Memory, and Cognition, 26*, 1378–1391.

Janson, S., Luczak, T., & Rucinski, A. (2000). *Random graphs*. New York: Wiley.

Jescheniak, J. D., & Schriefers, H. (1998). Serial discrete versus cascaded processing in lexical access in speech production: Further evidence from the co-activation of near-synonyms. *Journal of Experimental Psychology: Language, Memory, and Cognition, 24*, 1256–1274.

Jiang, J., Yu, W., & Liu, H. (2019). Does scale-free syntactic network emerge in second language learning? *Frontiers in Psychology, 10*, 925.

Joanisse, M. F., & McClelland, J. L. (2015). Connectionist perspectives on language learning, representation and processing. *WIREs Cognitive Science, 6*(3), 235–247.

Johnson, N. F., & Pugh, K. R. (1994). A cohort model of visual word recognition. *Cognitive Psychology, 26*, 240–346.

Kane, E. A., & Higham, T. E. (2015). Complex systems are more than the sum of their parts: Using integration to understand performance, biomechanics, and diversity. *Integrative and Comparative Biology, 55*(1), 146–165.

Kapatsinski, V. (2006). Sound similarity relations in the mental lexicon: Modeling the lexicon as a complex network. *Speech Research Lab Progress Report, 27*, 133–152.

Karimi, H., & Diaz, M. (2020). When phonological neighborhood density both facilitates and impedes: Age of acquisition and name agreement interact with phonological neighborhood during word production. *Memory and Cognition, 48*, 1061–1072.

Katz, L. (1953). A new status index derived from sociometric analysis. *Psychometrika, 18*, 39–43.

Kauffman, S. A. (1993). *The origin of order: Self-organization and selection in evolution*. London: Oxford University Press.

Kaushanskaya, M., Yoo, J., & Van Hecke, S. (2013). Word learning in adults with second-language experience: Effects of phonological and referent familiarity. *Journal of Speech, Language, and Hearing Research, 56*(2), 667–678.

Keeling, M. J., & Eames, K. T. D. (2005). Networks and epidemic models. *Journal of the Royal Society: Interfact, 22*(4), 295–307.

Kephart, J. O., & White, S. R. (1991). *Directed-graph epidemiological models of computer viruses*. Paper presented at the Proceedings of the IEEE Computer Society Symposium on Research in Security and Privacy, Oakland, CA.

Kim, P. M., Korbel, J. O., & Gerstein, M. B. (2007). Positive selection at the protein network periphery: Evaluation in terms of structural constraints and cellular context. *Proceedings of the National Academy of Sciences of the United States of America, 104*, 20274–20279.

Kjaergaard, M., Brander, S., & Poulsen, F. M. (2010). Small but slow world: How network typology and burstiness slow down spreading. *Physical Review E, 83*(83), 602–608.

Klatt, D. H. (1981). Lexical representations for speech production and perception. *Advances in Psychology, 7*, 11–31.

Kleinberg, J. M. (2000). The small-world phenomonon: An algorithmic perspective. *Proceedings of the 32nd Annual ACN Symposium on Theory of Computing*, 163–170.

Kleinman, D., & Gollan, T. H. (2019). Inhibition accumulates over time at multiple processing levels in bilingual language control. *Cognition, 173*, 115–132.

Ko, K., Lee, K. J., & Park, C. (2008). Rethinking preferential attachment scheme: Degree centrality versus closeness centrality. *Connections, 28*(1), 4–15.

Kondrak, G. (2000). A new algorithm for the alignment of phonetic sequence. *Proceedings of the 1st North American Chapter of the Association for Computational Linguistics Conference*, 288–295.

Kong, J. S., & Roychowdhury, V. P. (2008). Preferential survival in models of complex ad hoc networks. *Physica A: Statistical Mechanics and its Applications, 387*(13), 3335–3347.

Koubkova-Yu, T. C.-T., Chao, J.-C., & Leu, J.-Y. (2018). Heterologous Hsp90 promotes phenotypic diversity through network evolution. *PloS Biology, 16*(11), e2006450.

Krapivsky, P. L., & Redner, S. (2001). Organization of growing random networks. *Physical Review E*, 6(2), 066123.

Kuperman, V., Stadthagen-Gonzalez, H., & Brysbaert, M. (2012). Age-of-acquisition ratings for 30,000 English words. *Behavior Research Methods, 44*(4), 978–990.

Landauer, T. K., & Streeter, L. A. (1973). Structural differences between common and rare words: Failure of equivalence assumptions for theories of word recognition. *Journal of Verbal Learning and Verbal Behavior, 12*, 119–131.

Lara-Martinez, P., Quintana-Obregon, B., Reyes-Manzano, C. F., Lopez-Rodriguez, I., & Guzman-Vargas, L. (2021). Comparing phonological and orthographic networks: A multiplex analysis. *PLoS ONE, 16*(2), e0245263.

Latora, V., & Marchiori, M. (2001). Efficient behavior of small-world networks. *Physical Review Letters, 87*, 198701.

Leach, L., & Samuel, A. G. (2007). Lexical configuration and lexical engagement: When adults learn new words. *Cognitive Psychology, 55*, 306–353.

Levelt, W. J. M. (1999). Models of word production. *Trends in Cognitive Science, 3*(6), 223–232.

Levelt, W. J. M. (2001). Relations between speech production and speech perception: Some behavioral and neurological observations. In E. Dupoux (Ed.), *Language, brain, and cognitive development: Essays in honor of Jacques Mehler* (pp. 241–256). Cambridge, MA: MIT Press.

Levelt, W. J. M., Roelofs, A., & Meyer, A. S. (1999). A theory of lexical access in speech production. *Behavioral and Brain Sciences, 22*, 1–38.

Levenshtein, V. I. (1966). Binary codes capable of correcting deletions, insertions, and reversals. *Soviet Physics Doklady, 10*, 707–710.

Levy, O., Kenett, Y. N., Oxenberg, O., Castro, N., De Deyne, S., Vitevitch, M. S., & Havlin, S. (2021). Unveiling the nature of interaction between semantics and phonology in lexical access based on multilayer networks. *Scientific Reports, 11*, 14479.

Li, C., Wang, M., & Davis, J. A. (2017). The phonological preparation unit in spoken word production in a second language. *Bilingualism: Language and Cognition, 20*(2), 351–366.

Li, D., Zhang, Q., Zio, E., Havlin, S., & Kang, R. (2015). Network reliability analysis based on percolation theory. *Reliability Engineering and System Safety, 142*, 556–562.

Li, L., Alderson, D., Doyle, J. C., & Willinger, W. (2005). Towards a theory of scale-free graphs: Definitions, properties, and implications. *Internet Mathematics, 2*(3), 431–523.

Li, X., & Chen, G. (2003). A local-world evolving network model. *Physica A: Statistical Mechanics and its Applications, 328*(102), 274–286.

Li, X., Jin, Y. Y., & Chen, G. (2003). Complexity and synchronization of the world trade web. *Physica A: Statistical Mechanics and its Applications, 328*(1–2), 287–296.

Linehan, J., Gross, M., & Finn, J. (1995). Greenway planning: developing a landscape ecological network approach. *Landscape and Urban Planning, 33*, 179–193.

Liu, J., Li, J., Chen, Y., Chen, X., Zhou, Z., Yang, Z., & Zhang, C.-J. (2019). Modeling complex networks with accelerating growth and aging effect. *Physics Letters A, 383*(13), 1396–1400.

Liu, J. S., & Kuan, C.-H. (2016). A new approach for main path analysis: Decay in knowledge diffusion. *Journal of the Association for Information Science and Technology, 67*(2), 465–476.

Luce, P. A. (1986). A computational analysis of uniqueness points in auditory word recognition. *Perception and Psychophysics, 39*, 155–158.

Luce, P. A., Goldinger, S., Auer, E. T., & Vitevitch, M. S. (2000). Phonetic priming, neighborhood activation, and PARSYN. *Perception and Psychophysics, 62*(3), 615–625.

Luce, P. A., & Pisoni, D. B. (1998). Recognizing spoken words: The neighborhood activation model. *Ear and Hearing, 19*, 1–36.

Luce, R. D., & Perry, A. D. (1949). A method of matrix analysis of group structure. *Psychometrika, 14*, 95–116.

Luef, E. M. (2022a). Phonological neighborhood complexity and sound change. *Language Dynamics and Change, 13*(1), 132–160.

Luef, E. M. (2022b). Growth algorithms in the phonological networks of second language learners: A replication study. *Journal of Experimental Psychology: General*, 151(12), e26-e44.

Luef, E. M. (2023). Obsolescence effects in second language phonological networks. *Memory and Cognition, 52*, 771–792.

Luef, E. M. (2024). Community structure in the phono-lexical network of child-directed speech. Paper presented at the 24th International Congress of Infant Studies (ICIS), Glasgow, Scotland.

Luef, E. M. (2025). Modeling the bilingual lexicon as a multiplex phonological network. *Canadian Journal of Experimental Psychology*, https://doi.org/10.1037/cep0000351.

Luef, E. M., Ghebru, B., & Ilon, L. S. (2018). Apps for language learning: their use across different languages in a Korean context. *Interactive Learning Environments, 28*(8), 1036–1047.

Lugosi, G., & Pereira, A. S. (2019). Finding the seed of uniform attachment trees. *Electronic Journal of Probability, 24*(18), 1–15.

Macklin-Cordes, J. L., & Round, E. R. (2020). Re-evaluating phoneme frequencies. *Frontiers in Psychology, 11*, 3181.

Maddieson, I. (2009). Calculating phonological complexity. In F. Pellegrino, E. Marsico, I. Chitoran, & C. Coupe (Eds.), *Approaches to phonological complexity* (pp. 83–110). Berlin, New York: de Gruyter Mouton.

Maechler, M. (2013). Package 'diptest'. R Package Version 0.75-5. R: A language and environment for statistical computing. Vienna, Austria: R Foundation for Statistical Computing.
Magnuson, J. S., Dixon, J. A., Tanenhaus, M. K., & Aslin, R. N. (2007). The dynamics of lexical competition during spoken word recognition. *Cognitive Science, 31*, 133–156.
Mak, M. H. C., & Twitchell, H. (2020). Evidence for preferential attachment: Words that are more well connected in semantic networks are better at acquiring new links in paired-associate learning. *Psychonomic Bulletin and Review, 27*, 1059–1069.
Marecka, M., Szewczyk, J., Otwinowska, A., Durlik, J., Foryś-Nogala, M., Kutyłowska, K., & Wodniecka, Z. (2021). False friends or real friends? False cognates show advantage in word form learning. *Cognition, 206*, 104477.
Marian, V., Bartolotti, J., Chabal, S., & Shook, A. (2012). CLEARPOND: Cross-linguistic easy access resource for phonological and orthographic neighborhood densities. *PLoS ONE, 7*(8), e43230.
Marian, V., & Blumenfeld, H. K. (2006). Phonological neighborhood density guides: Lexical access in native and non-native language production. *Journal of Social and Ecological Boundaries, 2*(1), 3–35.
Marslen-Wilson, W. D. (1987). Functional parallelism in spoken word-recognition. *Cognition, 25*, 71–102.
Marslen-Wilson, W. D. (1990). Activation, competition and frequency in lexical access. In G. T. M. Altman (Ed.), *Cognitive models of speech processing: Psycholinguistic and computational perspectives* (pp. 148–172). Cambridge, M. A.: MIT Press.
Marslen-Wilson, W. D., Brown, C. M., & Tyler, L. K. (1988). Lexical representations in spoken language comprehension. *Language and Cognitive Processes, 3*, 1–16.
Marslen-Wilson, W. D., & Warren, P. (1994). Levels of perceptual representation and process in lexical access. *Psychological Review, 101*, 653–675.
Marslen-Wilson, W. D., & Welsh, A. (1978). Processing interactions and lexical access during word recognition in continuous speech. *Cognitive Psychology, 10*, 29–63.
Martin, C., & Niemeyer, P. (2020). On the impact of network size and average degree on the robustness of centrality measures. *Network Science*, 1–22.
Martindale, C., Gusein-Zade, S. M., McKenzie, D., & Borodovsky, M. Y. (1996). Comparison of equations describing the ranked frequency distributions of graphemes and phonemes. *Journal of Quantitative Linguistics, 3*, 106–112.
McClelland, J. L., & Rogers, T. T. (2003). The parallel distributed processing approach to semantic cognition. *Nature Reviews Neuroscience, 4*(4), 310–322.
McClelland, J. L., Rumelhart, D. E., & Hinton, G. E. (1986). The appeal of parallel distributed processing. In D. E. Rumelhart & J. L. McClelland (Eds.), *Parallel distributed processing: Explorations in the microstructure of cognition* (pp. 3–44). Cambridge, MA: MIT Press.
McEnery, T., Brezina, V., Gablasova, D., & Banerjee, J. (2019). Corpus linguistics, learner corpora, and SLA: Employing technology to analyze language use. *Annual Review of Applied Linguistics, 39*, 74–92.
Mendes, G., & Da Silva, L. (2009). Generating more realistic complex networks from power-law distribution of fitness. *Brazilian Journal of Physics, 39*(2A), 423–427.
Mendes, J. F. F. (2003). Effect of accelerated growth on network dynamics. In R. Pastor-Satorras, M. Rubi, & A. Diaz-Guilera (Eds.), *Statistical mechanics of complex networks*. Berlin, Heidelberg: Springer.
Metcalf, L., & Casey, W. (2016). *Cybersecurity and applied mathematics*. Amsterdam: Elsevier.
Meyer, A. S. (1991). The time course of phonological encoding in language production: Phonological encoding inside a syllable. *Journal of Memory and Language, 30*(1), 69–89.
Midgley, K. J., Holcomb, P. J., & Grainger, J. (2011). Effects of cognate status on word comprehension in second language learners: An ERP investigation. *Journal of Cognitive Neuroscience, 23*(7), 1634–1647.
Milli, L., Rossetti, G., Pedreschi, D., & Giannotti, F. (2018). Active and passive diffusion processes in complex networks. *Applied Network Science, 3*, 42.
Milojević, S. (2010). Power law distributions in information science: Making the case for logarithmic binning. *Journal of the American Society for Information Science and Technology, 61*(12), 2417–2425.
Mirman, D., & Magnuson, J. S. (2008). Attractor dynamics and semantic neighborhood density: Processing is slowed by near neighbors and speeded by distant neighbors. *Journal of Experimental Psychology: Learning, Memory, and Cognition, 34*(1), 65–79.

Moreira, S., & Hamilton, M. (2010). Goats don't wear coats: An examination of semantic interference in rhyming assessments of reading readiness for English language learners. *Bilingual Research Journal, 30*(2), 547–557.

Mulík, S., Carrasco-Ortiz, H., & Amengual, M. (2018). Phonological activation of first language (Spanish) and second language (English) when learning third language (Slovak) novel words. *International Journal of Bilingualism, 23*(5), 1024–1040.

Naug, D. (2008). Structure of the social network and its influence on transmission dynamics in a honeybee colony. *Behavioral Ecology and Sociobiology, 62*, 1719–1725.

Navarrete, E., Pastore, M., Valentini, R., & Peressotti, F. (2015). First learned words are not forgotten: Age-of-acquisition effects in the tip-of-the-tongue experience. *Memory and Cognition, 43*(7), 1085–1103.

Neergaard, K. D., Britton, J., & Huang, C.-R. (2019). *Neighborhood in decay: Working memory modulates effect of phonological similarity on lexical access.* Paper presented at the 41st Annual Conference of the Cognitive Science Society.

Neergaard, K. D., Luo, J., & Huang, C.-R. (2019). Phonological network fluency identifies phonological restructuring through mental search. *Scientific Reports, 9*, 15984.

Newman, M. E. J. (2001). The structure of scientific collaboration networks. *Proceedings of the National Academy of Sciences of the United States of America, 98*, 404–409.

Newman, M. E. J. (2002). Assortative mixing in networks. *Physical Review Letters, 89*(20), 208701.

Newman, M. E. J. (2003a). Properties of highly clustered networks. *Physical Review E, 68*, 026121.

Newman, M. E. J. (2003b). The structure and function of complex networks. *SIAM Review, 45*(3), 167–256.

Newman, M. E. J. (2004). Coauthorship networks and patterns of scientific collaboration. *Proceedings of the National Academy of Sciences of the United States of America, 101*, 5200–5205.

Newman, M. E. J. (2005). Power laws, Pareto distributions and Zipf's law. *Contemporary Physics, 46*(5), 323–351.

Newman, M. E. J. (2006). Modularity and community structure in networks. *Proceedings of the National Academy of Sciences of the United States of America, 103*, 8577–8582.

Newman, M. E. J. (2010). *Networks: An introduction.* Oxford, UK: Oxford University Press.

Newman, M. E. J., & Girvan, M. (2004). Finding and evaluating community structure in networks. *Physical Review E, 69*(2), 026113.

Newman, M. E. J., Strogatz, S. H., & Watts, D. J. (2002). Random graph models of social networks. *Proceedings of the National Academy of Sciences of the United States of America, 99*, 2566–2572.

Nguyen, T. A. S., Castro, N., Vitevitch, M. S., Harding, A., Teng, R., Arciuli, J., Leyton, C. E., Piguet, O., & Ballard, K. J. (2022). Do age and language impairment affect speed of recognition for words with high and low closeness centrality within the phonological network? *International Journal of Speech-Language Pathology, 25*(6), 915–928.

Nooteboom, S. G. (2005). Lexical bias revisited: Detecting, rejecting and repairing speech errors in inner speech. *Speech communication, 47*, 43–58.

Nusbaum, H. C., Pisoni, D. B., & Davis, C. K. (1984). Sizing up the Hoosier mental lexicon: Measuring familiarity of 20,000 words. *Research on Speech Perception Progress Report, 10*, 357–376.

O'Séaghdha, P. G., & Frazer, A. K. (2014). The exception does not rule: Attention constraints form preparation in word production. *Journal of Experimental Psychology: Learning, Memory, and Cognition, 40*(3), 797–810.

O'Séaghdha, P. G., Chen, J.-Y., & Chen, T.-M. (2010). Proximate units in word production: Phonological encoding begins with syllables in Mandarin Chinese but with segments in English. *Cognition, 115*(2), 282–302.

Oldfield, R. C. (1966). Things, words, and the brain. *Quarterly Journal of Experimental Psychology, 18*, 340–353.

Oppermann, F., Jescheniak, J. D., & Schriefers, H. (2010). Phonological advance planning in sentence production. *Journal of Memory and Language, 63*(4), 526–540.

Opsahl, T., Agneessens, F., & Skvoretz, J. (2010). Node centrality in weighted networks: Generalizing degree and shortest paths. *Social Networks, 32*, 245–251.

Pachon, L., Sacerdote, L., & Yang, S. (2018). Scale-free behavior of networks with the copresence of preferential and uniform attachment rules. *Physica D: Nonlinear Phenomena, 371*, 1–12.
Page, L., Brin, S., Motwani, R., & Winograd, T. (1998, January). The PageRank citation ranking: Bringing order to the web (technical report). *Proceedings of the 7th International World Wide Web Conference.*
Papadopoulos, F., Kitsak, M., Serrano, A., Boguna, M., & Krioukov, D. (2012). Popularity versus similarity in growing networks. *Nature, 489*, 537–540.
Payne, J. L., & Wagner, A. (2014). The robustness and evolvability of transcription factor binding sites. *Science, 343*, 875–877.
Peel, L., Delvenne, J.-C., & Lambiotte, R. (2018). Multiscale mixing patterns in networks. *Proceedings of the National Academy of Sciences of the United States of America, 115*(16), 4057–4062.
Perline, R. (2005). Strong, weak and false inverse power law. *Statistical Sciences, 20*(12), 68–88.
Peterson, R. R., & Savoy, P. (1998). Lexical selection and phonological encoding during language production: Evidence for cascaded processing. *Journal of Experimental Psychology: Language, Memory, and Cognition, 24*, 539–557.
Pham, T., Sheridan, P., & Shimodaira, H. (2015). PAFit: A statistical method for measuring preferential attachment in temporal complex networks. *PLoS ONE, 10*(9), e0137796.
Phoneverter (n. d.). Retrieved August, 10, 2022, from http://phonetictools.altervista.org/phonverter/
Phonotactic Probability Calculator (n. d.). Retrieved August 6, 2022, from https://calculator.ku.edu/phonotactic/about
Piantadosi, S. T. (2014). Zipf's word frequency law in natural language: A critical review and future directions. *Psychonomic Bulletin & Review, 21*, 1112–1130.
Piantadosi, S. T., Tily, H. J., & Gibson, E. (2012). The communicative function of ambiguity in language. *Cognition, 122*, 280–291.
Pigliucci, M. (2008). Is evolvability evolvable? *Nature Reviews Genetics, 9*, 75–82.
Pisoni, D. B., Nusbaum, H. C., Luce, P. A., & Slowiaczek, L. M. (1985). Speech perception, word recognition and the structure of the lexicon. *Speech Communication, 4*(1), 75–95.
Poltrock, S., Chen, H., Kwok, C., Cheung, H., & Nazzi, T. (2018). Adult learning of novel words in a non-native language: Consonants, vowels, and tones. *Frontiers in Psychology, 9*, 1211.
Porter, M. A., Onnela, J.-P., & Mucha, P. J. (2009). Communities in networks. *Notices of the American Mathematical Society, 56*, 1082–1097.
Quillian, R. (1967). Word concepts: A theory and simulation of some basic semantic capabilities. *Behavioral Science, 12*, 410–430.
Quinn, G. P., & Keough, M. J. (2002). *Experimental designs and data analysis for biologists.* Cambridge, UK: Cambridge University Press.
Ravasz, E., & Barabási, A. (2003). Hierarchical organization in complex networks. *Physical Review E, 67*, 026112.
Redner, S. (2005). Citation statistics from 110 years of Physical Review. *Physics Today, 58*, 49–54.
Ren, H.-P., Song, J. Y., Yang, R., Baptista, M. S., & Grebogi, C. (2016). Cascade failure analysis of power grid using new load distribution law and node removal rule. *Physica A: Statistical Mechanics and its Applications, 442*, 239–251.
Ren, J., Yang, X., Yang, L.-X., Xu, Y., & Yang, F. (2012). A delayed computer virus propagation model and its dynamics. *Chaos, Solitons and Fractals, 45*(1), 74–79.
Rickles, D., Hawe, P., & Shiell, A. (2007). A simple guide to chaos and complexity. *Journal of Epidemiology and Community Health, 61*(1), 933–937.
Rigney, D. (2010). *The Matthew effect: How advantage begets further advantage.* New York: Columbia University Press.
Roach, P. (2004). British English: Received Pronunciation. *Journal of the International Phonetic Association, 34*(2), 239–245.
Roberts, F. S. (1976). *Discrete mathematical models.* New Jersey: Prentice-Hall.
Rodriguez, F. A. (2019). Network centrality: An introduction. In E. Macau (Ed.), *A mathematical modeling approach from nonlinear dynamics to complex systems.* (Vol. Nonlinear Systems and Complexity 22, pp. 177–196). Cham: Springer.

Roelofs, A. (2006). The influence of spelling on phonological encoding in word reading, object naming, and word generation. *Psychonomic Bulletin and Review, 12*, 33–37.
Rogers, E. M. (2003). *Diffusion of innovations (5th ed.)*. New York: Free Press.
Romani, C., Galuzzi, C., Guariglia, C., & Goslin, J. (2017). Comparing phoneme frequency, age of acquisition, and loss in aphasia: Implications for phonological universals. *Cognitive Neuropsychology, 34*(7–8), 449–471.
Schaub, M. T., Delvenne, J.-C., Rosvall, M., & Lambiotte, R. (2017). The many facets of community detection in complex networks. *Applied Network Science, 2*, 1–13.
Saavedra, S., Reed-Tsochas, F., & Uzzi, B. (2008). Asymmetric disassembly and robustness in declining networks. *Proceedings of the National Academy of Sciences of the United States of America, 105*, 16466–16471.
Sadat, J., Martin, C. D., Costa, A., & Alario, F.-X. (2014). Reconciling phonological neighborhood effects in speech production through single trial analysis. *Cognitive Psychology, 68*, 33–58.
Salavati, C., Abdollahpouri, A., & Manbari, Z. (2019). Ranking nodes in complex networks based on local structure and improving closeness centrality. *Neurocomputing, 336*, 36–45.
Salem, N., & Hussein, S. (2019). Data dimensional reduction and principal components analysis. *Procedia Computer Science, 163*, 292–299.
Sanders, R. (1987). The Pareto principle: Its use and abuse. *Journal of Services Marketing, 1*(2), 37–40.
Scarborough, R. (2013). Neighborhood-conditioned patterns in phonetic detail: Relating coarticulation and hyperarticulation. *Journal of Phonetics, 41*(6), 491–508.
Schank, T., & Wagner, D. (2005). Approximating clustering coefficient and transitivity. *Journal of Graph Algorithms and Applications, 9*(2), 265–275.
Schriefers, H., & Vigliocco, G. (2015). Psychology of speech production. In J. D. Wright (Ed.), *International Encyclopedia of the Social and Behavioral Sciences* (pp. 225–258). Amsterdam et al.: Elsevier.
Schulpen, B., Dijkstra, T., Schriefers, H., & Hasper, M. (2003). Recognition of interlingual homophones in bilingual auditory word recognition. *Journal of Experimental Psychology: Human Perception and Performance, 29*(6), 1155–1178.
Schur, E. (2007). Insights into the structure of L1 and L2 vocabulary networks: Intimations of small worlds. In H. Daller, J. Milton, & J. Treffers-Daller (Eds.), *Modelling and assessing vocabulary knowledge* (pp. 182–204). Cambridge: Cambridge University Press.
Schweppe, J., Grice, M. & Rummer, R. (2011). What models of verbal working memory can learn from phonological theory: Decomposing the phonological similarity effect. *Journal of Memory and Language, 64*(3), 256–269.
Scott, J. (1991). *Social network analysis: A handbook*. London: Sage.
Sebastián Gallés, N., Cuetos Vega, F., Carreiras Valiña, M. F., & Martí Antonin, M. A. (2000). *Lexesp: Léxico informatizado del español*. Barcelona: Publicacions i Edicions de la Universitat de Barcelona.
Sevald, C. A., & Dell, G. S. (1994). The sequential cuing effect in speech production. *Cognition, 53*, 91–127.
Shai, S., Stanley, N., Granell, C., Taylor, D., & Mucha, P. J. (2017). Case studies in network community detection. In R. Light & J. Moody (Eds.), *The Oxford handbook of social networks*. Oxford, UK: Oxford University Press.
Shao, Z.-G., Zou, X.-W., Tan, Z.-J., & Jin, Z.-Z. (2006). Growing networks with mixed attachment mechanisms. *Journal of Physics A: Mathematical and General, 390*(9), 2035.
Sheridan, P., & Onodera, T. (2018). A preferential attachment paradox: How preferential attachment combines with growth to produce networks with log-normal in-degree distributions. *Scientific Reports, 8*, 2811.
Shoemark, P., Goldwater, S., Kirby, J., & Sarkar, R. (2016). Toward robust cross-linguistic comparisons of phonological networks. *Proceedings of the 14th ACL SIGMORPHON Workshop on Computational Research in Phonetics, Phonology, and Morphology*, 110–120.
Siegenfeld, A. F., & Bar-Yam, Y. (2020). An introduction to complex systems science and its applications. *Complexity, 2020*, 6105872.
Siew, C. S. Q. (2013). Community structure in the phonological network. *Frontiers in Psychology, 4*, 553.
Siew, C. S. Q. (2019). An R package to simulate spreading activation in a network. *Behavioral Research, 51*, 910–929.

Siew, C. S. Q., Chern, J., & Castro, N. (2023). Evidence of community structure in phonological networks of various languages. *Proceedings of the Annual Meeting of the Cognitive Science Society*, 45. Retrieved from https://escholarship.org/uc/item/4j2652dp

Siew, C. S. Q., & Vitevitch, M. S. (2016). Spoken word recognition and serial recall of words from components in the phonological network. *Journal of Experimental Psychology: Learning, Memory, and Cognition, 42*(3), 394–410.

Siew, C. S. Q., & Vitevitch, M. S. (2020a). An investigation of network growth principles in the phonological language network. *Journal of Experimental Psychology: General, 149*(12), 2376–2394.

Siew, C. S. Q., & Vitevitch, M. S. (2020b). Investigating the influence of inverse preferential attachment on network development. *Entropy, 22*, 1029.

Siew, C. S. Q., Wulff, D. U., Beckage, N. M., & Kenett, Y. N. (2019). Cognitive network science: A review of research on cognition through the lens of network representations, processes, and dynamics. *Complexity, 2019*, 2108423.

Simmons, E. S., & Magnuson, J. S. (2018). Word length, proportion of overlap, and phonological competition in spoken word recognition. In C. Kalish, M. Rau, J. Zhu, & T. Rogers (Eds.), *Proceedings of the Cognitive Science Society* (pp. 1062–1067).

Smits, E., Sandra, D., Martensen, H., & Dijkstra, T. (2009). Phonological inconsistency in word naming: Determinants of the interference effect between languages. *Bilingualism: Language and Cognition, 12*, 23–39.

Stamer, M. K., & Vitevitch, M. S. (2012). Phonological similarity influences word learning in adults learning Spanish as a foreign language. *Bilingualism: Language and Cognition, 15*(3), 490–502.

Stella, M. (2020). Multiplex networks quantify robustness of the mental lexicon to catastrophic concept failures, aphasic degradation and ageing. *Physica A: Statistical Mechanics and its Applications, 554*, 124382.

Stella, M., Beckage, N. M., Brede, M., & de Domenico, M. (2018). Multiplex model of mental lexicon reveals explosive learning in humans. *Scientific Reports, 8*, 2259.

Stella, M., & Brede, M. (2015). Patterns in the English language: Phonological networks, percolation and assembly models. *Journal of Statistical Mechanics: Theory and Experiment, 2015*(5), P05006.

Steyvers, M., & Tenenbaum, J. B. (2005). The large-scale structure of semantic networks: Statistical analyses and a model of semantic growth. *Cognitive Science, 29*(1), 41–78.

Storkel, H. L. (2001). Learning new words: Phonotactic probability in language development. *Journal of Speech, Language, and Hearing Research, 44*, 1321–1337.

Storkel, H. L. (2002). Restructuring of similarity neighbourhoods in the developing mental lexicon. *Journal of Child Language, 29*, 251–274.

Storkel, H. L., Armbruster, J., & Hogan, T. P. (2006). Differentiating phonotatic probability and neighborhood density in adult word learning. *Journal of Speech, Language, and Hearing Research, 49*, 1175–1192.

Storkel, H. L., & Lee, S.-Y. (2011). The independent effect of phonotactic probability and neighborhood density on lexical acquisition by preschool children. *Language and Cognitive Processes, 26*(2), 191–211.

Stumpf, M. P. H., & Porter, M. A. (2012). Mathematics: Critical truths about power laws. *Science, 335*(6069), 665–666.

Suarez, L., Tan, S. H., Yap, M. J., & Goh, W. D. (2011). Observing neighborhood effects without neighbors. *Psychonomic Bulletin and Review, 18*, 605–611.

Sun, E. D., Michaels, T. C. T., & Mahadevan, L. (2020). Optimal control of aging in complex networks. *Proceedings of the National Academy of Sciences of the United States of America, 117*(34), 20404–20410.

Tambovtsev, Y., & Martindale, C. (2007). Phoneme frequencies follow a Yule distribution. *SKASE Journal of Theoretical Linguistics, 4*, 1–11.

Tanaka, M., & Takahashi, R. (2019). The dynamic characteristics in the L2 mental lexicon (technical report). *IEICE, 119*, T2019–2023.

Tang, J., & Liu, P. (2014). Synchronization in a novel local-world dynamical network model. *Mathematical Problems in Engineering, 2014*, 851403.

Telesford, Q. K., Joyce, K. E., Hayasaka, S., Burdette, J. H., & Laurienti, P. J. (2011). The ubiquity of small-world networks. *Brain Connectivity, 1*(5), 367–375.

The British National Corpus, v. B. X. E. (2007). Distributed by Bodleian Libraries, University of Oxford, on behalf of the BNC Consortium. URL: http://www.natcorp.ox.ac.uk/

Treiman, R., & Danis, C. (1988). Short-term memory errors for spoken syllables are affected by the linguistic structure of the syllables. *Journal of Experimental Psychology: Learning, Memory, and Cognition, 14*, 145–152.

Trubetzkoy, N. (1939). *Grundzüge der Phonologie*. Göttingen: van der Hoeck & Ruprecht.

Turnbull, L., Huett, M.-T., Ioannides, A. A., Kininmonth, S., Poeppl, R., Tockner, K., . . . Parsons, A. J. (2018). Connectivity and complex systems: Learning from a multi-disciplinary perspective. *Applied Network Science, 3*, 11. doi:https://doi.org/10.1007/s41109-018-0067-2

Turnbull, R. (2021). Graph-theoretic properties of the class of phonological neighbourhood networks. *Proceedings of the Workshop on Cognitive Modeling and Computational Linguistics*, 233–240.

Turnbull, R., & Peperkamp, S. (2017). What governs a language's lexicon? Determining the organizing principles of phonological neighbourhood networks. In H. Cherifi, S. Gaito, W. Quattrociocchi, & A. Sala (Eds.), *Complex networks and their applications V* (pp. 83–94). Cham, Switzerland: Springer.

Ullman, M. T. (2007). The biocognition of the mental lexicon. In M. G. Gaskell, G. T. M. Altmann, P. Bloom, A. Caramazza, & P. Levelt (Eds.), *The Oxford handbook of psycholinguistics* (pp. 267–288). Oxford, UK: Oxford University Press.

Van Hell, J. G., & Dijkstra, T. (2002). Foreign language knowledge can influence native language performance in exclusively native contexts. *Psychonomic Bulletin and Review, 9*(4), 780–789.

van Hemmen, J. L., & Schulten, K. (1995). *Models of neural networks I*. New York: Springer.

Van Heuven, W. J. B., Dijkstra, T., & Grainger, J. (1998). Orthographic neighborhood effects in bilingual word recognition. *Journal of Memory and Language, 39*, 458–483.

Van Rensbergen, B., Storms, G., & De Deyne, S. (2015). Examining assortativity in the mental lexicon: Evidence from word associations. *Psychonomic Bulletin and Review, 22*, 1717–1724.

Velleman, S. L., & Vihman, M. M. (2007). Phonology development in infancy and early childhood: Implications for theories of language learning. In M. C. Pennington (Ed.), *Phonology in context* (pp. 25–50). London: Palgrave Macmillan.

Vitevitch, M. S. (1997). The neighborhood characteristic of malapropisms. *Language and Speech, 40*, 211–228.

Vitevitch, M. S. (2002a). Influence of onset density on spoken-word recognition. *Journal of Experimental Psychology: Human Perception and Performance, 28*(2), 270–278.

Vitevitch, M. S. (2002b). The influence of phonological similarity neighborhoods on speech production. *Journal of Experimental Psychology: Learning, Memory, and Cognition, 28*, 735–747.

Vitevitch, M. S. (2002c). Naturalistic and experimental analyses of word frequency and neighborhood density effects in slips of the ear. *Language and Speech, 45*, 407–434.

Vitevitch, M. S. (2007). The spread of the phonological neighborhood influences spoken word recognition. *Memory and Cognition, 35*, 166–175.

Vitevitch, M. S. (2008). What can graph theory tell us about word learning and lexical retrieval? *Journal of Speech, Language, and Hearing Research, 51*, 408–422.

Vitevitch, M. S. (2021). What can network science tell us about phonology and language processing. *Topics in Cognitive Science, 14*(1), 127–142.

Vitevitch, M. S., Armbruster, J., & Chu, S. (2004). Sub-lexical and lexical representations in speech production: Effects of phonotactic probability and onset density. *Journal of Experimental Psychology: Learning, Memory, and Cognition, 30*, 514–529.

Vitevitch, M. S., & Castro, N. (2015). Using network science in the language sciences and clinic. *International Journal of Speech-Language Pathology, 17*, 13–25.

Vitevitch, M. S., Chan, K. Y., & Goldstein, R. (2014). Insights into failed lexical retrieval from network science. *Cognitive Psychology, 68*, 1–32.

Vitevitch, M. S., Chan, K. Y., & Roodenrys, S. (2012). Complex network structure influences processing in long-term and short-term memory. *Journal of Memory and Language, 67*(1), 30–44.

Vitevitch, M. S., Ercal, G., & Adagarla, B. (2011). Simulating retrieval from a highly clustered network: Implications for spoken word recognition. *Frontiers in Psychology, 2*, 369.
Vitevitch, M. S., & Goldstein, R. (2014). Keywords in the mental lexicon. *Journal of Memory & Language, 73*, 131–147.
Vitevitch, M. S., Goldstein, R., & Johnson, E. (2016). Path-length and the misperception of speech: Insights from network science and psycholinguistics. In A. Mehler, A. Lücking, S. Banisch, P. Blanchard, & B. Job (Eds.), *Toward a theoretical framework for analyzing complex linguistic networks: Understanding complex systems* (pp. 29–45). Berlin: Springer.
Vitevitch, M. S., & Luce, P. A. (2004). A web-based interface to calculate phonotactic probability for words and nonwords in English. *Behavior Research Methods, Instruments, and Computers, 36*, 481–487.
Vitevitch, M. S., & Luce, P. A. (2016). Phonological neighborhood effects in spoken word perception and production. *Annual Review of Linguistics, 2*, 75–94.
Vitevitch, M. S., & Rodriguez, E. (2004). Neighborhood density effects in spoken word recognition in Spanish. *Journal of Multilingual Communication Disorders, 3*(1), 64–73.
Vitevitch, M. S., & Sale, M. (2023). Identifying the phonological backbone in the mental lexicon. *PLoS ONE, 18*(6), e0287197.
Vitevitch, M. S., & Sommers, M. (2003). The facilitative influence of phonological similarity and neighborhood frequency in speech production. *Memory and Cognition, 31*, 491–504.
Vitevitch, M. S., & Stamer, M. K. (2006). The curious case of competition in Spanish speech production. *Language and Cognitive Processes, 21*, 760–770.
Vlachos, D. S., Parousis-Orthodoxou, K. J., & Simos, T. E. (2008, September). Winner-takes-all strategies for complex network evolution. In *AIP Conference Proceedings* (Vol. 1048, No. 1, pp. 1030–1033). American Institute of Physics.
Wagner, A. (2007). Robustness and evolvability: A paradox resolved. *Proceedings of the Royal Society B: Biological Sciences, 275*(1630).
Walsh, M., & Gluck, K. A. (2015). Mechanisms for robust cognition. *Cognitive Science, 39*, 1131–1171.
Wang, D., Wen, Z., Tong, H., Lin, C.-Y., Song, C., & Barabási, A. L. (2011, March). *Information spreading in context*. In *Proceedings of the 20th international conference on World wide web* (pp. 735–744).
Wang, T., & Zhang, P. (2021). Directed hybrid random networks mixing preferential attachment with uniform attachment mechanisms. *arXiv*. doi:https://arxiv.org/abs/2101.04611
Wasserman, S., & Faust, K. (1994). *Social network analysis*. Cambridge, UK: Cambridge University Press.
Watts, D. J., & Strogatz, S. H. (1998). Collective dynamics of 'small-world' networks. *Nature, 393*, 440.
Weaver, I. S. (2015). Preferential attachment in randomly grown networks. *Physica A: Statistical Mechanics and its Applications, 439*, 85–92.
Weber, A., & Scharenborg, O. (2012). Models of spoken-word recognition. *Wiley Interdisciplinary Reviews: Cognitive Science, 3*, 387–401.
Wells, J. C. (1997). SAMPA computer readable phonetic alphabet. In D. Gibbon, R. Moore, & R. Winski (Eds.), *Handbook of standards and resources for spoken language systems*. Berlin, New York: Mouton de Gruyter.
Wilks, C., & Meara, P. (2002). Untangling word webs: Graph theory and the notion of density in second language word association networks. *Second Language Research, 18*, 303–324.
Wilks, C., Meara, P., & Wolter, B. (2005). A further note on simulating word association behaviour in an L2. *Second Language Research, 21*(4), 359–372.
Xu, Y., Feng, Z., & Qi, X. (2021). Signless-laplacian eigenvector centrality: A novel vital nodes identification method for complex networks. *Pattern Recognition Letters, 148*, 7–14.
Yang, Z., Algesheimer, R., & Tessone, C. J. (2016). A comparative analysis of community detection algorithms on artificial networks. *Scientific Reports, 6*, 30750.
Yates, M. (2009). Phonological neighbourhood spread facilitates lexical decisions. 62(1304–1314).
Yates, M. (2013). How the clustering of phonological neighbors affects visual word recognition. *Journal of Experimental Psychology: Learning, Memory, and Cognition, 39*(5), 1649–1656.
Yelland, G. W. (1994). Word recognition and lexical access. In A. Bowers (Ed.), *Encyclopedia of language and linguistics* (pp. 1–11). Edinburgh: Pergamon Press.

Ying, D. (2011). Scientific collaboration and endorsement: Network analysis of coauthorship and citation networks. *Journal of Infometrics, 5*(1), 4633–4636.

Zhang, X., & Gan, C. (2018). Global attractivity and optimal dynamic countermeasure of a virus propagation model in complex networks. *Physica A: Statistical Mechanics and its Applications, 490*, 1004–1018.

Zhao, J., & Xu, K. (2009). Enhancing the robustness of scale-free networks. *Journal of Physics: Mathematical and Theoretical, 42*(19), 195003.

Zhou, B., Meng, X., & Stanley, H. E. (2020). Power-law distribution of degree-degree distance: A better representation of the scale-free property of complex networks. *Proceedings of the National Academy of Sciences of the United States of America, 117*(26), 14812–14818.

Zhu, H., Wang, X., & Zhu, J.-Y. (2003). Effect of aging on network structure. *Physical Review E, 68*(5), 056121.

Zhu, Q., & Cen, C. (2017). A novel computer virus propagation model under security classification. *Discrete Dynamics in Nature and Society, 2017*, 8609082.

Ziegler, J. C., Muneaux, M., & Grainger, J. (2003). Neighborhood effects in auditory word recognition: Phonological competition and orthographic facilitation. *Journal of Memory and Language, 48*, 779–793.

Zipf, G. K. (1935). *The psycho-biology of language*. Boston, MA: Houghton-Mifflin.